Okta Administration Up and Running

Drive operational excellence with IAM solutions for on-premises and cloud apps

HenkJan de Vries

Lovisa Stenbäcken Stjernlöf

BIRMINGHAM—MUMBAI

Okta Administration Up and Running

Copyright © 2023 Packt Publishing

Group Product Manager: Pavan Ramchandani
Publishing Product Manager: Khushboo Samkaria
Book Project Manager: Neil D'Mello
Senior Editors: Sujata Tripathi and Runcil Rebello
Technical Editor: Yash Bhanushali
Copy Editor: Safis Editing
Proofreader: Safis Editing
Indexer: Hemangini Bari
Production Designer: Shankar Kalbhor
DevRel Marketing Coordinators: Marylou De Mello and Shruthi Shetty

First published: December, 2020
Second edition: December, 2023

Production reference: 1231123

Published by
Packt Publishing Ltd.
Grosvenor House
11 St Paul's Square
Birmingham
B3 1RB, UK

ISBN 978-1-83763-745-4

www.packtpub.com

I dedicate this book to my wife and family, whose encouragement kept me going during this endeavor. To my mentors, who have been the compass in my lifelong journey of growth. A heartfelt thanks to Lovisa, whose collaboration and friendship were indispensable in the creation of this work (again). Additionally, I extend my gratitude to the diverse array of individuals I've encountered during my time associated with Okta—each interaction has contributed a unique thread to the fabric of my professional life. To all of you, your influence has been instrumental, and for that, I am profoundly thankful.

HenkJan de Vries

Contributors

About the authors

HenkJan de Vries is a seasoned Okta specialist with over a remarkable decade of immersion in the Okta universe. As a dedicated Okta partner engineer, he's cultivated an impressive track record, offering unwavering support to a multitude of Okta clients. HenkJan's profound expertise extends beyond the immediate, encompassing a keen understanding of long-term strategic requirements and the nitty-gritty of day-to-day organizational management.

His credentials include certification as a consultant, and he proudly holds a coveted spot within Okta's prestigious SME group. But HenkJan's passion transcends the professional sphere; he's a committed contributor to Okta's user community, where his invaluable assistance earned him the esteemed titles of "Okta Advocate" in 2019 and "Okta Community Leader" in 2020.

Currently, HenkJan is making waves in the identity management landscape as a consultant with Atlas Identity. While being part of the team, the firm has achieved significant recognition, being honored as the "Delivery Partner of the Year EMEA 2023." This accolade is a testament to HenkJan's knowledge and his dedication to solid delivery and customer success, further establishing his and Atlas Identity's reputation for excellence in the field.

Lovisa Stenbäcken Stjernlöf has helped customers identify identity-related pains and implemented Okta for various organizations for over 5 years. Starting out as a project manager, gaining certifications within Google and Salesforce, it was a natural step to start helping customers with their complete cloud setup, including Identity and Okta. She has been leading various teams selling and implementing Okta for the Swedish market for the last few years.

About the reviewer

With over 20 years of IT experience, **Alex Voermans** is an expert in the field of **Identity and Access Management (IAM)**. He focuses on (Workforce) identity, automation and HR as a source, helping his current employer to manage their digital identities and access rights. He also has a keen interest in cybersecurity, where he collects and reports information to raise awareness and train end users. He is proficient in designing and delivering internal training courses for both IT professionals and end users, covering various aspects of IAM and cybersecurity best practices.

I appreciate HenkJan and Lovisa for giving me the opportunity to review their new book on Okta and provide them with feedback. I recommend this book to anyone who is interested in IAM and who is using or planning to use Okta. Each chapter explains with examples how to get the most out of your Okta environment. I also learned new things by reading this book. I hope you enjoy reading this book as much as I did. #learningisfun

Table of Contents

Part 1: Getting Started with Okta

1

2

3

4

5

9

Preface

Welcome to the first revision of *Okta Administration Up and Running*. If you've ever wondered how to manage user identities and secure access to your organization's resources effortlessly, you're in the right place. In this book, we'll guide you through the exciting world of Okta administration, breaking down complex concepts into plain, everyday language. You'll learn the ins and outs of Okta's features, from user provisioning and single sign-on to multifactor authentication and group management. So, whether you're a tech enthusiast or a seasoned IT pro, get ready to empower your organization's identity and access management with this clear, engaging, and informative journey through Okta's capabilities. Let's get started!

Who this book is for

Okta Administration Up and Running – Second Edition is tailored for individuals and professionals who are eager to enhance their identity and access management skills using Okta. This book is your indispensable companion if you are the following:

- **IT administrators and managers**: If you're responsible for maintaining user accounts, ensuring secure access, and managing applications within your organization, this book will equip you with the knowledge and tools to streamline these tasks efficiently.

- **Security enthusiasts**: For those passionate about securing digital identities and safeguarding data, this book provides a comprehensive understanding of Okta's security features, including multifactor authentication and adaptive policies.

- **System integrators and consultants**: Whether you're helping organizations implement Okta solutions or seeking to deepen your expertise in identity management, this book offers valuable insights and practical guidance.

- **Small business owners and entrepreneurs**: Even if you don't have a dedicated IT team, this book simplifies Okta administration, making it accessible for small business owners looking to bolster their organization's security and efficiency.

- **IT students and aspiring professionals**: If you're just starting your journey in the world of IT, you should know that Okta is a widely used tool in the industry. This book will serve as an excellent resource to build your foundational knowledge.

- **Anyone interested in modern identity management**: Whether you're curious about how identity and access management works or simply interested in staying informed about the latest technology trends, this book offers an accessible entry point into the world of Okta.

Throughout these pages, you'll find practical examples, step-by-step instructions, and real-world scenarios that will empower you to harness the full potential of Okta's capabilities. So, dive in, and let's demystify the world of Okta administration together. Your journey to becoming an Okta expert starts here!

What this book covers

Chapter 1, IAM and Okta, dives into the foundational principles of IAM, where you'll uncover why it's the bedrock of modern IT and security, ensuring the safeguarding of digital assets and seamless user access. But that's just the beginning. We'll unravel Okta's intriguing origin story, tracing its evolution into a powerhouse of IAM solutions. What truly sets this chapter apart is the compelling exploration of Okta's array of base and advanced products. Discover how these tools can revolutionize your organization's identity management, authentication, and access control.

Chapter 2, Working with Universal Directory, delves into the core of Okta's directory functionality. This chapter is your gateway to connecting your infrastructure seamlessly through directory integrations, efficiently managing user identities, and ensuring secure access. You'll master the art of importing and creating users, optimize productivity with groups, bolster security by managing devices, and even extend user profiles to tailor them to your unique needs. Get ready to unlock the secrets of Okta's Universal Directory and elevate your identity management game.

Chapter 3, Using Single Sign-On for a Great End User Experience, is your gateway to unleashing the full potential of Okta's **Single Sign-On (SSO)** functionality. Get ready to discover how to use SSO seamlessly with Okta, utilize the convenience of FastPass for easy sign-on, and navigate the Okta dashboard with finesse. We'll also delve into the agentless Desktop SSO setup, explore the Okta Integration Network, harness the power of Secure Web Authentication and **Security Assertion Markup Language (SAML)**/OpenID Connect applications, and master the art of managing inbound SSO and **identity provider (IdP)** discovery. Your journey to a superior end user experience begins here!

Chapter 4, Increasing Security with Adaptive Multifactor Authentication, prepares you to uncover the depths of Okta's **Multifactor Authentication (MFA)** capabilities. In this chapter, we'll explore diverse factor types, authenticators, and enrollment methods. Discover the power of contextual access management and the art of enrolling end users seamlessly in MFA. Dive into the world of heightened security and user authentication as we delve deep into the heart of Okta's MFA functionality. Your journey to fortified security begins here – get ready to unlock the secrets of adaptive MFA!

Chapter 5, Automating Using Lifecycle Management, dives deep into the world of user provisioning automation, enabling you to streamline and enhance your identity management processes. Discover how to effortlessly automate user provisioning, create rich user profiles, and establish group rules for efficient management. We'll also explore the setup of self-service options, putting control in the hands of your users. Join us on this journey to harness the power of automation and make identity management a breeze.

Chapter 6, Customizing Your Okta GUI, delves into the realm of personalized user experiences. This chapter explores the fundamental aspects of end-user functionality and customization. Gain insights into configuring the user dashboard and fine-tuning Okta plugin settings. We'll also navigate the intricacies of custom domain setup and the creation of bespoke pages, enabling you to mold Okta to suit your unique requirements. This chapter offers a gateway to a world of tailored solutions and heightened user engagement through Okta's customizable features. Let's dive in and uncover the limitless possibilities of customization.

Chapter 7, Okta Workflows, steps into the world of Okta Workflows within Okta administration, where innovation meets efficiency. This chapter uncovers the power of Okta Workflows – a transformative tool designed to simplify complex processes. Explore its versatility in integrating applications and functions seamlessly. Learn how to safeguard your workflows with export backups, and delve into the realm of delegated admin workflows. In this chapter, we'll unveil the capabilities of Okta Workflows, opening doors to enhanced automation and process optimization. Get ready to unlock the potential of this dynamic feature, revolutionizing the way you manage identity and access.

Chapter 8, API Access Management, demystifies API terminology and explores the ins and outs of managing Okta with APIs. Get ready to dive into the fundamentals of API access management, empowering you to safeguard your digital assets. Plus, we'll delve into the nitty-gritty of API administration, ensuring you have the tools and knowledge to master this vital aspect of identity and access management. Let's unravel the secrets of effective API access control together!

Chapter 9, Managing Access with Advanced Server Access, provides you with a comprehensive understanding of Advanced Server Access (ASA). We'll explore the setup of ASA, empowering you to configure it effectively. Dive into the world of managing your ASA environment, and discover how automation can elevate your access management game. This chapter is your key to mastering advanced access control with Okta, opening doors to heightened security and streamlined operations.

To get the most out of this book

To maximize the benefits of this book on Okta administration, it's advantageous to have a foundational understanding of **identity and access management (IAM)** principles, as well as basic familiarity with Okta's core features and functionality. We assume readers are eager to deepen their expertise in IAM and Okta, aiming to leverage its advanced capabilities effectively. To get the most out of this resource, actively engage with the chapters, practice hands-on exercises, and explore the practical use cases provided.

Conventions used

There are a number of text conventions used throughout this book.

`Code in text`: Indicates code words in text, database table names, folder names, filenames, file extensions, pathnames, dummy URLs, user input, and Twitter handles. Here is an example: "input your host and port in `host:port` format."

A block of code is set as follows:

```
{
  "kty": "RSA",
  "alg": "RSA",
  "kid": "e86a0cf3-0df6-4c5e-aeeb-7fab2b1dfe15",
  "use": null,
  "e": "AQAB",
  "n": "w21EOpj1Mnm6jqLaM2FtfjR9cZU0u3agvA
Ts1EDuucEUW0-I52U3sN8n4MYGZCODRiwtOhtVEt_
u7aXqKo2roUR3N11uced5sCQW9AaUT35lvKVVUKgvccS_VO7k9Zkn8qGYVBv72vTnH1QW
nsSAP3sHykNpK1hyziYBe2DbldO4ZmJE7nPIStWz160C-dccPbei4azYWyVOgHcYSZtg-
by0L4QLezkOShloSnZ_ZzDrjSkAI3FZefr-GFBYufNSSzclJRrMxe7zy-D0cpTdOHQ-7NB
o0Ar2cbBYIbQsH18EjKGR28NjT2OkC829w3JVJlMbGr1LLHMS9ZFtDLMVQQ"
}
```

Any command-line input or output is written as follows:

```
# Run this command in your project root folder.npm install @okta/okta-
signin-widget -save
```

Bold: Indicates a new term, an important word, or words that you see on screen. For instance, words in menus or dialog boxes appear in **bold**. Here is an example: "An organization in this stage typically has an **Active Directory (AD)** or some other on-premises structures as a user directory."

> **Tips or important notes**
> Appear like this.

Get in touch

Feedback from our readers is always welcome.

General feedback: If you have questions about any aspect of this book, mention the book title in the subject of your message and email us at `customercare@packtpub.com`.

Errata: Although we have taken every care to ensure the accuracy of our content, mistakes do happen. If you have found a mistake in this book, we would be grateful if you would report this to us. Please visit www.packtpub.com/support/errata, selecting your book, clicking on the **Errata Submission Form** link, and entering the details.

Piracy: If you come across any illegal copies of our works in any form on the internet, we would be grateful if you would provide us with the location address or website name. Please contact us at copyright@packtpub.com with a link to the material.

If you are interested in becoming an author: If there is a topic that you have expertise in and you are interested in either writing or contributing to a book, please visit authors.packtpub.com.

Share Your Thoughts

Once you've read *Okta Administration Up and Running – Second Edition*, we'd love to hear your thoughts! Scan the QR code below to go straight to the Amazon review page for this book and share your feedback.

https://packt.link/r/1837637458

Your review is important to us and the tech community and will help us make sure we're delivering excellent quality content.

Download a free PDF copy of this book

Thanks for purchasing this book!

Do you like to read on the go but are unable to carry your print books everywhere?

Is your eBook purchase not compatible with the device of your choice?

Don't worry, now with every Packt book you get a DRM-free PDF version of that book at no cost.

Read anywhere, any place, on any device. Search, copy, and paste code from your favorite technical books directly into your application.

The perks don't stop there, you can get exclusive access to discounts, newsletters, and great free content in your inbox daily

Follow these simple steps to get the benefits:

1. Scan the QR code or visit the link below

https://packt.link/free-ebook/9781837637454

2. Submit your proof of purchase
3. That's it! We'll send your free PDF and other benefits to your email directly

Part 1: Getting Started with Okta

In the first six chapters of *Okta Administration*, we embark on a comprehensive journey through the realm of **identity and access management** (**IAM**), using Okta's powerful tools. Starting with *IAM and Okta*, we explore the core principles of IAM and Okta's origins. We then dive into the *Working with Universal Directory, Using Single Sign-On for a Great End User Experience, Increasing Security with Adaptive Multifactor Authentication, Automating Using Lifecycle Management*, and *Customizing Your Okta GUI* chapters. These chapters cover key aspects of identity management, security, automation, and customization, laying the foundation for a robust Okta administration skillset.

This part has the following chapters:

- *Chapter 1, IAM and Okta*
- *Chapter 2, Working with Universal Directory*
- *Chapter 3, Using Single Sign-On for a Great End User Experience*
- *Chapter 4, Increasing Security with Adaptive Multifactor Authentication*
- *Chapter 5, Automating Using Lifecycle Management*
- *Chapter 6, Customizing Your Okta GUI*

1
IAM and Okta

Okta is a premium, platform-agnostic set of services that helps organizations with efficient and modern **identity and access management (IAM)**. One of Okta's biggest strengths is its ability to work with a variety of platforms and integrate its features and services into these platforms' own solutions to provide seamless IAM. This strength has made Okta the leader in the IAM field, as it's valuable in helping us manage our organization's systems to ensure easy and efficient user account management.

In this chapter, we'll learn about Okta and its features. This information will serve as the foundation with which to approach this book and pick up the skills we require to integrate Okta with our systems and learn how to use it in the best way possible. In this chapter, we'll explore the following topics:

- The origins of Okta
- Exploring Okta
- Okta's basic features
- Okta's advanced features
- Okta and NIST

Exploring the origins of Okta

Okta was founded by Todd McKinnon (CEO) and Frederic Kerrest (COO), two former Salesforce employees. They saw that the cloud wasn't just a product for the big leagues and predicted it would be necessary for anyone who wanted to grow their business. They started the business in the middle of the 2008 recession, with Andreessen Horowitz investing as one of the first capital injections for Okta in 2010. In 2017, Okta went public with its IPO and valuation of $1.2 billion.

The name *Okta* is derived from the unit of measurement for clouds covering the sky at any given moment. On the scale, 0 okta is a clear blue sky and 8 oktas means complete overcast. The wordplay in Okta (in Greek, *octa* is 8) and the fact that Okta wanted to cover all cloud access by becoming the identity standard, thus creating a complete overcast (8 oktas), is well thought out. As of 2022, Okta has grown its clouds by specifically creating two offerings: the **Workforce Identity Cloud (WIC)** and the **Customer Identity Cloud (CIC)**. This book will only cover WIC.

Since Okta arrived in the IAM space, it has steadily grown to become the leading vector and has been in the leading segments of market investigation firms (Gartner, Forrester, etc.), bypassing giants such as Oracle, IBM, and Microsoft. Their take on being completely vendor-neutral has allowed them to gain customers, big and small, across all verticals. This particular focus makes sure that Okta can serve all applications, without being tied to or biased toward any relationship or partnership. It gives the customer complete freedom in choice, setup, and tools.

In recent years, Okta has been socially active, taking the 1% pledge; committing to giving back time, product, and equity to the community and supporting non-profit efforts in different ways. As Okta understands what it is like to start up and grow, during its annual conference in 2019, it announced an investment fund of 50 million dollars under the name **Okta Ventures** to help other start-ups in the identity and security sector ramp up and grow. Currently, over two dozen start-ups have benefitted from this venture seeding.

Understanding IAM and Okta

IAM is usually utilized to do the following:

- Manage the roles of users within an organization
- Manage the privileges that users have to access company resources while using user context
- Configure scenarios to determine whether access is granted or denied

Beyond these actions, IAM can do much more, such as the following:

- Orchestrate the user's lifecycle during their time within the company
- Constantly determine whether access is allowed according to company policies and rules to gain access to needed resources, content, and data using the best available security features

The time of perimeters is behind us. Organizations can no longer just trust their networks and secure access mainly through their infrastructure. Nowadays, access is needed by every device and every application, at any given moment, with any reason or intent. This shows that security needs are dynamic and their requirements are continuously evolving.

Outdated directories are being replaced by different tools, and they all have to be maintained, secured, and fortified outside of the comfort of the company's network. This is bringing a lot of extra consolidation and rethinking of the concept of using the cloud and also how to manage it all for the workforce.

This brings us to the start of a new era where new IAM solutions were born in the cloud and existing solutions started a shift toward the cloud. This didn't mean every organization all of sudden dropped its network and pushed everything and everyone to the cloud. Vendors had to become hybrid, delivering tools to connect the ground to the cloud with integrations. By consolidating the two, the shift slowly started to pick up pace and organizations began to understand the possibilities of using tools such as Okta as their IAM solution of choice.

Exploring Okta

A complete user and system management setup isn't just in one product, nor is it dependent upon a single vendor. A complete view of all sections within and outside of the organization is best done by utilizing different tools.

This combination and their deep integrations make it possible to create a fine-knit layer of security and insights on top of everything, flexible enough to allow exceptions, but strong enough to fight off anything considered harmful to the user, content, data, systems, or organization.

An IAM system can be seen as a collection of different elements and tools to deliver this. It can be considered that the following functionalities are part of, but not limited to, an organization's toolkit:

- A password vault to store and maintain access to applications and systems. This can be advanced by using protocols that allow **single sign-on** (**SSO**).

- Provisioning integrations to create and manage user identities within directories, applications, databases, and infrastructures.

- Security enforcement applications to secure access to applications, as well as securing the data of these systems and others.

- Unified reporting systems allow fine-grained insight into the array of tools to create oversight and provide better knowledge of what is happening within and outside of the corporate network.

Okta is capable of delivering all of these functionalities, to some degree, for organizations large and small across any business vertical and within cost-effective boundaries.

By staying true to their form, they are capable of excelling in being an agnostic system. By allowing any application vendor to create integrations with Okta and delivering applications broadly on request from customers, Okta has been able to grow its reach to over 7,000 pre-built and maintained integrations in the public catalog **Okta Integration Network** (**OIN**). While creating these integrations, Okta also invested heavily in delivering more and more functionality to ground-to-cloud visibility and launched their Okta Access Gateway product. On top of these out-of-the-box integrations, Okta has added their no/low-code Workflows engine, allowing any identity-driven event to use Okta's abilities internally and even on applications not in their integrations library.

Looking further than users, the world consists of more and more IoT applications, and the need for machine-to-machine management is becoming a much larger element within organizations' business models. By offering API access management and **Advanced Server Access (ASA)**, Okta creates more functionality to fill the needs of every aspect of the IAM situation within any organization.

Let's now take a look at the things that set Okta apart in the IAM space.

Zero trust

As organizations shift away from on-premises applications by making sure the workforce can decide how and when they access the data they need, Okta makes it possible to incorporate forward-thinking concepts, such as **zero trust**. Zero trust is the framework where no physical or non-physical entities within or outside of the corporate perimeter are trusted at any given moment in time. This allows for insight and control to manage users, identities, infrastructure, and devices accessing business resources and data. Threat detection and remediation are a part of the cycle that makes sure that this concept is enforced.

The zero trust principle of least-privileged access can be incorporated into the organization's security policies. It allows users and machines to only get enough access for that given moment and that task. This can be hard to manage on a case-by-case scenario (for example, allowing and denying access to individual corporate content and files), but by understanding the concept, it can be used as a rule of thumb to only give out need-to-access privileges. A couple of examples are as follows:

- A support agent needs administrator rights in a system but might not need full super admin rights. Role-based access can be applied here.
- A machine reading data from a database needs read-only access, not write access. This would reduce the risk of an attacker being able to change or delete data.

Acquiring an IAM tool is not enough by default to make sure your organization lives up to a zero trust approach, but it is a starting point for many organizations. When it comes to IAM and zero trust, Okta divides the journey into four stages of maturity.

Stage zero – fragmented identity

An organization in this stage typically has an **Active Directory (AD)** or some other on-premises structures as a user directory. Cloud applications might be used, but there is no integration into the directory. Passwords are not consolidated, but rather separate logins are everywhere. Security is done on a case-by-case basis, or rather, app by app. In stage zero, most services and devices will reside within the corporate infrastructure, as seen in *Figure 1.1*:

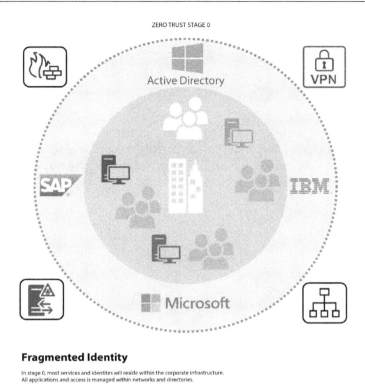

Fragmented Identity

In stage 0, most services and identites will reside within the corporate infrastructure.
All applications and access is managed within networks and directories.

Figure 1.1 – All applications and access are managed with networks and directories

Once users break free from or break through the corporate firewall, the need for more control over who can access what and when, where, and how allows the organization to move to the next stage.

Usually, more traditional organizations fall into this category. Their history is based more upon older infrastructure, and the move toward the cloud is slowly happening. Companies with on-premises servers, fierce reliance on firewalls, and VPN access are often found in this stage.

Stage one – unified IAM

Once you open the gates, there is no coming back to a perimeter-based security practice. It's important to make sure certain access is managed for employees, partners, and contractors. Delivering unified SSO relieves the user of the responsibility to create, maintain, and manage strong passwords per application, portal, and infrastructure. By adding **multifactor authentication** (**MFA**), the organization is capable of creating more policies that incorporate different activities to confirm the user's identity while accessing corporate content.

Examples of this are as follows:

- Using an application such as Google Authenticator or Okta's own application, Okta Verify, to receive a one-time code

- Using SMS to receive a one-time code

- Biometrics such as a fingerprint reader or a YubiKey

In stage one, you will see a shift. Users will access corporate data outside of the network. Slowly, SaaS will make its way into the organization. Even so, old structures will still stay in place to maintain legacy and non-cloud access as follows:

Unified IAM

In stage 1, you will see a shift. Users will be access corporate data outside of the network. Slowly SaaS will make its way into the organization. Evenso old structures will still stay in place to maintain legacy and non cloud access.

Figure 1.2 – An outline of what stage one might look like

You will find organizations of every trade in this stage. Moving to the cloud is part of their strategy. They will most likely start to embrace **Software-as-a-Service (SaaS)** options over their own capabilities. This is where perimeters start to fade and the call for more flexible security and management is needed.

Stage two – contextual access

Context-based access plays a large part when you want to expand your zero trust initiative. Understanding your users, their devices, location, systems, and even time and date can be of importance to accelerate your dynamic zero trust parameters. By incorporating all these components, you now allow your security team to widen their view of a user's posture and activities and set fine-grained policies and rules that are applicable to that user.

Having such deep control and the capability to interact on such a low level with users fits perfectly with the concept of zero trust. Of course, automation is the magic sauce. Using all these different elements in your security risk assessment is the first step, setting policies on top of that is step two, but automating it all and having the systems grow stronger is what adds even more value. This is step three.

Within this stage, usually, you will observe that corporate APIs and systems have, or leverage, APIs that need to be protected as well. Allowing API management ensures that even your systems are only allowed access based on the least-privilege framework.

Contextual Access

In stage 2, organizations will mostly likely adopt more and more cloud services. The identity will become the perimeter and identity providers will become part of the primary components. Outside access to corporate content and data is no longer a complimentary, it has become mandatory.

Figure 1.3 – An outline of what stage two might look like

Organizations might have a complete roadmap for themselves set out with regard to their zero trust initiative. Cloud-driven, cloud-native, and cloud-born organizations will quickly adopt it, and there are many of them in this stage. Traditional organizations that have made it to this stage have come a long way; they truly were able to reinvent themselves.

Stage three – adaptive workforce

When system automation increases, risk-based analysis can be added. This is when we are capable of creating a fully flexible and adaptive workforce. The incorporation of more security systems becomes a large addition to the whole security practice. Usually, external values from third-party applications such as **mobile device management (MDM)**, **cloud access security broker (CASB)**, **security information and event management** (SIEM), and other connected systems will deliver even more user and machine context that can be used within policies.

Unknown vectors are detected, and policies start to act upon these discoveries. Adding alternative access controls when it's needed or required allows for more security. While security might go up, the users' access can now be more controlled with the help of seamless access methods. Passwordless and dynamic authentication policies become a more common situation in which users are prompted to show who they are based on the risk they present to the systems that are controlling the access:

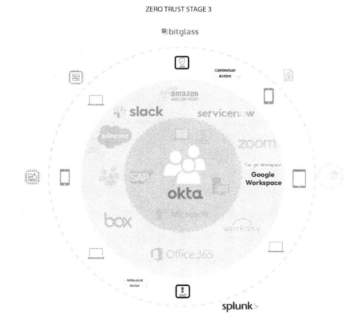

Adaptive workforce

In stage 3, interconnectivity towards everything will become the norm. Automation added on top of data and content security. Least privileged access can be maintain based on log consolidation and API management.

Figure 1.4 – An outline of what stage three might look like

Organizations that fall into this category will be front-runners in this initiative. They not only understand it, but they have also implemented it and made it their mantra. High-tech organizations with global workforces and dynamic management will fit this picture perfectly.

So, how would you start your own organization's journey towards zero trust?

- Start by researching the concept
- Assess your own organization
- See what solutions you can keep and what needs to change and mitigate the gaps in your solutions
- Get your users on board

Now that we've learned about the steps to take with your organization to move toward a zero trust approach, let's look at the basic features in Okta that we can use to start our journey.

Discovering the basic features of Okta

Okta has a lot of different products, and organizations can pick and choose as they see fit. The most commonly used are the following:

- **Universal Directory (UD)**
- **SSO**
- **Adaptive Multifactor Authentication (AMFA)**
- **Lifecycle Management (LCM)**

It's not always obvious in the administrator portal where one product starts and another one ends. This will be clarified in this book. The products will all be explained with practical examples in the coming chapters, but here is an initial overview.

Universal Directory

UD can be considered the foundation of any Okta setup. UD is the directory of your users, groups, and devices. Users can be sourced by Okta, other directories, an HR system, or even any source that contains user data. For organizations with multiple directories, such as AD, LDAP, G Suite, and an HR system, Okta can offer a complete 360-degree view of the users and their attributes consolidated into one system. Users can be sorted into groups created in Okta and imported from a directory or an application. With Okta's attribute sourcing feature, the attributes of any user can be sourced by different sources.

Single sign-on

SSO lets us connect applications and lets our users access them through Okta. End users will only have to log in to Okta once and can thereafter access any application they have assigned to them. This is done with integrations based on SAML, WS-Federation, or OpenID Connect or with a simple **Secure Web Authentication** (**SWA**), where Okta stores credentials and passes them along to the application in a secure way. In the OIN, more than 7,000 integrations are available, and more are added every day. If the required application isn't available in the OIN, customers can create their own integrations. This will be described in depth in *Chapter 3, Using Single Sign-On for a Great End User Experience*.

Multifactor authentication and adaptive multifactor authentication

Included in Okta's SSO product are basic MFA features. You can easily set up policies to let your users utilize different kinds of authenticators after entering their password. Using the basic IP settings, you can set up network zones that protect your users and block bad actors from the outside.

Many third-party MFA solutions can be integrated with Okta, allowing you to leverage existing and perhaps currently deployed solutions into your Okta MFA policies.

If the basic features of MFA aren't enough for you, Okta's **Adaptive MFA** (**AMFA**) product brings even more advanced options. With AMFA, you can set and use the context in your MFA policies. The context can be location awareness, device fingerprinting and posture, or impossible velocity. Okta's device trust options allow you to integrate with your third-party MDM systems to generate even more context around your users and devices.

Lifecycle management

So far, the Okta products we've looked at have focused a lot on end user experience and security. LCM is all about automation, easing up the friction between HR and IT. With LCM, organizations are better set up for audits. For instance, with your Okta instance set up—with groups, rules, integrations, and system logs—and access given, it's easy to show when a user had access to what. With the group rules feature, automation takes over access given, removing the risk of manual errors. This will streamline work for the HR and IT departments, allowing them to do the work by creating the user only once in the organization's systems. The creation, management, and deletion of users and accounts has never been this easy. Automatic account creation also minimizes mistakes caused by human error. A predetermined setup allows the organization to invest time upfront to create and set up the provisioning, and after that, it will automatically run based on the user's identity and profile.

With Okta's LCM functionality, you can also automate access control in certain applications. This allows you, with minimal interaction, to manage users with the correct role, license, entitlement, and group access.

Advanced features of Okta

If your organization needs to go deeper than general IAM, you might need to look at Okta's more advanced features. Let's look at them now.

Okta Advanced Server Access

Okta ASA lets us extend our zero trust practices toward server accounts. Okta can manage access to both user or service accounts to Linux or Windows servers across different cloud vendors, such as GCP, AWS, and Azure, or on-premises servers. In Okta, your admins get a great overview of who has access to what and can see individual logins in log reports. ASA works with a lightweight agent and is installed in your infrastructure landscape.

Workflows

With Workflows, you can automate many business processes using a simple *if this, then that* methodology with no-code configurations. Okta provides a library of connections to many popular cloud applications, and Workflows can also integrate with custom APIs. Some examples of where Workflows can be used include the following:

- On and off-boarding enhancements
- Resolving conflicts when new users are created
- Sharing reports on a monthly basis

Okta Access Gateway

Okta Access Gateway (**OAG**) makes it possible to implement modern cloud-based access management to on-premises legacy applications. With this product, you can gather all your identity needs in one place, making them easier to manage. It's easy to integrate, with templates and native on-premises integrations. By replacing your current **web access management** (**WAM**) system, you can bring your applications to your users in a modern and non-restrictive way. Additionally, you can also secure those apps even more with extra MFA functionality.

API Access Gateway

Leveraging Okta's API Access Gateway allows the developer of your tools, systems, and platforms to be securely managed by Okta, while they can focus on their primary tasks. The processes of adding security and allowing scopes to grant access to your own systems are managed by Okta. The shift of responsibility goes from the developer to the security and operations team. Focusing on management with out-of-box integrations and authorization servers is core to Okta's API Access Management.

Okta and NIST

To be continuously compliant with today's regulations and tomorrow's rules and recommendations, Okta will help organizations follow new frameworks and guidelines that are accepted as the (new) norm.

While you might be working on your zero trust initiative, many organizations will also refer to the cybersecurity framework from the **National Institute of Standards and Technology (NIST)**. As with all guidelines and frameworks, there is no miracle product to implement for compliance. Okta doesn't cover all aspects that are included in the framework but can indeed help organizations manage the elements relating to IAM and access control.

The five core values of NIST are as follows:

1. Identify
2. Protect
3. Detect
4. Respond
5. Recover

What the framework is basically saying is that organizations need full visibility and control to be secure. As we have seen from the introduction to Okta's features, by implementing the core features, you get a full 360-degree view of all users, their roles, and their accesses. By implementing AMFA, you can fulfill the requirement of context-based MFA with factors that suit each type of user for each situation.

To find a complete list of the NIST controls that Okta can help with, visit `https://www.okta.com/sites/default/files/pdf/Meeting-the-Latest-NIST-Guidelines-Okta-Final.pdf`.

Summary

In this chapter, we learned basic details about IAM and how Okta works as a great solution to any IAM needs. We've learned about the scenarios in which Okta emerges as an IAM solution. Finally, we learned about the features of Okta and how they work with various platforms to give us dynamic control over user accounts within our organizations. All of this information forms the basis of our understanding for the rest of the book, where we will take a deeper look at Okta and how to make use of all its features.

In the next chapter, we will learn how to work with UD by setting it up and configuring it. We will learn how to add or import users and explore the most important features and policies to help us use UD efficiently.

2

Working with Universal Directory

Universal Directory (**UD**) is the base of Okta, the foundation on which other pieces are built. Your users and applications will be an intricate part of UD. Groups will be vital for you to keep organized and make your Okta org as low maintenance as possible. In this chapter, you'll learn everything you need to know to integrate other directories and configurations for users, understand device registrations, and set up groups.

Let's jump right in and look at what companies might have been using before, and how that can work with Okta.

We will explore the following topics:

- Connecting your infrastructure with directory integrations
- Importing and creating users
- Using groups to be productive
- Managing devices for more security context
- User profiles and how to extend them

Directory integrations

If your organization is fairly new, there is a big chance that it was born in the cloud. You may be only using cloud services and your UD might be in one of your applications, perhaps your collaboration platform. You will probably want to use Okta as your new identity directory going forward. But for other organizations, your users may have been living in a separate directory for ages, and you might have multiple hardware and infrastructure connections to that directory. The most common directory services are Microsoft **Active Directory** (**AD**) and **Lightweight Directory Access Protocol** (**LDAP**), and many organizations like this are not ready to leave them behind. Don't worry – Okta can integrate with multiple directories and synchronize users, groups, attributes, and passwords.

Previously, this directory setup was sufficient, but with the shift in perimeter that was explained in *Chapter 1*, this can become a problem when companies are moving toward cloud applications. Many cloud applications have their own directory, but the administrator's overview of who has access to what might be lost. It is possible to still use AD or LDAP, but with custom API integrations, the upkeep will become harder to manage.

Instead, organizations can keep their AD/LDAP integration and use Okta as a directory for their cloud applications by using out-of-the-box standard integrations maintained by Okta.

AD and various LDAP directories are handled differently, and in the following sections, we will guide you through how to install and configure some of them.

Microsoft AD integration

For Microsoft AD, three different components can be used for different use cases:

- The Okta AD agent
- The Okta (agentless) Desktop Single Sign-On functionality
- The Okta AD Password Sync agent

In this chapter, we will discuss the AD agent and the Password Sync agent. The agentless Desktop Single Sign-on functionality will be discussed in *Chapter 3, Using Single Sign-On for a Great End User Experience*.

Importing users and groups with the Okta AD agent

The Okta AD agent is a lightweight agent to be installed on any Windows domain server to handle user authentication, provisioning, and deprovisioning between AD and Okta.

To set up the AD agent, start by logging into Okta from a browser on the Windows server where your directory lives. Go to the **Directory** tab in the admin console and choose **Directory Integrations**. If you have had previous directory integrations, you will see them listed here. Choose **Add Active Directory**. In the next window, you will see the requirements:

- Install on Windows Server 2012 or later
- Must be a member of your AD domain
- Consider the agent a part of your IT infrastructure to maintain
- Run this setup wizard from the host server

When going through the installation, you will enter your Okta URL and your AD credentials. The best practice is to use a service account that has administrative rights on the domain controller. The agent creates a read-only integration account and connects to Okta through an outbound port 443 SSL connection. Usually, no firewall or network changes will be needed. Please make sure you've added required proxies if your network does require these to gain access to the internet.

> **Tip**
>
> Test logging into the host machine with AD credentials and accessing the internet via a browser. If that works, no change is needed in terms of the firewall or network settings.

From the Okta side, setup requires Okta super administrator access and will establish a security token. The token is only valid for one agent and can be revoked whenever needed. The token that's created at setup is authenticated by Okta, and the agent verifies the service by validating the **Secure Sockets Layer** (**SSL**) certificate for the URL. In terms of the domain controller, the agent will be authenticated using the read-only account for integration that was created during its installation.

Once your agent has been installed and verified, you can start importing your users into Okta. By going to **Directory | Directory Integrations | Active Directory**, you can set your preferences.

Now, let's look at the integration settings and options that are available. Go to **Directory | Directory Integrations | Active Directory | Provisioning | Integration**. In the **Import settings** section, you will see the following options:

- **User OUs connected to Okta**: Here, you can add or remove **organizational units** (**OUs**) that are used to import users.

- **User Filter**: This will allow you to set filters on users within the OU you wish to import from. The default filter is **sAMAccountType=805306368**. Make sure you test filters in AD before adding them here as it could result in users being deactivated in AD.

- **Group OUs connected to Okta**: You can add or remove OUs that are used to import groups.

- **Group Filter**: This will allow you to filter your group OU import down to the specified list of groups you prefer to import into Okta. The default filter is **objectCategory=group**. Make sure you also test any custom filter in AD to make sure it does what you want in Okta.

> **Note**
>
> Both **User Filter** and **Group Filter** are early access features, which we usually do not discuss, but in this case, they have been around for a long time and Okta does discuss the items themselves too.

If you select the **Enable delegated authentication (DelAuth) to Active Directory** option in the **Delegated Authentication** section, you will relay authentication from Okta to AD when users sign into Okta. You can find this section by going to the **Provisioning** tab and selecting **Integration**. For organizations using AD for other services as well, this is an easy way for users to manage fewer passwords. It also makes for easier onboarding and adoption of Okta, where users don't have to remember anything new. When DelAuth is turned on, users who use AD for access will no longer have a password in Okta.

If we move to the other menu option, **To Okta**, we will find the following settings:

- **Schedule import**: In this section, you can select with what frequency you want to import users from your directory. You can use **Do not import users** to only allow manual importing and not have the schedule run at all.

- **Okta username format**: The format of the username must match the username you used when you imported users; otherwise, it might cause errors for active users. You can do this by selecting one of the options in the drop-down menu:

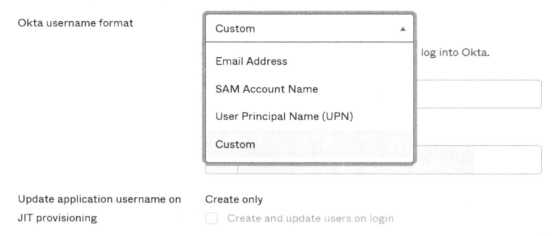

Figure 2.1 – Okta username format options

- **Update application username on**: Here, you can decide if the username in the previously given format will only be created or if the conditions change, the username will be updated in AD.

- **Just in Time (JIT) provisioning**: If you click **Create** and update users on login, a user's account in Okta is automatically created the first time they sign into Okta using their AD credentials. For existing users, any account and group updates will be synchronized during new logins.

- **Universal Security Group (USG) support**: Select this option to avoid domain boundaries when importing group memberships. This requires JIT provisioning to work.

- **Do not import users**: Turn this option on to allow synchronization to take place for groups, but not import users. This can be done by using JIT instead.

- **Activation email**: By checking this box, you avoid sending out an email to end users to activate their account upon import. This should be your default setting on your first import since you might have other items to set up in your new Okta instance before you're ready for active users.

In the **User Creation & Matching** section, you manage the settings that decide whether a user imported from AD is matched with an existing user in Okta. With the matching rules, you will establish how to map an imported user to an existing user. This is an important step to ensure you don't get duplicates of the same user in Okta; it is especially important if you import users from other places, such as applications.

To determine that an imported user is matched, you can choose from the following options:

- **Okta username format matches**.
- **Email matches**.
- **The following attribute matches**: You can choose an attribute from the drop-down list. The chosen attribute must match for it to be deemed an exact match.
- **The following combination of attribute matches**: You can choose combinations of attributes from a list; each combination you choose must match for it to be deemed an exact match.

You can also set rules so that partial matches will be considered matches. For example, it could happen when a user's first and last name match but the username or email doesn't.

Lastly, you have to decide what will happen when these matches are identified; there are two options for this. If you have a matched user, you can select **Auto-confirm exact matches** and/or **Auto-confirm partial matches**. If you don't select any of them, you have to manually confirm each import. In this section, you also decide what to do to the new users that were imported, without being matched with an existing user in Okta. Here, you can select **Auto-confirm new users** and/or **Auto-activate new users**. If you leave both unchecked, the users will be confirmed once they are manually activated by an administrator.

These parameters can be set up to your own needs and preferences in regards to your setup:

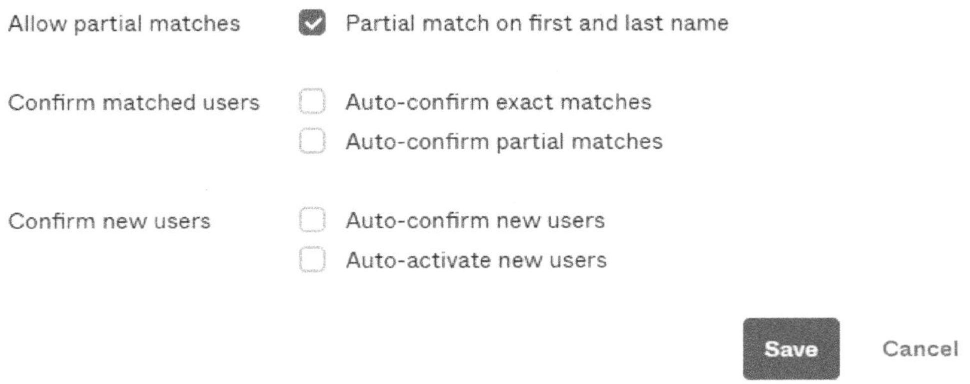

Allow partial matches	☑ Partial match on first and last name
Confirm matched users	☐ Auto-confirm exact matches
	☐ Auto-confirm partial matches
Confirm new users	☐ Auto-confirm new users
	☐ Auto-activate new users

Save Cancel

Figure 2.2 – Options of Okta username format

Now, let's move on to the final section that we will discuss on this **To Okta** page. Import safeguards ensure a smooth import process by setting a limit on unassigned users, helping to prevent any disruptions due to excessive unassignments during the import. They act as a safety net, halting the import if the percentage of unassigned users crosses a pre-specified threshold, thereby ensuring that the integrity and functionality of apps within an organization remain uncompromised:

- **App unassignment safeguard**: Apply to apps with over 100 users, default at a 20% unassignment threshold, and are specific to applications assigned by groups imported from (AD, excluding AD user deactivation from the unassignment calculation

- **Org-wide unassignment Safeguard**: Encompass all users and app assignments across the organization, activate with a minimum of 100 app assignments, and have a default 20% unassignment threshold, including deactivated users in the unassignment calculation, irrespective of their import lifecycle state

Now that we're done with these steps, let's see how we can sync passwords from AD to other downstream applications.

Easily logging into apps with the Okta AD Password Sync agent

Earlier, we looked at the **Delegated Authentication** feature. In this scenario, passwords are not passed over to Okta; AD simply handles the authentication of users when they log into Okta. But in some cases, a downstream application needs a password to authenticate users (usually Secure Web Authentication apps). In this scenario, Okta checks the password that's been entered with AD and also checks whether the user is assigned an application using the synchronized password. If the user doesn't have any applications in need of the password, Okta caches the password for 5 days. If the user has an application that uses the synchronized password, the password is synchronized to the application and also stored in Okta for the application; the password is cached in Okta for 5 days.

If you have installed **(A)DSSO agent**, which we will discuss in more detail in *Chapter 3, Using Single Sign-On for a Great End User Experience*, the Password Sync agent makes sure any changes of the password in AD are synchronized in Okta. If a user changes their password on the computer sign-on screen, the password has to be synced between AD and Okta. The user might have to sign out and then sign into Okta again to be able to access the application with the synchronized password.

To install, go to the admin console, then **Security | Delegated Authentication**. On the menu on the right-hand side, scroll down and click the link to download the synchronize password agent. After that, do the following:

1. Start the installation and follow the steps provided.

2. You will have to enter your domain name in `https://mycompany.okta.com` format. Don't forget the `https://` part!

3. At the end, you must pick your installation location and then hit **Install**. After that, click **Finish**.

4. Restart the server.

So, how do you configure the agent? On the server, navigate to **Start | All Programs | Okta | Okta AD Password Sync | Okta AD Password Synchronization Agent Management Console**. There, you can validate the URL. If it's valid, a success message will appear under the field. If you want, you can also set the level of logging for the agent.

> **Note**
> The Password Sync agent must be installed on all domain controllers. Also, don't forget to enable delegated authentication!

Okay, that's all for any basic AD integration. Now, let's look at how it's done for an LDAP directory.

LDAP integration

For other LDAP directories, there is a separate agent. Let's look at how to install it. The instructions are different, depending on whether it's a Linux or Windows server. We will go through the Windows installation. Make sure you are logging into Okta on the host server and with a super administrator account. Within the admin console, go to **Directory | Directory Integrations**. Choose **Add Directory | Add LDAP Directory**. As with the AD integration, the requirements will be listed on the first page. Once you've fulfilled them, click **Set up LDAP**:

1. Click on **Download Agent**, then choose the **Download EXE installer** and download it to your server.

2. Double-click the file and run the installer. If you get prompted to allow the agent to make changes on the computer, answer **Yes**.

3. Click **Next**, then agree to the license agreement, then click **Next** again.

4. Pick your location to install the agent, then click **Install**.

After that, you get to insert information on the configuration side:

- **LDAP Server**: Input your host and port in `host:port` format
- **Root DN**: The distinguished root name of the directory, where users and groups are searched
- **Bind DN**: Administrator login credentials to bind the integration
- **Bind Password**: Administrator login credentials to bind the integration

Click **Next**. In the next window, you get to enter a proxy server for your LDAP agent, if you wish. After that, you need to register your agent with your Okta service by entering your Okta subdomain. Hit **Next**. After that, you must enter the username and password of your Okta admin account, then click **Sign in**. You will have to allow API access, then click **Finish**!

Now, it's time to apply the settings. Navigate to **Directory | Directory Integrations**. The agent for the integration you just installed should be listed as **Not yet configured**:

- **LDAP Provider**: In this dropdown, you can select what provider you have, and the fields will be automatically filled. If the one you use isn't on the list, you must enter information in the fields manually.

- **Unique Identifier Attribute**: This value gives you the unique immutable value for the users and groups imported; only objects with this value will be imported from LDAP to your Okta org.

- Verify that it's auto-populated correctly by picking the LDAP provider.

- **DN attribute**: This one comes for free if you pick an LDAP provider; it gives the attribute of all objects that contain the **distinguished name (DN)** value.

Go down to the user section to continue the configuration:

- **User Search Base**: In this field, you enter the DN of the base user subtree – that is, where you want to import your users from.

- **User Object Class**: Okta needs the object class of the users it should import.

- **User Object Filter**: You get this for free when selecting an LDAP provider at the top. The default is **Object Class**.

- **Account Disabled Attribute**: Input the attribute used to indicate whether a user is active or disabled.

- **Account Disabled Value**: This is used to input the value that indicates whether the account is locked (for instance, **TRUE**).

- **Password Attribute**: In this field, you enter the user password attribute.

- **Password Expiration Attribute**: This is usually a Boolean value and it's inserted for you if you pick an LDAP provider. If yours isn't on the list, check your LDAP server documentation for this value.

- **Extra User Attributes**: This is optional, but you get the chance to enter any other user attributes to import.

You will then finish the group or role section; typically. only one of them is used. In the **Validation** configuration section, you want to configure the following:

- **Group Search Base**: This is the root of the group structure that Okta will search in using the DN – for example, `ou=groups`, `dc=example`, or `dc=com`.

- **Group Object Class**: By adding this to Okta's query, it will filter what type of groups you want to import – for example, `groupofnames`, `groupofuniquenames`, or `posixgroup`.

- **Group Object Filter**: By default, Okta prefills this with the object class of the group.

- **Member Attribute**: Here, you can specify the attribute containing all the member DNs.

- **User Attribute**: Normally, this field is empty. Okta will classify user memberships at runtime. If you explicitly use `posixGroup`, it is recommended to configure the value with `memberUID` and the user attribute with `uid`.

In the role section, the following fields are available:

- **Object Class**: The object class of a role

- **Membership Attribute**: The attribute indicator as part of the DN string – for example, `cn=ADMIN`, `ou=roles`, `dc=example`, or `dc=com`

To make sure your setup is correct, you can validate the settings by taking the following steps:

1. Fill in the **Okta username format** field. What you enter here generates the username your users will use when they sign into Okta. This needs to be in the format of an email.

2. Enter a username to validate your setup. Okta will query the LDAP and you can validate that all returned data is correct.

3. Click **Test Configuration**. You will get a **Validation Successful!** notification regarding the username you entered.

4. Click **Next**, then **Done** – with that, your LDAP integration configuration is done!

Now that we've learned about directory integrations, let's look at users and other means of sourcing them.

Everything about users

In Okta, there are three different kinds of users: Okta-sourced, directory-sourced, and application-sourced. They have some different characteristics, so let's have a look at them.

The basics with Okta-sourced users

If you don't have any external directory, your users might be created and sourced in Okta. There are different available options to create users: one-on-one in the administrator console, via a CSV upload, or via the API.

Let's start with adding a single user:

1. In the admin console, navigate to **Directory | People**.

    Before we move on and add our users, let's look at the **People** section. At the top, you have some quick actions, such as adding a user, resetting passwords, or **More actions**, which contains even more options, such as the following:

    - **Import users from CSV**

    - **Activate**

    - **Deactivate**

    - **Disconnect from AD**

    - **Expire passwords**

    - **Unlock people**

    Under these top buttons, you get an overview of your users, along with two filtering options:

    - A search panel to search in. With an added advanced search option.

    - A status selector that allows you to filter the user list based on any status users can be in.

    Click **Add Person**; a new dialog box will appear. Let's go through the fields:

Figure 2.3 – Add Person

By default, the only available option for **User type** is **User**. If you have other kinds of users in your Okta directory, such as contractors or partners, you can set this here.

> Creating a new user type
>
> To create a user type, go to **Directory | Profile Editor**. In the top-right corner, you will see a green button for **Create Okta User Type**. Adding the new user type name and its variable name creates a copy of the default **User** user type and its 31 default attributes.

Let's get back to creating a new user. An Okta-sourced user has four required attributes, which you enter in the following boxes:

- **First name**
- **Last name**
- **Username**
- **Primary email**

You also have the option to add a secondary email. This can be used as a backup if the user loses access to their primary email and needs to reset their Okta account.

If you have groups set up in your Okta org, you can assign the user to multiple groups in the next field. In the **Activation** dropdown, you get to select whether you want the user to be activated now or later; the latter will put the user in a staged state. Lastly, you have the option to preset their password when you activate now. If you select this option, you get to enter a password, and also choose whether the user is required to set a new password on their first login. Once you are done, don't forget to click **Save**!

Another option to create users is with a CSV.

> Tip
>
> Using the CSV upload method is most useful for creating multiple users at once.

In the **People** section under **Directory**, you can find the option to use a CSV under the **More Actions** dropdown. From the dialog box that appears, you get a template to use for the import. The CSV contains columns for a lot of attributes, but when you create a user from the **Add Person** button, you need to enter at least the required four base attributes. In the CSV, the variable names, rather than the attribute names, are displayed. If you want a translation between the two, you can check it out in **Profile Editor** and pick respective the Okta profile. But for the four base attributes, it looks like this:

- `login`: Username
- `firstName`: First name
- `lastName`: Last name
- `email`: Primary email

After you're done with the CSV, import it through the dialog box. If you have any errors, it will let you know, and you can go back and correct the file. If the import runs successfully, you can click **Next**. In the next window, you get to pick how to import the users. You can choose to either automatically activate new users or **Do not create a password and only allow login via Identity Provider**. Click **Import users**. You will see a list of new, updated, and unchanged users. If there are any errors, you can see what they are by downloading the offered error report. As mentioned previously, it's also possible to create users through Okta's APIs. This will be explored further in *Chapter 8, API Access Management*.

Enriching user profiles with attributes

As mentioned previously, you can see a user's complete list of attributes in **Profile Editor**. There, you can also add attributes to the Okta default user. Navigate to **Directory | Profile Editor**, select the profile you want to edit, and then click the pencil icon. You will see the full list of attributes. Use the **Add Attributes** button to prompt a new window:

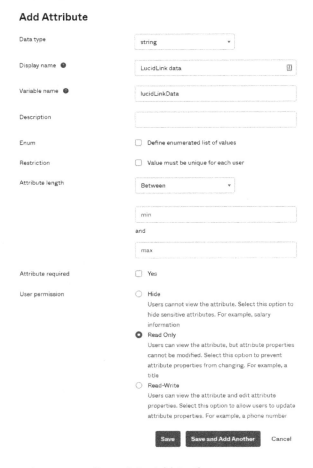

Figure 2.4 – Add Attribute

Let's input some information:

- **Data type**: Here, you can choose from 10 options:

    - **string**: Zero or more characters, such as letters, numbers, and punctuation marks

    - **number**: Floating-point decimal in Java's 64-bit double format

    - **boolean**: True, false, or null

    - **integer**: Whole numbers in Java's 64-bit long format

    - **string array**: Collection of strings in the sequence

    - **number array**: Collection of numbers in the sequence

    - **integer array**: Collection of integers in the sequence

    - **country code**: A code representing the country of origin of the user

    - **Language code**: A code representing the user's language

    - **linked object**: A code representing the user's relationship with another attribute

- **Display name**: What the admins will read.

- **Variable name**: The attribute name that will be used for mapping.

- **Description**: Enter a description for your attribute.

- **Enum**: You can create an enumerated list – for instance, small, medium, or large if your attribute is T-shirt size.

- **Restriction**: By checking this box, you require this attribute entry to be unique.

- **Attribute Length**: As its name suggests, you can decide how long and/or short the attribute entry can be.

- **Attribute required**: Check this if this attribute must be filled to be able to create a new user.

- **User permission**: This setting allows you to change the attribute's visibility on the end user side. The options are as follows:

    - **Hide**: The attribute is not visible on the end user's settings page

    - **Read Only**: The attribute is visible on the end user's settings page, but it is not editable

    - **Read-Write**: The user can see the attribute on its settings page, and can also alter the value in that attribute

Lastly, hit **Save**, or **Save and Add Another** if you want to create more attributes.

That's the basics for Okta-sourced users. Let's move on and look at directory-sourced users.

Another look at directory-sourced users

In the previous chapter, we looked at how to integrate Okta with various directories. Apart from an AD or LDAP directory, users can also be sourced by an HR system. We will dig into this in *Chapter 5, Automating Using Lifecycle Management*.

Users that are imported and synchronized from AD are based on the OU(s) you've chosen to import from. If you want to go back and check your settings or change them, you can navigate to **Directory | Directory Integration** and choose your directory. Under **Provisioning**, in the pane to the left, you will see that you can set it up both to and from Okta. Under the **To Okta** section, you will find the settings you made during the integration configuration, such as **Matching rules**. The last option, **Integration**, is where you can see what OUs you are importing both users and groups from.

If you want to trigger a new import, you can go to the **Import** tab in the current view and click **Import now**. You can select **Incremental import** or **Full import**. For an incremental import, the scan will only be for users that have been created or updated since the last import. For a full import, all current data on a user is replaced with what's in the directory. Users not found in the scan (for instance, removed from the OU) will be denied access to Okta, but not deactivated.

Attributes for a user that have been sourced by your directory can be found in the user's profile, and are read-only when sourced by an external directory.

Now, you know everything about how directories are integrated, and also how users are sourced there. Let's check how that works for users from applications – new ways of working with application-sourced users.

If your organization has been using an application such as Google Workspace as your directory before introducing Okta, you can import your users from there. To be able to start the import, you need to integrate Okta with your application environment through **Okta Integration Network (OIN)**.

With your application integrated, you must start by navigating to the **Provisioning** tab of that application. In the **To Okta** section, you will be able to configure settings for imports and matches:

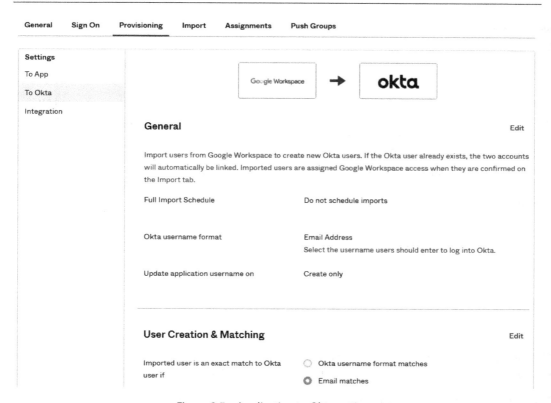

Figure 2.5 – Application to Okta settings

As with the AD integration, you get to select how to match users that are imported from the application with existing users in Okta. You can also check what you want to do with matches and new users:

- Auto-confirm exact matches
- Auto-confirm partial matches
- Auto-confirm new users
- Auto-activate new users

By clicking **Edit** in the top section, you can choose an interval for how often you want to automatically import users. If you'd rather import manually, select **never**. Then, navigate to the **Import** tab. By simply clicking **Import users**, the integration will search for new or updated users. In Okta, you will see a division of exact and partial matches, as set in the previous tab.

If your users are living in an HR application such as Workday or BambooHR, they can be sourced by that. This flow will be explained in more detail in *Chapter 5, Automating Using Lifecycle Management*.

Now that we have looked at what to do with different types of sources, we will look at how to set profile and attribute sources.

Profile and attribute sourcing

With profile sourcing, it's possible to decide what source of truth a user's attributes are dictated by. A user can only be sourced by one environment (AD, application, Okta) at any given time. Different groups or types of users can, however, be sourced by different sources. If you have an integrated application that can act as a source of truth, such as AD or Google Workspace, as in our previous examples, you can specify that the application can be used as a profile source in the provisioning settings:

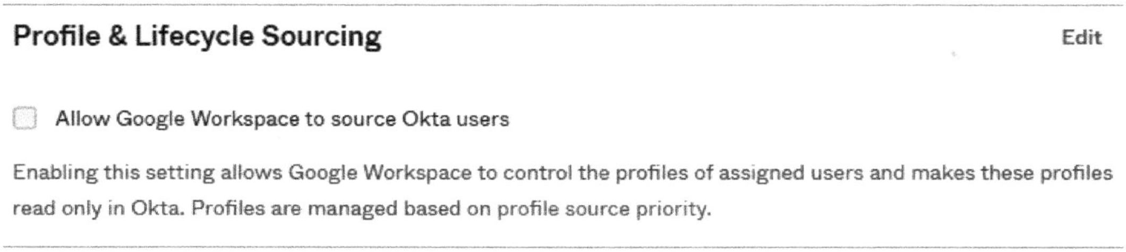

Profile & Lifecycle Sourcing   Edit

☐ Allow Google Workspace to source Okta users

Enabling this setting allows Google Workspace to control the profiles of assigned users and makes these profiles read only in Okta. Profiles are managed based on profile source priority.

Figure 2.6 – Enabling Google Workspace to source users

Simply click **Edit** and check the box to allow Google Workspace to source users. Note that it can be a problem for an application to source users if you also have the **Update User Attribute** feature in play.

Now, let's learn how to set profile sources. Navigate to **Directory | Profile Sources**. If you have more than one profile source, you will be able to set the priority order:

Profile Sources

Profile Source	Priority	
BambooHR BambooHR	1	↑ ↓
Active Directory labs.oktaadministration.local	2	↑ ↓
Google Workspace Google Workspace	3	↑ ↓

Figure 2.7 – Different profile sources and their priorities

To change the order of the priority, simply click the arrows. For users assigned to BambooHR, their profiles will be sourced by BambooHR. For users not assigned to BambooHR, their profiles will be sourced by Google Workspace. If a user is assigned to both, the highest source will be the leading one.

If this is not fine-grained enough for your organization, you can also use **attribute-level sourcing (ALS)**. With this feature, you can let data such as a name and email be sourced by an HR application, while the phone number will be sourced by AD and the secondary email will be sourced by the user.

There are a few requirements for using **ALS**:

- Profile sourcing is enabled

- You have prioritized the different profile sources

- Mapping has been set through UD mapping

You've already done the first two, so let's look at the latter. Navigate to **Directory | Profile Editor**. Go to your Okta profile and find the attribute you want to change the source of. Click the **i** icon of the attribute and, under **Source priority**, select the source of that attribute. This will only determine the source of that specific attribute; others might have different sources to abide by:

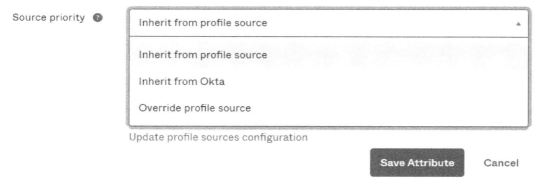

Figure 2.8 – Different options for attribute sourcing

To override the inherited source, choose **Override profile source**. You will then get to pick an alternative source. When you are done, click **Save Attribute**. Once you've done this, you will have changed the source of that specific attribute.

Now that you've learned about users, let's move on and learn how to work with groups.

Using groups

Every user needs to gain access to mail accounts, file servers, Wi-Fi, applications, and so on. Managing this on an individual case-by-case basis can become very time-consuming and repetitive work. Using groups solves this problem by allowing users to be managed in bulk. Access rights can be updated and changed, and all users within the group receive these updates as one. It simplifies the work, delivers more insight into the management of the directory, and issues are more quickly resolved in larger pieces.

Groups have existed for a long time, and the concept is still very relevant. That's why you can find group management in almost every application currently available. Okta is no exception and relies heavily on group management to consolidate user structures, application assignments, and policy enforcement.

Types of groups in Okta

An Okta org is always created with one default group – the **everyone** group. Even though this is a good name, the fact that it can't be deleted or renamed results in the group itself becoming hard to use in several instances. Assigning applications to this group allows everyone within Okta to gain access to the app. This includes any outside or third-party users that aren't part of the organization. Policies that use this group means that there is no distinction between users. In the hierarchy of policy setup, these policies should be considered last in the row as they will catch everyone. Okta can manage several different types of groups:

- Okta groups
- Directory groups
- Application groups

Okta groups are the standard grouping method within Okta Universal Directory. These groups can be created from within Okta and can be managed to do multiple things. Users can be assigned to groups. Applications can be assigned, and any provisioning for the assigned users can be managed. Directories can be attached to the groups, allowing users to be provisioned into the directory:

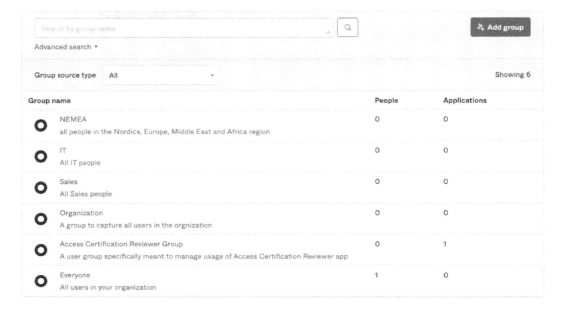

Figure 2.9 – Group interface in Okta

Creating an Okta group can be done via the admin interface. You can name the group and add additional information to clarify the group's function. Once the group has been created, it will receive a unique ID. This can't be changed but can be used in functions and API calls.

Let's create an Okta group to understand the different sections and elements. Creating an Okta group is relatively simple. Here are the steps you need to follow:

1. In the **Group** section under **Directory | Groups**, click on the blue **Add Group** button in the main window.

2. In the opened window, give the group a name that helps you understand the needs of the group.

3. Add a description to further explain the usage of the group.

4. Click **Save** to store your new group.

Right now, these attributes of the group are limited. There are just two – **Name** and **Description** – but it is possible to add more attributes to groups for further enrichment. As we explained earlier in this chapter, you can add attributes to user profiles, but in the same section under **Directory | Profile Editor**, you can also choose to add and update group attributes by clicking the **Add Attribute** button directly in the group:

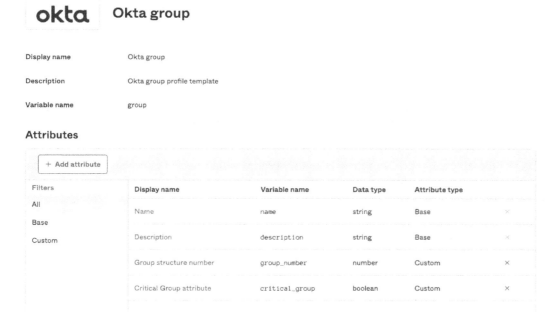

Figure 2.10 – Group Profile Editor in Okta

These attributes can be useful for adding more metadata to groups. You can use this metadata to further advance the search for groups in the **Groups** section:

Figure 2.11 – Okta's Advanced search using a custom attribute

Groups can also be created by using Okta's API. Using the API allows you to quickly create groups, especially if you need to create a lot of them in a short amount of time. We will go through this in more detail in *Chapter 8, API Access Management*.

Okta can hold different types of groups. Directory groups will be shown once you have set up the group's OU within the directory integration. These groups will be visualized with a different icon in the group list than Okta groups. These groups don't allow user assignments from Okta; it is a visual of the group in AD and can only be managed by AD. In the overview pane, you will find that the groups are prepopulated with users:

Group name		People	Applications
Sales labs.oktaadministration.local/Organization/Sales/Sales		0	0
IT labs.oktaadministration.local/Organization/IT/IT		0	0
Marketing labs.oktaadministration.local/Organization/Marketing/Marketing		0	0

Figure 2.12 – Layout of an AD group in Okta's Groups section

The users shown in those groups are users who are also in Okta. These identities have been connected, with the import and matching we went through earlier, and therefore, the group can show the corresponding users in the integrated directory. If users are not shown in the group but exist in the directory group within the directory itself, this means the user doesn't have a corresponding user identity in Okta. For instance, it can be that the user isn't in one of the OUs Okta is importing from.

Directory groups can be used to assign applications. This means that if you have a structure that works for you within your directory, you do not need to create Okta groups to recreate this structure. If you need to create more than the directory shows, adding Okta groups would be one choice; adding more groups through the directory is another. Depending on the situation, it can be advisable to leave the directory as-is and recreate the directory structure with Okta groups to have more options and capabilities. If you are thinking about replacing AD down the line, this can be a good approach.

Certain applications are capable of showing groups, just like directories do. By setting up provisioning and allowing group import, you can do this with applications such as the following:

- Google Workspace
- Office 365
- Slack
- Box
- BambooHR
- Workday
- Atlassian

The list is constantly growing, and Okta works hard to add more and more group integrations to allow even more and better management of users across all systems:

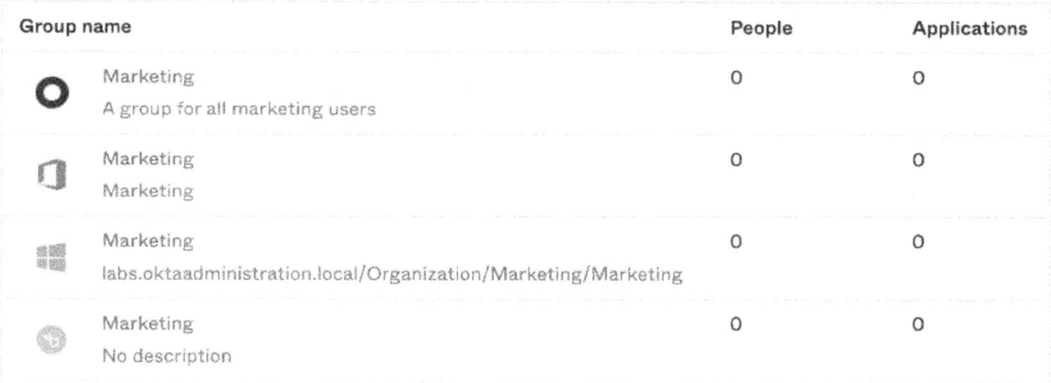

Group name		People	Applications
⬤	Marketing A group for all marketing users	0	0
◻	Marketing Marketing	0	0
▦	Marketing labs.oktaadministration.local/Organization/Marketing/Marketing	0	0
◉	Marketing No description	0	0

Figure 2.13 – Different types of groups showing the number of users in them

Application groups act the same way as directory groups do. User counts show the connected identities, and users can't be added to these groups. Applications can be assigned, but based on the fact that it's an application group, assigning other applications can be considered a bad practice.

Using AD groups

Okta has a deep integration with AD and handles AD groups based on their type:

- **Universal security groups (USGs)**
- **Distribution groups (DGs)**

These two groups are imported and handled differently when it comes to user assignments.

USGs

USGs can be imported through manual or periodic imports; when an unknown user signs in to Okta for the first time, JIT provisioning can be leveraged. Importing USGs can be done as full and incremental imports. If a user is unknown and signs in for the first time to Okta between imports, Okta will check whether the user is a part of the domain, import any USGs that the user is part of within the synchronized OUs, and import the user with its corresponding profile. This allows Okta to always be up to date on any changes during events triggered by users when logging in.

If a user logs into Okta and their USG is outside of the domain, the USG will not be imported, but the user will be added individually to Okta. If the second domain gets added later, or if the OU in which the USG resides is added for synchronization, any new USGs will be imported into Okta during the next scheduled import or manual import or added when a user is JIT provisioned.

Once domains have been added, Okta can see within them. With OUs that have been selected to synchronize, Okta is capable of joining users together that are part of different domains. Users who are manually moved out of the synchronized domain and/or OUs will no longer have access to Okta and integrated services. This method is commonly used by AD administrators.

Okta isn't capable of detecting nested groups within the synchronized groups. Okta will see the users of these nested groups as users within the parent group and treat them as such. If this happens accidentally, Okta will not be able to roll back the assignments. This can result in unwanted assignments. JIT provisioning will be able to resolve this problem and remove the user from the synchronized parent group. This does require oversight as users themselves need to log in; an admin cannot do this for them.

DGs

DGs are handled differently than USGs. Okta handles user assignments in this aspect.

The synchronization of users assigned to USG within a linked domain will occur during both scheduled and manual imports, as well as during JIT provisioning, as facilitated by the mentioned platform.

However, for DG', synchronization is only permitted during scheduled and manual imports, with JIT provisioning being an exception to this.

This will mean that if a user is eligible to sign into Okta and hasn't been imported, their DG assignment in Okta has not been updated. This will result in login problems. Having the periodic import schedule set to every hour, which is the shortest import schedule, will, in most cases, be sufficient to resolve this problem.

Users that are part of a DG, where the DG is a member of a USG, will not inherit Okta access if the USG is not imported into Okta via a regular import.

Okta will not see the child DG, and thus its users, while JIT provisioning is occurring. Regular imports will be needed to allow membership of parent groups to be reflected in Okta.

Creating users in AD through Okta groups

User management can also be done from Okta. You can provision users into AD by using dedicated Okta groups. This allows you to create group-assigned users in the corresponding OUs you set up synchronization with. This allows quick and bi-directional user management. It allows more granular management, and if AD has specific OUs you want your users to reside in, you can attach all of these OUs to corresponding Okta groups. Each of these can have different setups and reasoning to do so.

Additionally, you can synchronize the users with extra AD attributes filled with Okta profile attribute values. This will synchronize valuable details across all your profile environments. Simply put, you can make sure your users have the correct details from and to the AD and Okta during any moment in their lifecycle.

Pushing groups

Pushing groups is a functionality that lets you create or manage existing groups in directories and applications. To be able to do a group push, the target application has to be set up with provisioning. While some applications have good integrations, others are limited. If the target app supports group push, new groups can be created. If the target app also supports enhanced group push, Okta can take control of existing groups in the app and there is no need to recreate the group structure. During this overtake of groups, Okta will overwrite the existing app group name with the Okta pushed group name. This might need further investigation within the application to see whether this is a desired outcome.

Here are some elements to consider while setting up group push:

- The group push requires application provisioning.
- Group members assigned to the synchronized group have to be previously provisioned and assigned to the target application.
- Pushing AD groups requires permission to create and manage users within groups based on the AD service account used in the integration.

- Okta won't allow groups to be pushed that are also used to provision users in the same target application.

- Usage of other application groups is allowed. However, be careful with using other application groups or directory groups as these can change based on internal management.

You can set up pushed groups within the **Push Groups** tab of a target application. Upon clicking the **Push Groups** tab, you will be presented with a configuration window:

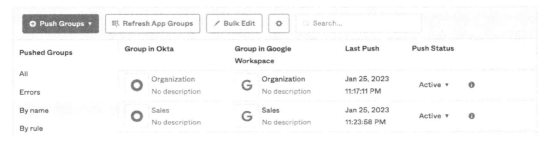

Figure 2.14 – Push group for an application

Clicking on the blue **Push Groups** button allows you to start setting up a pushed group. Okta allows you to do this manually by selecting a group by name, or even by using rule-based automation to add groups based on conditions:

Push Groups to Google Workspace

Figure 2.15 – The Push Groups button

Let's set up a group push rule. First, we will explain how to do it manually. After that, we'll learn how to set up a rule-based group push.

You can set up a group push manually by following these steps:

1. Click **Push Groups**.
2. Select **Find groups by name**.
3. Search for the desired group to push.
4. Optionally, select **Push group membership immediately**.

This allows you to work with different options. Depending on your integration, you can have either the option to create a group or the option to choose between creating or linking to an existing group. In both scenarios, the options are the same:

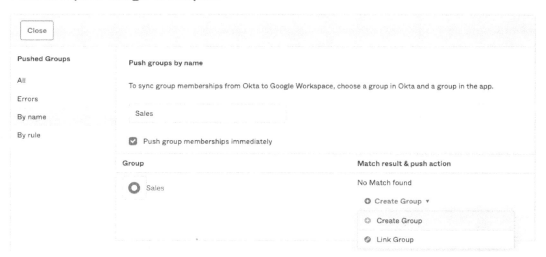

Figure 2.16 – Push groups matching options

Choose to either create a new group or a link group.

If you selected **New Group**, do the following:

1. Create the new group.
2. Set the desired application group name.

If you selected **Link Group**, do the following:

1. Select the desired group you want to link to.
2. Click **Save**.

If you are going to use the group push with rules, the setup differs slightly. Let's see how that is done. Click **Push Groups** and then follow these steps:

1. Select **Find Groups by rule**.

2. Give the rule a name.

3. Create the rule with either name conditions or description conditions – for example, *Push all groups with "Sales" in the name to the target app*.

4. Optionally, you can select **Immediately push groups found by this rule**. If you do not choose this option, groups added to the list will be inactive until they are set to active.

This will only allow new groups to be pushed.

Group push rules will find all groups across all applications and directories. This means it can have a huge impact if certain applications have similar group names that are found by the group push rule.

> Tip
>
> If you have multiple groups with the same name from incoming directories or groups, place those named groups into a new Okta group with a more unique name, and synchronize that into the target application. Alternatively, you can utilize the group description to be even more granular and filter those values for mass group push actions.

It can be that groups that have been pushed to the target app won't respond or have trouble synchronizing users. Turning the push rule off and on will trigger a new synchronization. It is a common mistake that users are added to the pushed group but not to the provisioned group and are therefore not visible in the target app or directory.

Sometimes, new groups in the target app don't appear for linking. Using the **Refresh App Groups** function will do a fresh import of the groups from the target app:

Push Groups to Google Workspace

Figure 2.17 – The Refresh App Groups button

If, for some reason, you want to delete a pushed group, you can choose to deactivate the group push. This will stop any further synchronization of the group toward the target app or directory, but the current pushed group in the app or directory will keep existing with its current set of users. You can also choose to unlink the group; this will present you with the extra option of deleting the group in the target app or directory:

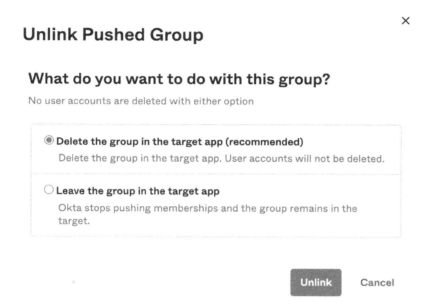

Figure 2.18 – Dialog window with options to unlink pushed groups

By selecting the recommended option, Okta will delete the group, and users in that group will not be deprovisioned or lose access to the application or directory. The group itself will no longer be available and functionalities within the application or directory will no longer apply to those users based on the group that's been pushed.

You can also bulk edit groups by selecting the **Bulk Edit** option. Additional tick boxes will appear beside the groups. You can then either choose to deactivate the group sync or delete the groups from the target application or directory:

Push Groups to Google Workspace

Figure 2.19 – How to bulk edit pushed groups

When setting up a pushed group, Okta allows linking groups from within Okta to the target application or directory. By default, the group will be named as the group it's linked to. Optionally, you can turn that off and allow the original name to exist within the target application or directory. It can be somewhat troublesome to find the correct links if those names differ a lot, but if there are justified reasons not to change them, this option will be your method of choice:

Push Groups to Google Workspace

Figure 2.20 – Icon to access settings

Turning off this feature after you have already linked groups will not reinstate the original names of the target groups. These will stay changed. Only new groups that have been pushed will follow this option:

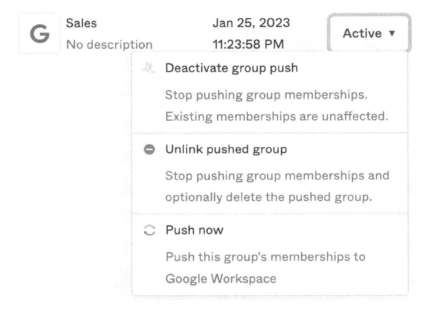

Figure 2.21 – Options for pushed groups

If you choose not to push immediately during the setup of a group push, you can force it to push in the main screen after saving the group push. This will trigger a forced push to the target group.

Deleting groups

Deleting a group can sometimes be a good habit to keep your directory clean. Having all these groups in the group list can create unwanted double entries and longer loading times, and make it harder to find groups using search.

The different types of groups can be deleted in different ways, but there are some common elements to consider:

- Okta groups can be deleted regardless of applications and user assignments.

- Application groups can be deleted in bulk through the **Integrations** tab of the provisioning settings, by unticking the **Import Groups** box.

- Application groups won't be deleted if they're still in use by group rules, policies, and push group mappings.

- Directory groups can be deleted by deleting or removing them from synchronized OUs in the directory. Okta will update accordingly during an upcoming import.

- Using the API, Okta and application groups can be deleted if previous steps are considered.

- Application groups that are deleted through the API will be re-imported by the application on the next import.

By not being too dependent on imported groups, application groups won't have too much impact on the directory setup of Okta.

> **Important note**
> Additionally, nowhere in the group interface is it clear if the group is used for policies. When you have workflows, you can use cards to list the group usage. Deleting groups can have an impact on how policies behave. Be aware of this and double-check whether the group is used in any way before deleting a group from Okta.

Assigning applications to groups

Setting up applications can be quite daunting, and doing it on a per-person basis is simply tedious work. Using groups can alleviate the pain and allow for more structural management of app assignments. Any type of application can be added to any type of group in Okta. This allows granular management based on Okta, directory, and application groups.

Applications that have been assigned to groups have no hierarchical priority, and management is done in one simple interface. Depending on the type of application being provisioned, or the sign-on settings being configured, the group can be used in different and combined methods.

The simplest method is to add **single sign-on** (**SSO**) applications. Users are assigned to the application based on their group membership, and will therefore follow the needed sign-on method, configured for that specific application.

Applications that have been assigned to groups with provisioning will ask for more group-based configurations to make sure all assigned users receive the same provisioning in the application.

Lastly, you can combine sign-on methods with provisioning in an assigned application in a group.

As applications might need more than one group to configure their users, multiple groups can allow more granular management of the following (you are not limited to these options):

- Profile attributes

- Licenses

- Roles

In certain cases, a combination of groups can be used to add multiple attribute values to the user while provisioning the user into the target application. Think of combining license types for Office 365 by using and assigning them through different groups, or combining multiple permission sets in Salesforce by having users be part of different groups to do just that.

Setting up the various provisioning methods will be discussed in more detail in *Chapter 5, Automating Using Lifecycle Management*.

Now that we've learned about different types of groups and how to use them, we will look at some best practices.

Some best practices for group usage

Here are some best practices on how to use the different types of groups in Okta:

- **Structuring the groups**: Creating structure in groups helps with better oversight, organization, and management of what they do and what they are used for. Reflecting on your organization will make it easy to understand what access is based on, and normally, that organizational structure will be the cornerstone for any application setup needed. Trying to map out the deepest and smallest end groups will allow you to be as granular as possible.

- **Using the groups**: Setting up a policy for how you will be using groups that make sense to your organization will help in your overall group usage in other ways as well. The same group that's used to assign sales applications can also be used for sales policies, and be pushed into applications as the sales group. This means that one group can do multiple things.

- **Specific application groups**: In some scenarios, you can't simply automate within the organizational structure. But by numbering a group range specifically for applications, you can always find and structure it in a way that shows the different groups that are used for different applications. Usually, these are used for provisioning different licenses or roles. Creating a group prefix that separates the groups, such as `APP - Salesforce - sales team -US`, helps with distinguishing the groups from each other. Having that prefix will keep the Okta groups together, and make them easier to find in the search functionality. Import only as necessary.

If you are setting applications up with provisioning, but you see no need for the groups to be imported, don't turn it on. Okta will be able to import quicker and the groups will not show up in your search queries. If you want to do this from AD, you can filter just the groups you want to import by using the **Group Filter** function. This will not import all groups. Group filtering is only available for directories.

- **Using directory groups**: If you are heavily reliant on your directory, it may be the best move not to recreate the group structure again with Okta groups. Even though they might have some more benefits, managing two sides of the coin will allow more error and more interpretation when troubleshooting. As AD and LDAP have a special relationship with Okta, it might be wise not to do so.

  On the other hand, if you are looking for a way to divert from your directory, or legacy decisions have resulted in a messy structure, recreating a fresh and strong Okta group structure can be very helpful for your usage toward applications and other possible directories.

- **Using application groups**: Usually, application groups already exist before Okta integrates with the app. Most of the time, the structure of the app has been owned by someone other than the IT or security team that is going to manage Okta. This can lead to fragmented and possible overuse of groups within that application. Using that as a structure to manage your users in Okta and toward other applications and directories is not considered a wise method; especially when the groups are used for policies, the application owner might *unknowingly* scramble the groups and in doing so remove access management.

  Using the application groups to allow group push or group rules to synchronize users from an application group to an Okta group is considered the best way to use these. Alternatively, if the import simply adds to many groups, but you still want to manage users in those, workflows might be the second-best thing. We discuss this in more detail in *Chapter 7, Okta Workflows*.

  If you are setting up the structure with specific naming conventions, consider turning off the overwrite application group names function since this can have an impact on the application. This is highly dependent on your situation and setup.

- **Removing deactivated users from groups**: For a simple overview of users in any one group, it's good to make sure you clean out deactivated users from them. The smartest way to do this is by setting up an Okta workflow, which goes through Okta groups and removes deactivated users on a schedule.

We will discuss these features and more in *Chapter 7, Okta Workflows*.

Now that we've covered how to work with groups and some best practices, let's look at the last thing that can be managed by UD – devices.

Overview of devices

With the **Devices** section in UD, organizations can get a better picture of which devices have access to Okta. It adds end user context and can be used in contextual-based access policies. Lastly, the use of Fastpass provides an opportunity to leverage a passwordless experience on an Okta-connected device. Fastpass will be discussed in more detail in *Chapter 3, Using Single Sign-On for a Great End User Experience*. It's important to note that this is not a replacement for any **mobile device management** (**MDM**) system. It's a function to connect a certain device to Okta and cross-connect that device to a user to give more security to the organization. Let's discover what we can do.

Registering a device

An administrator can't register a device in the Okta administration portal. Instead, the device is registered when a user uses a device to enroll with Okta Verify. If you navigate to **Directory** > **Devices**, you will see a list of all devices that have been registered in your Okta org. Any user can be associated with multiple devices, and vice versa. When you go to a user profile in Okta, you can find the associated devices there too:

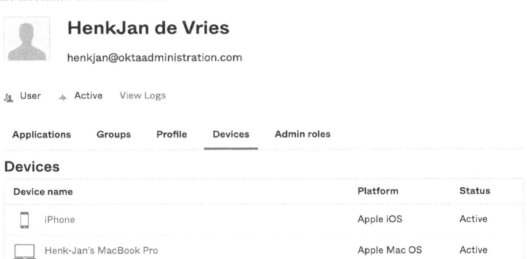

Figure 2.22 – Registered device in a user profile

In the list of devices, you can see if the device is **Managed** or **Not managed**. This status indicates whether a separate MDM system is integrated with Okta, and if the device is managed by that MDM. With this integration in place, management hints (for mobile devices) or management attestation certificates (for desktops) are deployed to the devices and checked when needed for access to Okta and/or applications.

Additionally, the device overview section will show what type of platform the devices are being used on. Lastly, it will allow you, as an admin, to suspend or deactivate a device. This can be useful when a device might be compromised or when the user switches devices.

Summary

In this chapter, we learned about UD and what we can do with it. We looked at how to integrate with existing directories, and you now have a good understanding of how to install and configure the different agents you might need. We also looked at the different kinds of users that Okta handles, and how to work with their attributes using profile sourcing. Then, we took a deep dive into the different types of groups available, and how to use them to make workloads easier – for instance, for assignments. Additionally, we highlighted some best practices for when you set up and work with your groups. Lastly, we described the **Devices** section and how it can be interpreted and used from an administrator's perspective.

In the next chapter, we will dive into Okta's SSO capabilities, showing how to utilize OIN and custom applications.

3

Using Single Sign-On for a Great End User Experience

Single sign-on (**SSO**) is a very end user friendly feature. But it also has great security benefits that will make any IT administrator happy. Bringing all authentication into one place doesn't only make it easier for end users; it also delivers a single pane of glass for administrators with ease.

In this chapter, we will look at Okta's SSO functionalities and how they will help your end users. We will look at how you can utilize the **Okta Integration Network** (**OIN**), but before that, we will look into the different connections you can make with various applications. We will also look at the difference between Okta and application-initiated sign-on flows, as well as IdP discovery.

We will look at the following topics in this chapter:

- Using single sign-on with Okta
- Using Fastpass for easy sign-on
- Using the Okta dashboard
- Setting up Agentless Desktop single sign-on
- The Okta Integration Network
- Using Secure Web Authentication applications
- Using SAML and OpenID Connect applications
- Managing inbound SSOIdP discovery

Using single sign-on with Okta

While we will talk a lot about logging into different types of applications and their security steps, Okta, of course, has its own sign-in options. This is, in general, the cornerstone of every end user's experience. When a user signs into Okta, it won't require any further password inputs in any application. This first encounter with Okta's SSO ensures that the user has identified themselves according to the global session policies. They are now allowed to sign in to any integrated applications assigned to them unless specific application policies have been set up.

The login process for Okta is straightforward and doesn't ask for any high-level understanding of the process. Signing in is as simple as any other application, but on the backend, you will see that Okta allows for a much more granular methodology, making sure all sign-ins are checked against any policy that has been set up.

Every Okta **organization** (**org**) is created with an `Okta.com` subdomain. These subdomains are determined at the moment the contract is signed with Okta, and changing them is difficult for Okta to do. Making sure you have the right one that your users remember is key.

> **Note**
>
> You can also create your own (sub)domain for accessing Okta. This will allow it to be even more part of your organization's strategy, visibly attached to your corporate structure. We will discuss this in detail in *Chapter 6, Customizing Your Okta GUI*.

As Okta wants to keep security as strong as possible, you will find that any subdomain will show you a login screen. This is to fend off bad parties in search of Okta orgs to start doing password spray attacks. Your end users could therefore also end up on a dummy subdomain, so making sure that your org is identifiable to your end users is important. Using Okta's option to set a sign-in background and login widget logo will help to identify the correct Okta org.

The sign-on policies are created in hierarchical order. When the Okta org is created, a default login policy is added to ensure anyone can log in from the start. Adding more policies to reflect your organization is highly preferable. Okta can offer different policies for different needs. Let's take a look at the different policy options and their settings.

Understanding global session policies

In the **Okta Identity Engine** (**OIE**), passwords are no longer a central requirement to access Okta. The access policy for Okta itself is now under the **global session policy** (**GSP**) section. Even though it might seem logical to have separate policies for logging in to Okta and perhaps adding sign-on policies for applications, in OIE, every access is considered an application access. This means that the Okta dashboard, the Okta Admin Console, the Okta browser plugin, and applications can all have separate access policies.

GSPs are contextual policies that help the user advance to authentication policies depending on their requirements. They control how long the overall session will be valid. Controlling for authentication is done via authentication policies. We will go through the setup of these later in this chapter.

When in the admin console, go to **Security | Global Session Policy** to create, edit, and manage all your global session policies. Global session policies are set up in several steps.

First, you create a new GSP by clicking on the **Add Policy** button. You will be presented with the option to name the policy, add a description to it, and assign it to a group:

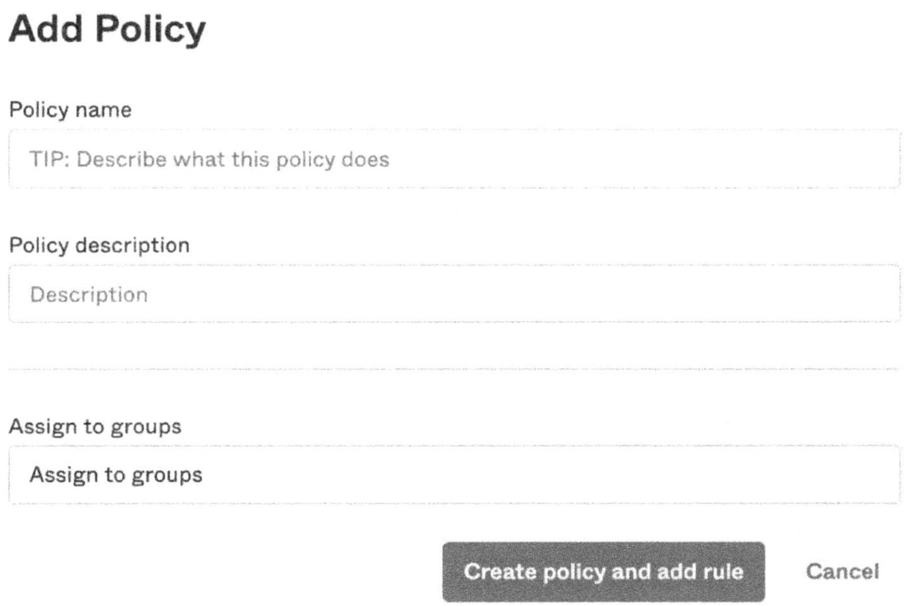

Add Policy

Policy name

TIP: Describe what this policy does

Policy description

Description

Assign to groups

Assign to groups

Create policy and add rule   Cancel

Figure 3.1 – Setting for Global Session Policy

After this is done, you can create a first rule in that policy. Without one, the policy will not be functional.

A rule contains three separate sections:

- General information
- Policy settings
- Session management

In the general section, you can set a descriptive **Rule name** and exclude any individual users who should bypass this rule. It is wise to be as descriptive as possible for the **Rule name**, as one policy can have multiple rules, understanding the meaning of each is of great value:

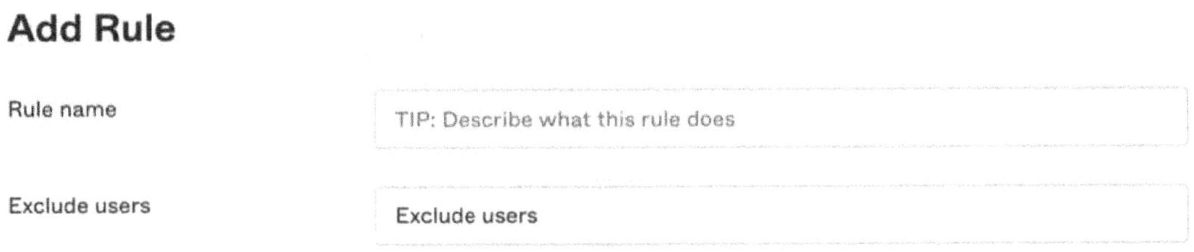

Add Rule

Rule name

TIP: Describe what this rule does

Exclude users

Exclude users

Figure 3.2 – Settings for adding a rule

In the policy settings, a simple `IF/AND/THEN` method is used to make sure users are correctly filtered through. The second part of the policy setup is creating the outcome a user needs to abide by. Here, we set the security elements for the users. Let's go through each part of this section:

- **IF User's IP is**: This is the option to select whether a user has to be part of a zone or whether the rule applies to users coming in from any specific IP

- **AND Identity Provider is**: This filter allows you to choose between any IdP, specifically Okta or an IdP you have set up

- **AND Authenticates via**: Additionally, a choice can be made for whether the users authenticates via any source or an LDAP interface

- **And Behavior is**: This is any behavior set up as part of the behavior detection that you want to add as a condition for this rule

- **THEN Access is**: Lastly, here you can choose whether the user is allowed access or is denied based on the combination of outcomes

In *Figure 3.3*, we see these settings with the dropdowns. They are not mandatory, but can help refine your policy rule:

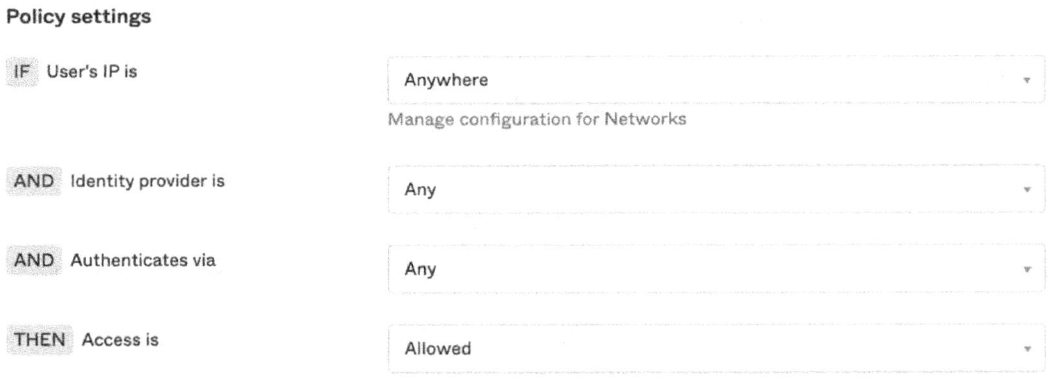

Policy settings

IF   User's IP is

Anywhere

Manage configuration for Networks

AND   Identity provider is

Any

AND   Authenticates via

Any

THEN   Access is

Allowed

Figure 3.3 – Policy settings

If access is allowed, that means we can determine how a user needs to authenticate. The next part of the **Policy settings** screen provides further options. With **Establish the user session with**, you can choose to allow any factor that meets the authentication policy for the access required. Alternatively, you can select **Password** as a requirement, regardless of any additional authentication policies. Let's go through these options:

> **Note**
>
> If a user hasn't set up a password, the user might be denied access based on this setting. We will go through the sign-in options later in this chapter.

- **Multifactor Authentication (MFA)**: Here, you determine whether MFA is required for access or if you allow the authentication policies to determine general access to Okta. If you set this setting to **Required**, the next setting will become available.

- **Users will be prompted for MFA**: This setting allows you to dictate when the user is prompted for MFA. It can be set to the following options:

  - **At every sign in**: This will prompt the user every time it is required to authenticate against Okta

  - **When signing in with a new device cookie**: This will challenge users when they try to log in with a new device or have cleared their browser cookies during the last session

> **Note**
>
> Using device cookie sign-in should be considered a low-risk use case setting.

The last section of this process is **Session management**. Here, we establish what a user needs to do to keep their Okta session alive.

- **Maximum Okta session lifetime**: You can decide to set no limit to the session or have the session expire after a certain period of time.

- **Expire session after user has been idle on Okta for**: This is a secondary expiry setting that makes sure the session is killed if the user has been inactive for a prolonged period.

> **Note**
>
> Okta considers inactivity to be the period in which the user is not active and doesn't click on an Okta page. For example, a user logs in in the morning and has the Okta dashboard open in a tab but never goes back to it.

- **Persist session cookies across browser sessions**: This will allow the use of cookies in the browser to make sure the user is not re-prompted to log in. Turning it off means that users might be prompted more often to sign in.

We will go through MFA and how to set this up in *Chapter 4, Increasing Security with Adaptive Multifactor Authentication*.

Now that we have added a Global Session Policy, let's look at adding authentication policies.

Authentication policies are rules that conditionally look for group assignments, applications, and rules that are used to grade the user's login attempts with a risk factor. Based on those conditions, a user is either allowed, denied, or required to step up their security.

To set up the policy, click on the blue **Add a policy** button:

Authentication policies   ❶ Help

Define how a user must authenticate to gain access to an app

Add a policy		Search...
Policy name	**Applies to**	
Any two factors Default Require two factors to access.	9 Apps View all Workflows *bamboo-ii Google Workspace	

Figure 3.4 – Adding a new Okta authentication policy

Then, you will be presented with a small window with a couple of text fields, as seen in *Figure 3.5*:

Add Authentication Policy

Name	
Description	

Save   Cancel

Figure 3.5 – Okta general sign-on policy settings

The window contains the following fields:

- **Name**
- **Description**

After you click on **Save**, you will be presented with an overview of the rules for that policy. A default rule is created, and you can't make any changes to the conditions in that rule. The actions are editable. We will go over that part in the next section, and it will apply to the default rule too. To create an additional rule, click **Add Rule**.

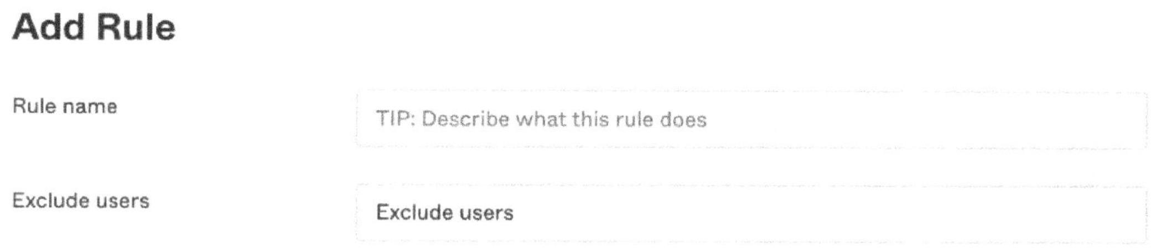

Add Rule

Rule name	TIP: Describe what this rule does
Exclude users	Exclude users

Figure 3.6 – Okta sign-on policy rule settings

In this window, you can use multiple conditions to check and set the security that is needed. This rule engine also works with an `IF/AND/THEN` methodology.

The options are as follows:

- **Rule Name**

The following options under **IF** are as follows:

- **User's user type is**: **Any usertype** or **One of the following user types** let you search any user types you have created in the **Profile Editor**

The options under **AND** are as follows:

- **User's group membership includes**: You can search for and select any groups that this rule should apply to.

- **User is**: Here, you select one or multiple users who are specifically required for this rule.

- **Device state is**: Select between **Any** or **Registered** (which requires Okta Verify as an enabled authenticator). When **Registered** is selected, the next option appears:

  - **Device Management is**: You can choose between **Not managed** or **Managed**. The actual settings for device management are changes in the device management menu. See *Chapter 4, Increasing Security with Adaptive Multifactor Authentication,* for details on how to do this.

- **Device Assurance policy is**: This can be set to **No policy** or **Any of the device assurance policies**. The predefined device assurance policies you have set up under the device assurance policy menu will be visible to choose from in a drop-down menu.

- **Device platform is**: This setting will be available if the previous is set to **No policy**. Here, you can select **Any** or **One of the following platforms**, where you get a dropdown with all available platforms (such as Windows, macOS, and iOS).

- **User's IP is**: **Any IP**, **In any network zone defined in Okta**, **In any of the following zones**, **Not in any network zone defined in Okta**, and **Not in any of the following zones** are options allowing you to select from zones you have set up (see how to do this in *Chapter 4: Increasing Security with Adaptive Multifactor Authentication*).

- **The following custom expression is true**: Here, add any statement with expression language. This will allow you to add even more specific device granularity by filtering or referencing device attributes that seem required for this authentication rule.

> **Note**
>
> See the following link for a detailed list of options, expressions, and device attributes you can add to your policy rule:
>
> `https://help.okta.com/oie/en-us/Content/Topics/identity-engine/devices/el-device-attributes.htm`

- Options under **THEN** are as follows

- **Access is**: **Allowed after successful authentication** or **Denied**

If access is allowed, the following **AND** statements will become available:

- **User must authenticate with**: Here, you can pick an option from a selection of combinations of passwords and factors. It will also allow you to have the user use any two factors the user is enrolled with. It can be that the types required to authenticate are not present for the user. A window will show you which factors would allow authentication to happen.

- **Possession factor constraints are** (optional): Select between **Phishing resistant**, **Hardware protected**, and **Exclude phone and email authenticators**. These constraints can help fortify your security measures for accessing applications. They allow you to be even more rigorous with regard to the type of device used, its posture, and its functionality.

- **If Okta FastPass is used**: Choose whether a user needs to approve a prompt on the desktop for Okta or, alternatively, use biometrics. This is seen in *Figure 3.7* (*Chapter 4* covers more on how to set up FastPass):

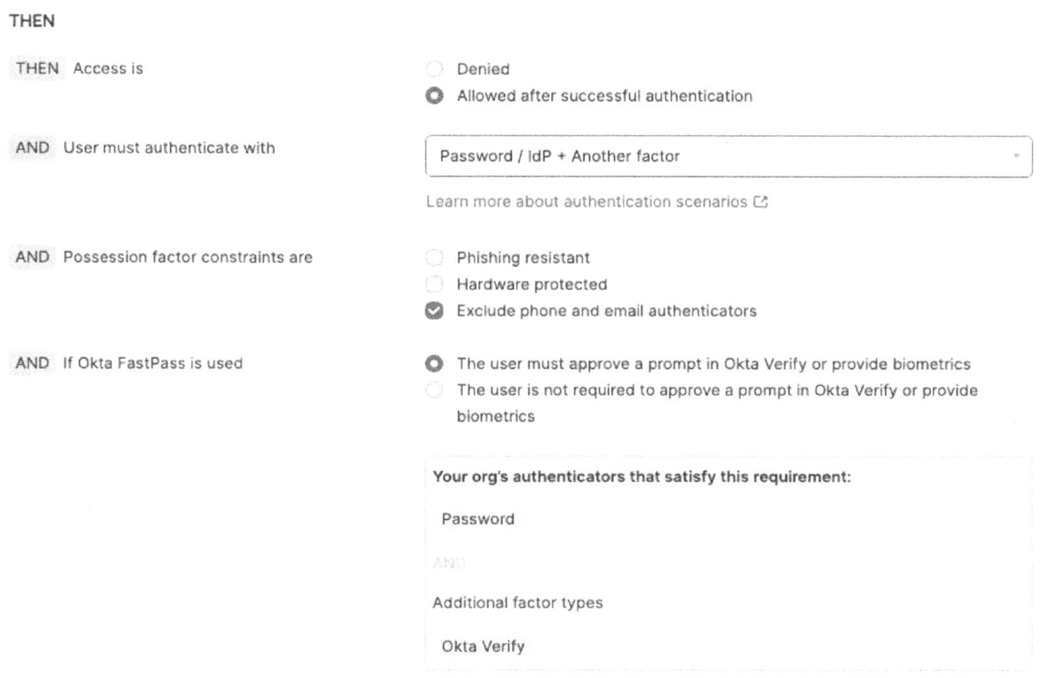

THEN

| THEN | Access is | ○ Denied |
| | | ● Allowed after successful authentication |

AND   User must authenticate with

> Password / IdP + Another factor

Learn more about authentication scenarios ☐

AND   Possession factor constraints are

○ Phishing resistant
☐ Hardware protected
✓ Exclude phone and email authenticators

AND   If Okta FastPass is used

● The user must approve a prompt in Okta Verify or provide biometrics
○ The user is not required to approve a prompt in Okta Verify or provide biometrics

Your org's authenticators that satisfy this requirement:

Password

AND

Additional factor types

Okta Verify

Figure 3.7 – Okta sign-on policy rule settings

Lastly, we have a couple of settings for re-authentication, which have **AND** statements. These are divided between passwords and all other factors, allowing you to have stricter rules for passwords compared to more secure factors:

- **Password re-authentications frequency is: Every sign-in attempt**, **Never re-authenticate if the session is active**, and **Re-authenticate after** where you set a number of minutes, hours, or days

- **Re-authenticate frequency for all other factors are: Every sign-in attempt**, **Never re-authenticate if the session is active** and **Re-authenticate after** where you set the number of minutes, hours, or days

You enter a number and select a unit in the drop-down menu, as shown in *Figure 3.8*:

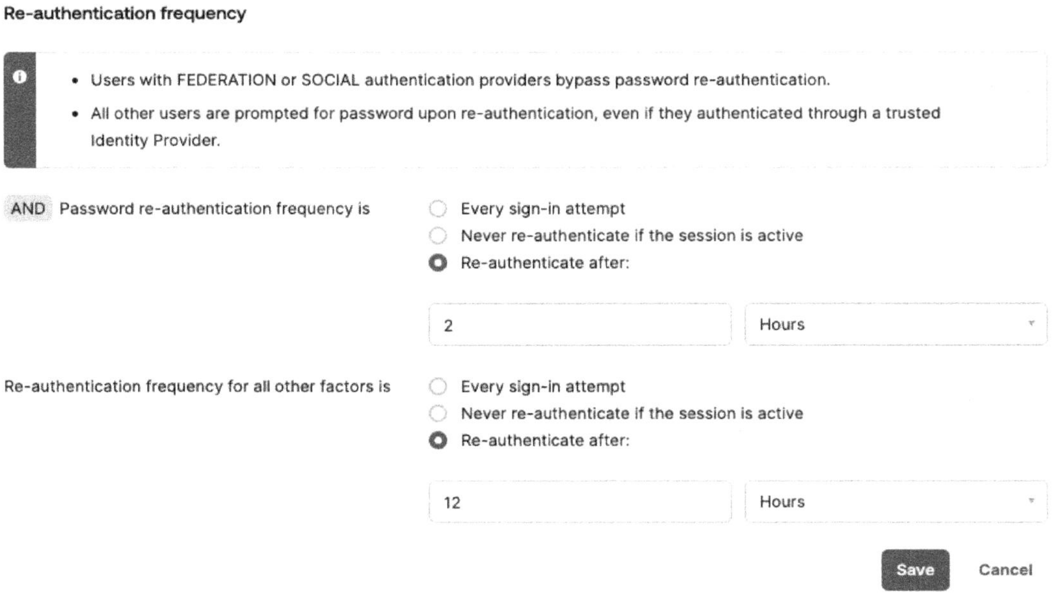

Re-authentication frequency

> ⓘ
> - Users with FEDERATION or SOCIAL authentication providers bypass password re-authentication.
> - All other users are prompted for password upon re-authentication, even if they authenticated through a trusted Identity Provider.

AND Password re-authentication frequency is

- ◯ Every sign-in attempt
- ◯ Never re-authenticate if the session is active
- ⦿ Re-authenticate after:

| 2 | Hours ▾ |

Re-authentication frequency for all other factors is

- ◯ Every sign-in attempt
- ◯ Never re-authenticate if the session is active
- ⦿ Re-authenticate after:

| 12 | Hours ▾ |

Save Cancel

Figure 3.8 – Okta sign-on policy rule settings

> **Tip**
> Since you set these rules per application, you can have stricter rules for business-critical systems and lower rules for non-critical systems.

These frequency settings are separate from the session times you might have set up in the Global Session Policy, so make sure you coordinate them in a way that makes sense to your security policies in general while also balancing the aspects of security versus friction for your end users.

There have been a lot of settings, but now you are ready to click **Save**. You can create more rules and have them apply to different groups, user types, or users. It's a good idea to list your applications and divide them into different categories and see if you can set the same authentication policy and rules for multiple apps. This will save you some work.

Using the Okta dashboard

Okta gives users a great experience by having a dashboard that all the user's applications are on. End users can arrange which apps go where and move them into different tabs to manage their environment even better. Okta's dashboard allows end users to set their personal passwords in applications and change and update these passwords later on. We will go through this in more detail later in this chapter.

Depending on the settings, they can also add personal applications through the personal application store, which has over 5,000 applications. This only includes applications with passwords because end users cannot integrate Okta with other applications themselves.

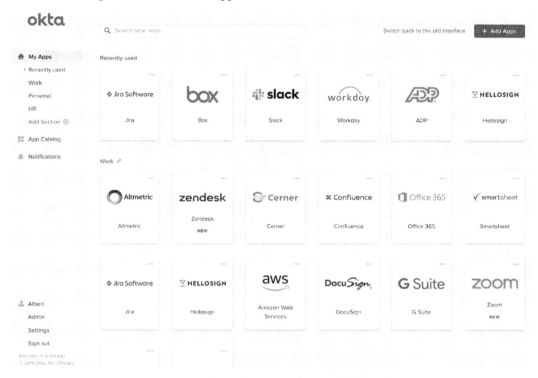

Figure 3.9 – An end user's application dashboard

Once a new application is added, the users will see a notification bubble after they get onto the dashboard. If they don't read it, the notification will stay available in the menu on the left under **Notifications**.

Within the same menu, the user can also edit their profile, which they can manage themselves. We will further deep-dive into this in *Chapter 6, Customizing Your Okta GUI*. Next, let's look how we can set up Agentless Desktop single sign-on.

Setting up Agentless Desktop single sign-on

To allow Desktop Single Sign On, **Agentless Desktop single sign-on** (**ADSSO**) is required in an Okta Identity Engine tenant. If you have a classic Okta tenant, you can use either the **Integrated Windows Authentication** (**IWA**) agent or ADSSO. For the IWA agent, we refer you to the Okta help pages.

To set up ADSSO, you are required to set up a service account and set up a **Service Principal Name** (**SPN**) for that account. The service account itself doesn't require additional privileges, but it will need permission to set the SPN.

Please read Microsoft's documentation on delegating authority to SPNs:

`https://learn.microsoft.com/en-us/previous-versions/windows/it-pro/`
`windows-server-2012-R2-and-2012`

> **Tip**
> ADSSO doesn't work if a user is a member of more than 600 security groups or if the Kerberos token is too large for Okta to consume. In those cases, the user will be redirected to the regular sign-in page with a 400 response.

Please follow the next steps to create a service account to set up ADSSO:

1. To open the **Active Directory Users and Computers** (**ADUC**), and then **Microsoft Management Console** (**MMC**) console on the Active Directory server, click **Start** > **Run**, enter dsa.msc, and press *Enter*.

2. Select the location where you want to create the service account and select **New** > **User**.

3. Fill in the minimum required fields according to your user policies and AD's requirements.

4. Click **Next**.

5. On the next screen, make sure you set a password, confirm your input, and untick the **User must change password at the next logon** box.

6. After that, click **Next** and **Finish**.

7. After *step 6*, go to the newly created users, right-click for properties, and select the **Account** tab. Here, select **This account supports Kerberos AES 128-bit encryption** or **This account supports Kerberos AES 256-bit encryption** check boxes in the **Account Options** area. Then, click **Apply**.

8. Additionally, create a group policy that enables AES encryption. This group policy can be set up on a domain controller or on the server the Okta agent is installed on. Policies such as these apply to the entire domain.

9. Lastly, we need to configure an SPN for the service account by opening a command prompt and running the following command:

   ```
   setspn -S HTTP/<oktasubdomain>.kerberos.<okta/
   oktapreview/okta-emea>.com <serviceaccount>
   ```

Once we have set up the service account with SPN privileges, we can now configure browsers to work with ADSSO on Windows and macOS.

In the following steps, we will explain how to set up Chrome on a Windows device. ADSSO does support multiple browsers and different operating systems. To make ADSSO available, you can follow the next steps:

1. Add a **Group Policy Object** (**GPO**) on a Windows server to apply IWA and URL settings to all domain-joined windows devices.

2. Enable IWA on the browser.

3. Add Okta's URLs to the local intranet in **Internet Explorer** (**IE**). Okta URLs added should be in the format: `https://subdomain.kereberos.okta.com`.

To make sure Chrome will work with the mentioned settings, we need to add the Okta URL to the Chrome allowlist. Simply add the following entry as a string value in the registry:

```
[HKEY_LOCAL_MACHINE\SOFTWARE\Policies\Google\Chrome]
"AuthServerAllowlist"=subdomain.kerberos.okta.com
```

For other browsers and OS types, the setup is likely to be similar, but follow this link to understand the steps for each of them if required:

```
https://help.okta.com/en-us/Content/Topics/Directory/ad-dsso-configure-browsers.htm
```

Now, let's turn on ADSSO. Follow the next steps to turn on ADSSO:

1. In Okta, go to **Security** > **Delegated Authentication**.

2. Go to the **Agentless Desktop SSO** section.

3. Click on **Edit** and select the desired ADSSO state:

   - **Off**: This means no active ADSSO service is running.

   - **Test**: This allows you to test the endpoint; for example `https://subdomain.okta.com/login/agentlessDsso`.

   - **On**: This will set ADSSO to active and allow users to sign in with ADSSO.

4. In the **Allowed Network** zones, add any zones that are used with machines accessing services combined with ADSSO. Identity Provider routing rules will overrule any zone rules if IdP Discovery is turned on.

5. In the section for **AD Instances**, select the AD in which you set up the SPN.

6. Complete the last steps to activate ADSSO:

- **Desktop SSO**: Enable this to turn DSSO in production.

- **Service account username**: Fill in the service account username with the SPN privileges you created. It needs to be a correct (and case-sensitive) **User Principal Name (UPN)** or **samAccountName**.

- **Service account password**: This is the password of the service account.

- **Validate service account credentials on save**: This will test the credentials. If the AD agent is down or has no connectivity, this step can be skipped.

7. Save your progress at this point.

We are almost there. Once the ADSSO has been turned on, we need to configure a newly created IdP routing rule specifically created for ADSSO.

1. In Okta, go to **Security | Identity Providers | Routing Rules**.

2. Select the ADSSO routing rule and click **Edit**.

3. Fill out the following fields to make sure the ADSSO will be used during authentication requests:

   User's IP is: Anywhere means no zone is selected. In zone means a specified zone is appointed to this rule. Not in zone refers to when you want this rule to kick in if the users are outside of any specified zones.

   User's device platform – here you can select a type of device you want the ADSSO agent to trigger on. This can be particularly interesting if you specifically want to exclude devices such as Linux machines or Macs.

   User is accessing – Here, you can specify whether the rule kicks in when accessing a specific application, all applications, etc.

4. Use the identity provider. Choose **AgentlessDSSO**.

5. Click **Update rule**.

6. When back in the overview, change the rule status to active to activate this rule for users that fit the profile of the settings we just filled out.

These settings can be as rigorous or user-friendly as you decide. By using device metrics, selection and filtering become much more granular.

Lastly, we need to validate the entire setup to make sure a user can use the ADSSO and that it does what it needs to do without any issues.

Log into a domain-joined device that is active within an Active Directory where you have enabled ADSSO. The user on the device needs to be active in Okta to proceed. We need to add the Kerberos URL to the security settings in the browser (if not already populated through the GPO setup earlier).

Now go to your Okta org, and if all settings are correct, the ADSSO will capture your authentication request and grant access without any interaction from the user. One last check is to go to the system logs of Okta and confirm the user logged in using ADSSO as the method.

That's it. We've set up an ADSSO service account, added SPN privileges, integrated the setup with Okta, and added the required IdP routing rule. Let's move on to learn more about the Okta Integration Network.

Simplifying administration with the Okta Integration Network

For many organizations, a reason to start using Okta is to avoid the upkeep of multiple integrations. This was a problem Okta saw early on, and the OIN has been an important cornerstone of Okta for a long time. At this time, the OIN is gathering over 7,500 integrations to applications within a variety of product types. What's unique about this collection is that all protocols for SSO and APIs for provisioning are maintained by Okta. Integrations are not only for cloud apps; a collection of on-premise, web-based applications are also represented within these integrations. The integrations are for **Secure Web Authentication** (**SWA**), **Security Assertion Markup Language** (**SAML**), and **OpenID Connect** (**OIDC**) integrations. For applications supporting any of these methods, even if it's on-premise or VPN services, it's possible to integrate with Okta, even though there is no existing integration in the OIN. All of this will be explained.

SAML has been around since 2002 and is the most commonly used SSO option by vendors and identity providers. SAML's protocols have gone through a few iterations, from 1.1 to the current standard, 2.0. There are still vendors that incorporated it when it was an earlier version. It's important to know that the older federations will work with Okta, but they are not cross-compatible with each other to set up and use.

As an administrator, there are two ways to interact with the OIN. You can go to Okta's website and search for different integrations, applications, or product segments. This is useful if you are thinking of selecting a new system, for instance, an HR system. Then you can easily go in and search for different applications and see what HR system has an integration that fits your needs.

The way you will most frequently interact with the OIN is through the admin console. From there, you will navigate to **Applications | Applications**. By clicking **Browse App catalog**, you will end up in what is basically a searchable catalog of all OIN-available integrations. The applications are divided into use cases:

Use Case	
All Integrations	7492
Apps for Good	9
Automation	26
Centralized Logging	11
Directory and HR Sync	19
Bot or Fraud Detection	3
Identity Proofing	10
Identity Governance and Administration (IGA)	7
Lifecycle Management	546
Multi-factor Authentication (MFA)	27
Risk Signal Sharing	7
Social Login	18
Single Sign-On	6967
Zero Trust	49

Figure 3.10 – Available OIN categories

Most applications are available in the **Single Sign-On** category. Under **Directory and HR Sync**, you will find applications you can use as a directory source. You will probably search for an application. The tile of the application you want to integrate shows what available integration options you have (for instance, SWA or SAML, which will be explained later) and whether provisioning is enabled, as you can see here:

Figure 3.11 – The application tile when finding an integration

Clicking on a tile will bring you to a complete page about the integration. Here, you can read more about its capabilities. You will find the following:

- **Overview**: A description of the application

- **Use case**: The OIN categories you will find this application under

- **Functionalities**: What access protocol the integration supports and what provisioning features are available

Now that we have looked into the OIN, we will deep dive into the two different kinds of SSO integration: SWA and federated (e.g., SAML or OIDC).

We will specifically talk about the standardized ways to add an application that doesn't already have a pre-configured setup. Applications available in the OIN mostly come with extensive integration documentation and usually are well managed by both Okta and the **Service Provider** (**SP**).

Setting up a basic integration with Secure Web Authentication

As mentioned earlier, there are a few different kinds of integrations, and one of them is SWA. This integration type was created for any application that doesn't support federated authentication. That means that the application does not support or allow an SSO flow where a user's authentication token is trusted across multiple systems or platforms. With SWA, Okta stores a user's credentials in a secure way, with strong encryption and a customer-specific private key. When an end user clicks on the application tile, the credentials are sent to the application login page over SSL. When setting up an SWA integration, you can configure the credentials settings in the following ways:

- The user sets the username and password

- The administrator sets the username and password

- The administrator sets the username and the user sets the password

- The administrator sets the username and the password is the same as the Okta password

- Users share a single username and password set by the administrator

The different configurations are quite self-explanatory, but we'll go through some things to think about.

The use case where users set their username and password might be used when an organization is already using an application and where the username and password already exist. It could also be for personal accounts you want to enable through Okta, such as LinkedIn.

The use case where the administrator sets both would be, for instance, when a company rolls out a new application. It provides strong administrator control, as the end user never sees their credentials. For this approach to work, the best thing would be to disable any possibility for end users to reset and change their password within the application.

The following are the steps to get this configuration to work:

1. Create the user and set a password in the application.
2. In Okta, create the integration via the OIN.
3. Navigate to the **Sign On** tab on the **Applications** page.
4. Edit the **SIGN ON** options.
5. Assign the application to the user and set the credentials.

It's good to know that, after this step, the password will never be visible in Okta again to either the end user or the administrator.

For the option where the password is the same as for Okta, the application must have provisioning capabilities. After the account is created in the downstream application, the username is connected through provisioning.

The last option is when multiple users share one account. This could, for instance, be an organization's social media account. As an administrator, you set the credentials, and by assigning the application to users, they get access without ever seeing the credentials. This adds multiple security measures, and when a user leaves the organization, they will not be able to access the application again after losing access to Okta.

For SWA applications to work, the user needs to install the Okta Browser Plugin. The plugin is available through the app stores of the main, commonly used browsers. The plugin is needed for security reasons. When an end user clicks on an SWA application, a new tab is opened. The credentials are collected from Okta through encrypted SSL and posted to the application. The plugin only works with trusted and verified sites:

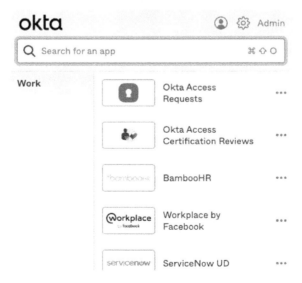

Figure 3.12 – Interface of the Okta Browser Plugin

The plugin can do a lot of things:

- **Initiate an Okta login**: If an end user clicks on an application in the Okta Browser Plugin but isn't logged in to Okta, the user will be prompted to log in to Okta on the application page.

- **Automatically sign-in to apps**: If the user is already signed in to Okta and navigates directly to the application's login page, the plugin will fill in the credentials and sign the user in.

- **Fill in credentials**: If the user previously hasn't used an SWA app and fills in the credentials and then navigates to that application, the user will get to enter the data and save it to Okta.

- **Update passwords**: If a user is in an application and changes the password, the plugin can save the new password. It can also enter the previous password if needed for the password update.

- **Switch users**: You can easily switch the active user by clicking the person symbol and choosing the account to see.

- **Admin console quick access**: For admins, there is a link to go directly to the admin console instead of the end user dashboard.

For applications without an SWA application in the OIN, you can easily create one yourself with the templates available. There are three main template types:

- Template App
- Template Plugin App
- Template Frame Plugin App

The Template Plugin App has the following subcategories:

- Template App 3 fields
- Template 2 Page Plugin App
- Template Basic Auth App

So, how and when should we use these? Navigate to **Applications | Applications**, and click **Browse App Catalog**. Search for `Template` and click **See All Results**.

Use the Template App if your application supports authentication via a form `POST`. On the **General** settings page, enter the following information:

- **Application label**: Enter the name you want for this new integration (usually the system name).

- **URL**: Enter the URL of the form you are posting to. Note that this is not the URL of the page where you see the form.

- **Username and password parameters**: Enter the parameters that contain the credential data.

- **Optional parameters**: Possibly more static data that is needed and sent during login.

- **Application visibility**: Select whether the application should be visible to users.
- **Browser plugin auto-submit**: Select this option if you want to submit the user's credentials immediately when a user navigates to the applications.

The **Template Plugin App** and its subcategory templates are configured similarly, so we'll go through them together. Start the same way by searching for the Template application you want to set up on the **Browse App Catalog** page. As before, in the **General** settings, make the following configurations:

- **Application label**: This is the name you want to be shown to your end users
- **Login URL**: This is the URL to the page where the sign-in form is visible
- **Redirect URL**: If the URL to the sign-in page redirects you, enter that URL here
- **Regular expression**: This is optional; you can define a pattern to restrict access to URLs
- **Username field**: This is the **Cascading Style Sheets** (**CSS**) selector for the username field
- **Password field**: This is the CSS selector for the password field
- **Login button**: This is the CSS selector for the login button
- **Checkbox**: This is the CSS selector for a checkbox (for example, this can be for a "Remember me" or "Agree to terms" checkbox on a login page)

As you might have noticed, the Template Plugin App is using the CSS selectors rather than providing parameters. So, how do you find these CSS selectors?

1. Open the page with the login form.
2. Click on one of the fields, right-click, and select **Inspect** in the menu that appears.

This opens the Chrome developer tool. In the **Elements** pane, you'll find the ID and type needed for your CSS selector:

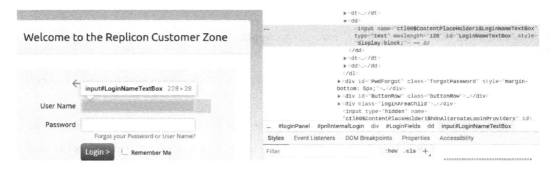

Figure 3.13 – An example of an input in a CSS selector

That's the basic configuration possibilities of the different SWA applications. Let's move on to look at how to set this up using the App Integration Wizard.

SWA with the App Integration Wizard

An easy way to get integration with an application with SWA is to use the App Integration Wizard by navigating to **Application | Application** and then clicking on **Create App Integration**. You will be prompted to choose SWA, SAML, OIDC, or API.

Choose **SWA**. After clicking **Next**, you will be prompted to fill in some information:

- **App name**: This is the name visible to your end users
- **App's login page URL**: This is the URL to the login page
- **App logo**: Optionally, you can upload a logo picture, which makes it easier for end users to navigate to the right icon on their dashboard
- **App visibility**: You can choose to not show the icon to end users on their dashboard
- **App type**: If this integration is with an internally created application that is not intended to be used outside of the organization, check this box

After these settings, you will be able to decide how the username and password are to be set, as per the earlier instructions. In general, if you want to find more information on adding applications, refer to `https://help.okta.com/en/prod/Content/Topics/Apps/Apps_Apps.htm`.

Let's look at the standard protocols of SAML and OIDC.

Using SAML and OpenID Connect applications

To fully embrace the capabilities of Okta's SSO, it is recommended to use federation protocols such as SAML and OIDC. Both handle and look at login flows differently, but they share one common feature; they allow an application to delegate their authentication to an IdP such as Okta. This means that there is no reason to have a password in your application anymore. The user is no longer responsible for a strong unused password, but the application will refer to the IdP for authentication. We will be looking at both to see what they have in common and where they differ.

SAML is a framework built upon XML and allows interactions between an IdP and SP to communicate user authentication, entitlement, and attribute information. The flexibility of the XML allows it to be modified and to send different relevant information based on the integration of the IdP and SP.

Every message is secured using a signed X.509. During the setup of the SSO integration, a public certificate is given to the SP to verify any incoming requests. A SAML response sent by the IdP will be signed with a private key and can be verified against the uploaded public certificate. This allows the SP to check the origin and trust the IdP.

An example of what a typical login flow from the SP looks like is shown in *Figure 3.14*:

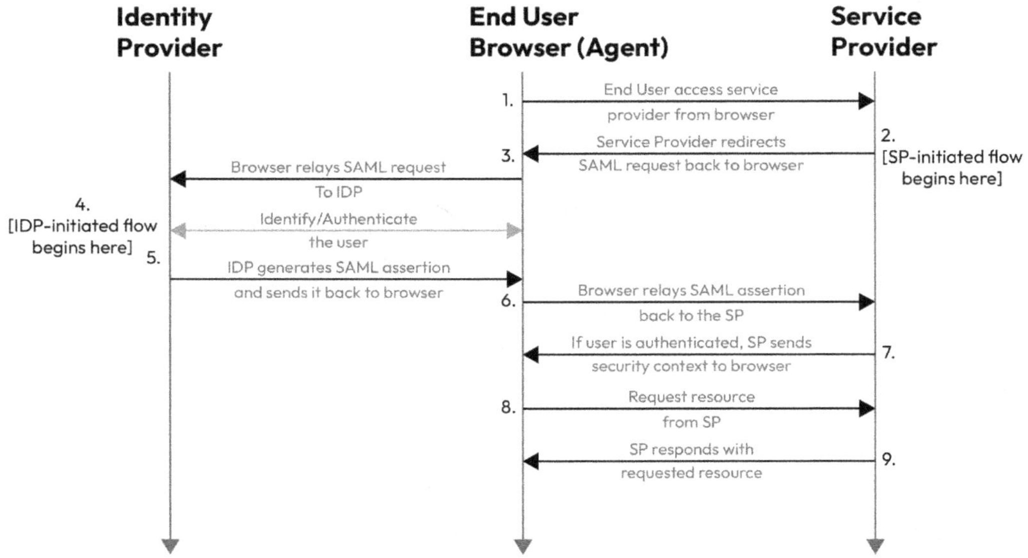

Figure 3.14 – An SP-initiated login flow

While the flow shown in the preceding figure starts with the user going to the SP (SP-initiated login flow), it can also be that a user starts at the IdP (IdP-initiated flow). They look similar, but the start of the request originates from the IdP side.

While nowadays it's more common that authentication flows also require consent requests (for example, to allow access to parts of the data in the underlying application), SAML doesn't have that built into its core. It can be custom-added into the login flow, but this only happens on the SP side and is usually not configurable for users and admins to turn on or set up.

In any application with SAML possibilities but without available integration options in the OIN, it's possible to set up your own integration with the **Application Integration Wizard** (**AIW**). What this kind of integration does is it creates the XML required for the SAML request. To set this up, you will need information from your application provider, either from the documentation or via their support. To start the setup, navigate to **Application | Application** and click **Create App Integration**. Select **SAML** and click **Next**. On the first page, you will only enter the **General** settings:

- **App name**: This is the name visible to your end users

- **App logo**: Optionally, you can upload a logo picture, which makes it easier for end users to navigate to the right icon on their dashboard

- **App visibility**: You can choose to not show the icon to end users on their dashboard

Next, configure the SAML settings:

- **Single sign-on URL**: This is the URL where the assertion is to be sent to with an HTTP POST. This can be called an SAML assertion consumer services URL in the application documentation.

- **Audience URI (SP Entity ID)**: This is the unique identifier defined by the application, usually called an SP Entity ID.

- **Default RelayState**: This field identifies a specific application resource if an SSO has been initiated from an IdP. It's usually left blank.

- **Name ID format**: These are the processing rules and constraints for the assertion's subject statement for SAML. Leave as the default **Unspecified** unless your application requires something specific:

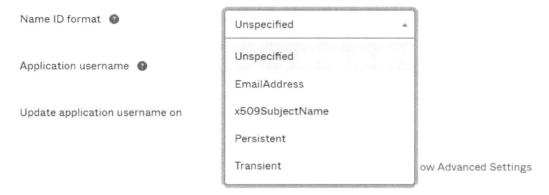

Figure 3.15 – Options for the Name ID format

- **Application username**: Select the format you want the username in, for this specific application – used for the assertion's subject statement.

- **Update application username on**: The only option is **Create and update**.

For **Application username**, there are a variety of options to choose from:

- **Okta username**
- **Okta username prefix**
- **Email**
- **Email prefix**
- **Custom**
- **(none)**

If needed there is an array of advanced settings:

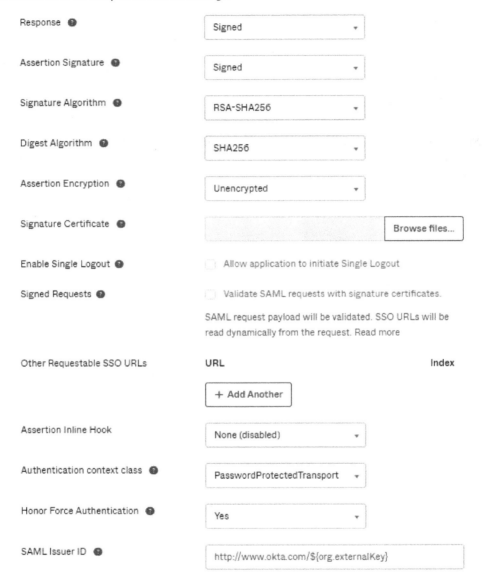

Figure 3.16 – Options for advanced settings

After that, you are able to set attribute statements, both per user and/or group. This can be used if the application needs any values set in a specific way or if any additional values are needed. To create these, you need to set **Name**, **Name format**, and **Value** or **Filter**:

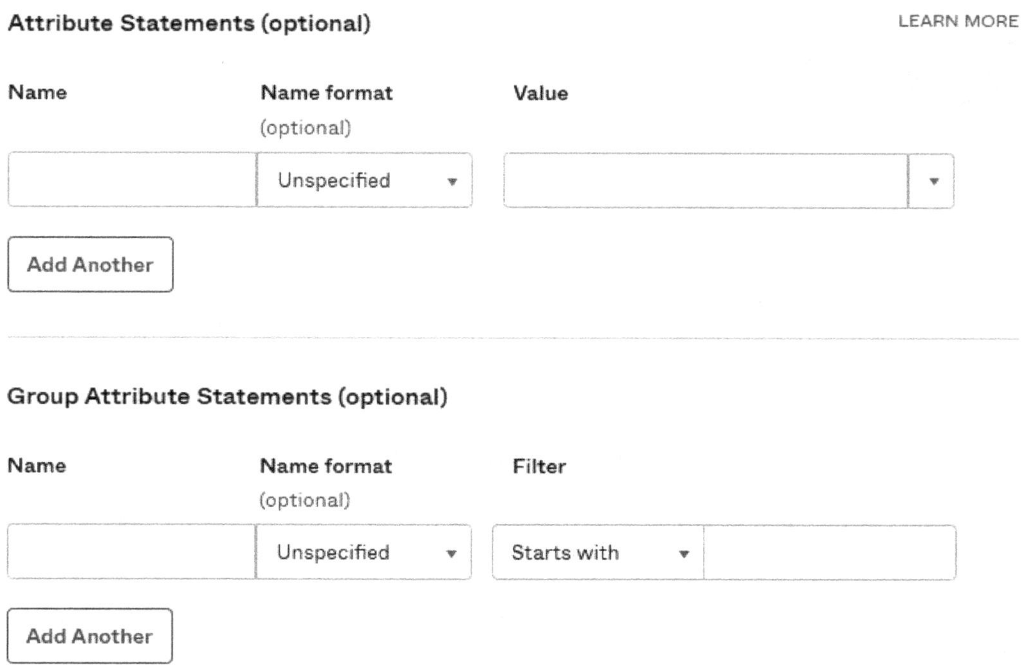

Attribute Statements (optional)   LEARN MORE

Name	Name format (optional)	Value
	Unspecified ▾	▾

Add Another

Group Attribute Statements (optional)

Name	Name format (optional)	Filter	
	Unspecified ▾	Starts with ▾	

Add Another

Figure 3.17 – Options to set attribute statements

It's possible to use Okta Expression Language to change the values. Read more about that in *Chapter 5, Automating Using Lifecycle Management*. If you need to set more than one statement, you can use the **Add Another** button. If you need help or more information to fill in the statements, you can use the **Learn More** link, which leads you to Okta's help site.

When you're done with all your settings, you can preview your SAML assertion before you start using it. If you have documentation from the application supplier, you can compare that against what you have set up the app with using this feature. If your application needs a certificate from Okta, you can download it from the right-side pane. When you're satisfied, click **Next** and you'll get the option to give feedback to Okta before you click **Done**.

Now let's take a look at OpenID Connect and how that is built and used.

OIDC is built on top of OAuth 2.0, which is a framework that grants limited access to scopes of data requested by one service to another service. Think of an email plugin in Gmail asking for access to read, write, and delete contacts. While this doesn't seem like an authentication process, OIDC was created to use OAuth 2.0 to ask for and give limited access to accounts, and by doing so, it creates a single sign-on method. Some very common and widely used OIDC methods are Google's Login with Google+ or almost any other main social login option:

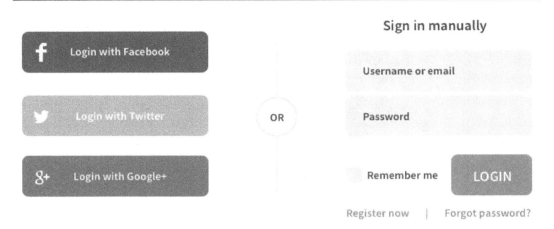

Figure 3.18 – Social logins using OIDC

The main idea is that identity tokens are used to authenticate with the IdP. This can be done through various OIDC flows (for example, implicit flow, authentication flow, and hybrid flow). All of these methods have distinct ways of allowing secure communication between the relaying party and the IdP. During this process, the flow will check, verify, and secure the data and information while authenticating the user.

As there is no other way to log into the application other than using the IdP as the authentication server, it cannot overstep any additional policies and security features added to the flow. Okta is capable of adding policies as we already discussed. But if there's already a session ongoing for Okta, Okta can even then use application policies to add conditional risk assessment and add multifactor authentication to secure access to the application. This allows for more checkpoints before someone accesses the requested application.

Setting up an OIDC application with the wizard can be done quite quickly. As before, you navigate to **Application | Application** and click **Create App Integration**. By selecting OIDC, you get additional choices: **Web application**, **Single Page application** or **Native application**. The setup, however, is similar:

- **App integration name**: Enter the application name.
- **Logo**: Optionally, upload a logo for the tile.
- **Grant type**: This option can vary depending on what type of app you are integrating, but the most common are authorization codes or refresh tokens. If you need more information on what to pick, click the **Learn More** link in the setup window.
- **Sign-in redirect URIs**: This is where Okta will send the OAuth responses to. Due to how OIDC works, the URIs must be absolute. You can set more than one.

- **Sign-out redirect URIs**: Optionally, you can also set URIs for logout. There can be more than one. It's the same here; they have to be absolute.

- **Base URI's**: This is an optional setting but is required if you plan to host the Okta sign-in widget yourself.

- **Controlled access**: Here, you can assign who should have access. This can be everyone or by group. You can also leave it blank and decide later.

By clicking **Save**, you have created the initial integration. You now enter additional configurations on the **General** settings page. The page opens automatically. There are a couple of different kinds of applications here where settings differ a little. For web apps and single-page apps, you have the following settings:

- **Login initiated by**: Here, you have some available selections:

  - **App Only**: There is no tile for the application for the end user to click; the application is instead started in the background

  - **Either Okta or App**: You get to choose the **Application visibility** option, then pick a **Login flow** option

  - **App Embed Link**: This is a link you can use to log into the OIDC client from outside of Okta

Then, you can move on to the following:

- **Initiate Login URI**: You can enter or change the existing link to initiate the sign-in request

Click **Save**. If you need to, you can generate a new client secret. Do so by clicking **Edit** in that section of the page, then click **Generate New Client Secret**.

For native apps, you have your initial configurations in the **General Settings** section. In the section for **Client Credentials**, you can select an option for **Client Authentication**:

- Use **Proof Key for Code Exchange** (**PKCE**) (for public clients): This ensures that only the client that initially requested the token can redeem it and is recommended for native applications.

- **Use client authentication**: With this, the client secret is included in the client and sent with requests to prove the identity. This is not recommended for native distributed applications since it's less secure.

As with web apps, you can generate a new client secret if needed.

That's all for integrations. Let's move on to inbound SSO.

Managing inbound SSO

Okta allows the users to use external identity providers to log in to Okta with their own user database and login methods. This can be a Microsoft, Google, or a generic OIDC or SAML application. You could have contractors or outside partners needing access to some of your applications that want their IdP to be the source to log in with. Using inbound SSO with Okta makes it possible to connect with other IdPs and have their users login.

Even though Okta can easily connect to one of the aforementioned methods, we will focus specifically on connecting with an SAML IdP, allowing users to log in and have additional options to use. This is shown in the following IdP list:

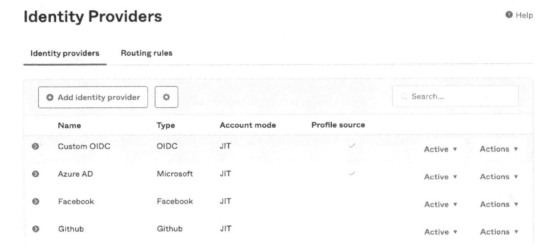

Figure 3.19 – An overview of the identity providers configured

When navigating to **Security | Identity Providers**, you end up on the overview page for all inbound SSO connections.

Clicking on the **Add Identity Provider** button allows you to choose the type of IdP. We will be setting up SAML 2.0 IdP:

Configure SAML 2.0 IdP

Select provider — Configure

General settings

Name

General settings

All fields are required to add this identity provider unless marked optional.

Authentication Settings

IdP Usage

SSO only

IdP username ❓

Enter expression or pick from list...

📖 Expression Language Reference

Filter ❓

◯ Only allow usernames that match defined RegEx Pattern

Match against ❓

Okta Username

Choose the user attribute to match against the IdP username.

Account Link Policy ❓

Disabled

If no match is found ❓

● Create new user (JIT)
◯ Redirect to Okta sign-in page

Authentication Settings

Expressions allow you to reference, transform, and combine attributes before you store them on a user profile or before passing them to an application for authentication or provisioning.

IdP Usage

Specifies how users from this IdP will be evaluated.

SSO only: Okta evaluates requests coming from the IdP as a password (knowledge factor).

Factor only: Okta evaluates requests coming from this IdP as a possession factor.

JIT Settings optional

Profile Source ❓

◯ Update attributes for existing users

Group Assignments ❓

None

JIT Settings

JIT account creation and activation only works for users who are not already Okta users.

Figure 3.20 – Adding an identity provider

You will get a new window with settings to go through:

- **Name**: This is a name for the integration.

- **IdP Usage**: Select between **SSO only** or **Factor only**. This specifies what Okta will look for from the IdP: a knowledge or possession factor.

- **IdP Username**: This is an open field to add condition expressions to determine the IdP login name of the inbound user. You can also just use the default values.

- **Filter**: This allows you to filter the inbound users using regex patterns.
- **Match against**: This allows you to choose the attribute you want the inbound username to be matched with to secure authentication.
- **If no match is found**: Let's look deeper into this one.

If no match is found, you get two options, where one has more features to it:

- **Redirect to Okta sign-in page**: This will send the user to manually authenticate to Okta
- **Create new user (JIT)**: This option will open up more options to set

Just-in-Time (JIT) provisioning was touched upon in *Chapter 2, Working with Universal Directory*. Let's look at the possibilities for how it works during IdP discovery:

- **Profile Master**: If JIT is allowed, you can allow users to be mastered by the inbound SSO and have their attributes updated every time they log in
- **Group Assignments**: This provisions users directly into the predefined groups they should be part of, based on their SAML insertion

For group assignments, we get the following options:

- **None**: This means no group assignment.
- **Assign to specific groups**: You can preset the groups users get added to.
- **Add user to missing groups**: If the SAML assertion has a SAML group attribute with groups, you can have Okta check and assign the user to groups that are in that filter.
- **Full sync of groups**: This is the same as the *Add user to missing groups* setting, but Okta will sync all the groups from **this** group filter. However, it will also remove the user from any Okta groups that are not in the filter.

Back to the initial set up, there are a few more settings to finish off:

- **IdP Issuer URI**: The inbound IdP issues this URI
- **IdP Single Sign-On URL**: The sign-on URL provided by the IdP to log into
- **IdP Signature Certificate**: A certificate provided by the IdP to upload into Okta

If advanced settings are needed, you can further set the values for **Request Binding, Request Signature, Request Signature Algorithm, Response Signature Verification, Response Signature Algorithm, Destination, Okta Assertion Consumer Service URL**, and **Max Clock Skew**.

Click **Finish** to save the configuration.

After saving, the added identity provider will be on the list and active immediately. To complete the setup, you need to copy the ACS URL and the Audience URI and possibly the SAML metadata. These details can be added to the IdP setup:

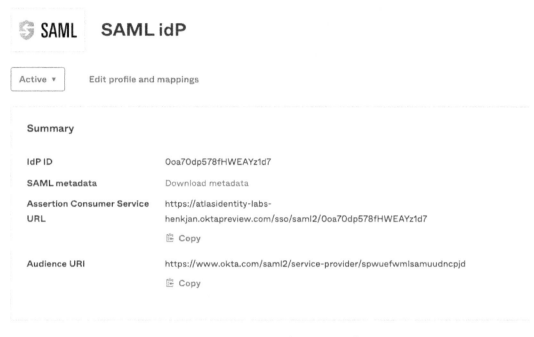

Figure 3.21 – An active identity provider

Depending on the inbound IdP, after configuration, it's wise to test the SSO into Okta by having a user that is either in both systems or pushed from the inbound IdP through JIT and test to login.

Once this works, you can also use IdP discovery and route how a user needs to log in to Okta. We will discuss that in the following section.

IdP discovery

IdP discovery can also be called IdP routing rules, which might be a more telling name. With these routing rules, end users can be routed to different IdPs depending on the context. The context can be, in this case, device-related, IP or network zone-related, or simply looking at the email subdomain. Rules can be set for each identity provider or combinations of user criteria. The rules are set in a hierarchy, and if there is more than one rule that matches the current situation, the topmost will be used. Let's look into how to set this up.

The first prerequisite is that at least one IdP needs to be set up. Navigate to **Security | Identity Providers**. If you don't have any set up, go back to the beginning of this section to set one up. Even without an additional IdP, you can still set up routing rules for networks, and if you have the IWA agent installed, you can set up rules for DSSO. The same goes for ADSSO. For both, an inactive rule is created once the integration is set up. If and when required, you can utilize the IdP routing rules to manage the way users are sent to the correct IdP. Go to the **Routing rules** tab. There is one set up by default where Okta is the IdP. Click **Add Rule** to create a new one:

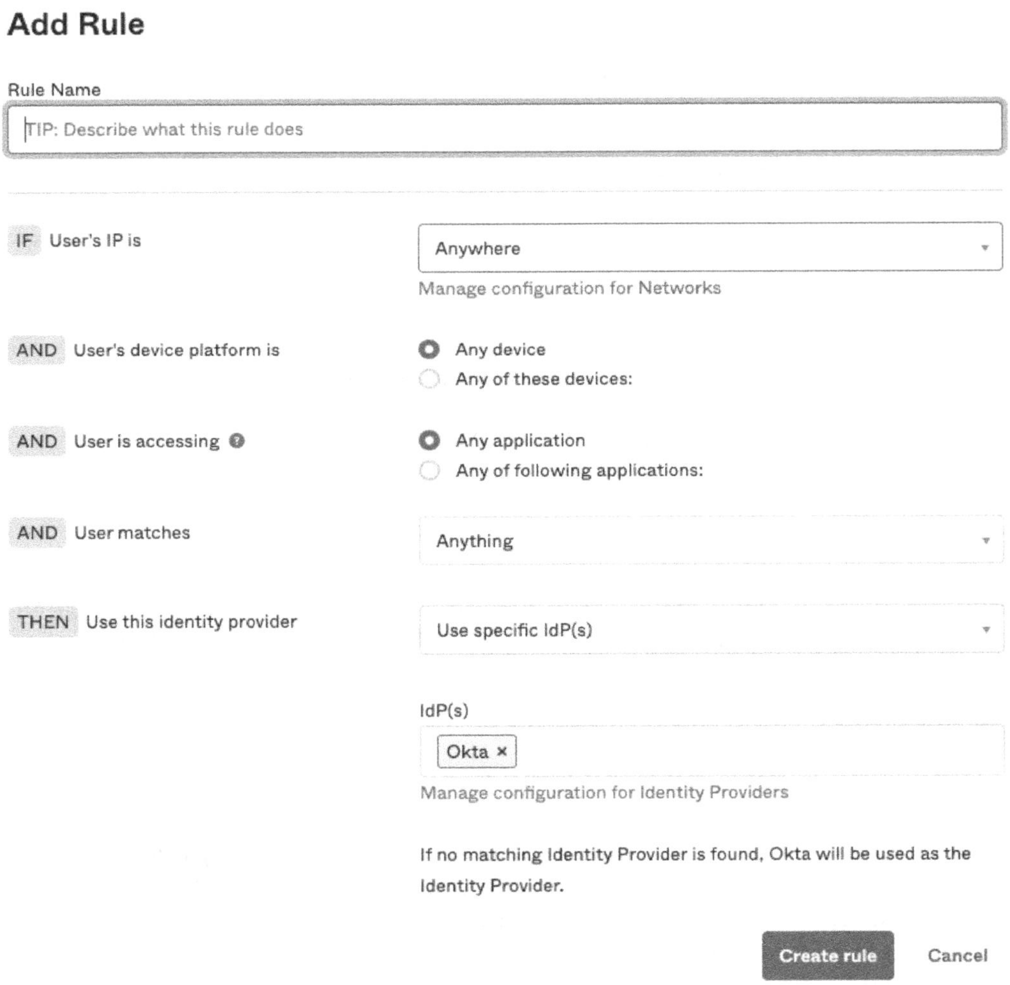

Add Rule

Rule Name

TIP: Describe what this rule does

IF   User's IP is

Anywhere

Manage configuration for Networks

AND   User's device platform is

○ Any device
○ Any of these devices:

AND   User is accessing ❼

○ Any application
○ Any of following applications:

AND   User matches

Anything

THEN   Use this identity provider

Use specific IdP(s)

IdP(s)

Okta ×

Manage configuration for Identity Providers

If no matching Identity Provider is found, Okta will be used as the Identity Provider.

Create rule   Cancel

Figure 3.22 – The configuration of routing rules

Routing rules are **IF**, **AND**, and **THEN** statements:

- **Rule Name**: Give your rule a name that makes it easy to understand what the rule entails

Under **IF**:

- **User's IP is**: If you want to use a zone here, you need to have that configured—see *Chapter 4, Increasing Security with Adaptive Multifactor Authentication*. Otherwise, you can set a rule that works in any zone (default).

Under **AND**:

- **User's device platform is**: Set any combination on mobile and desktop devices
- **User is accessing**: It's possible to select one or multiple applications that this rule is targeting
- **User matches**: Here, you select the login attribute that must match

You will have the following options:

- **Anything**: It will apply to anyone.
- **Domain list on login**: If you log in from a specific domain, this rule applies to you. As the name implies, you can enter a full list of domains.
- **User attributes**: Select a user attribute; for instance, you might want a rule for a specific department.
- **Regex on login**: If neither the domain nor attribute is enough, you can combine them with any valid regular expression.

Under **THEN**:

- **Use this Identity Provider**: Select one of your available IdPs from the dropdown

So, what are the use cases for these kinds of rules? For instance, if you use a hub-spoke model with multiple Oktas interconnected (or alternative directories such as Azure or Google) or have multiple domains in your organization, you can easily set different IdPs for them. If you have both on- and off-network users, you might need to keep legacy authentication for off-network but use Okta for on-network. The sky is the limit.

As mentioned before, you can also use other social logins as methods to sign into Okta. These options need to be set up in a similar way and require changes to be made on the login page of Okta to be used. Alternatively, you can use these routing rules to use the normal login page but have the user be transferred to their own social IdP for authentication. The choices are quite extensive.

Summary

In this chapter, you have been through the different integration methods supported by Okta and how to integrate your organization's applications using the tools available. For your end users to access these applications via SSO securely, we've also looked into how to set password and sign-on policies and rules. To simplify the login process and the end user experience, we also learned about inbound SSO and IdP discovery. We also lightly touched upon the user dashboard and Okta Mobile application to see how end users will integrate with Okta on a daily basis.

In the next chapter, we will go into the possibilities around multifactor authentication and the different settings and policies available.

4

Increasing Security with Adaptive Multifactor Authentication

Two-factor authentication (**2FA**) and **multifactor authentication** (**MFA**) are security features that are growing in many organizations to keep their users and data more secure. The two terms mentioned here are not the same, but rather an evolution from having two authenticators to having multiple authenticators. Instead of one type of authenticator, based on the context, users are asked to confirm who they are by presenting something they know, such as their username and password, something they have, such as a physical card, token, or soft token on a device, and/or something they are, such as using biometrics.

After introducing **single sign-on** (**SSO**) to your organization, MFA is the logical next step to increase security and progress in your journey to zero trust. You will learn different ways to implement this here.

In this chapter, we will look at Okta's capabilities within this field, as well as more advanced features such as Adaptive MFA. You will increase your skills in the following areas:

- Factor types
- Authenticators and enrollment
- Different types of authenticators
- MFA enrollment
- Contextual access management
- Enrolling end users in MFA
- Securing a VPN with MFA

Factor types

Factor types are the way a user can authenticate in Okta. They deliver an indication of the strength of the authenticators that are used with that type. Factor types in Okta have been aligned with standards from NIST to make sure that the options and functionality will abide by strict governmental rules and guidelines.

> **Info**
>
> To read more on NIST and the **Computer Security Resource Center** (**CSRC**), please go to `https://csrc.nist.gov/glossary/term/Multi_Factor_Authentication`.

Following the factor type standards, Okta has divided them into three categories. Let's take a look.

Knowledge factors

These are authenticators of *something you know*. The most typical knowledge factor would be a password, which we all use every day. However, a pin code, an answer to a security question, or security phrase authenticators can be used as knowledge factors. In all cases, it requires the characteristic of *user presence* – the user proves they have control of the authenticator (that is, the password) by actively authenticating (submitting it in a field).

Possession factors

These factors use physical or digital means to "unlock" access. Anything that you own (possess) can be a key to unlock and grant access. Nowadays, a lot of these authenticators are digital or have a digital method on a physical device. A combination of methods determines it is a possession factor. These are some of the characteristics:

- **User presence**: As explained earlier.
- **Device-bound**: This is a device that's dedicated to delivering the required authentication. This can be a physically small token, phone, or computer. It cannot be transferred unless a new device is re-enrolled.
- **Phishing-resistant**: This is an authenticator that cryptographically verifies the login server.
- **Hardware-protected**: This characteristic is offered by certain authenticators that safeguard secrets or private keys. These devices store the device key in either a secure enclave, the **Trusted Platform Module** (**TPM**), or on a separate hardware token. It's important to note that not all devices offer hardware protection.

Biometric factors

These factors are an additional layer on top of possession factors. They include physical characteristics of the user that can be scanned by a device, such as a fingerprint reader or facial scanner, to verify the user's identity. A scan is used to confirm that the individual requesting authentication is the same person who initially established this type of authentication. The characteristics associated with biometric factors are as follows:

- Device-bound

- User presence

- Phishing-resistant

- Hardware-protected

With this knowledge, let's continue to the specific authenticators Okta offers and how to enroll them.

Authenticators and enrollment

Authenticators are the actual methods and devices used to abide by the required factors to gain access. Okta has a section in the security menu called **Authenticators** where you can manage, add, and set up enrollment methods, as well as set policies for some of these authenticators.

When you land on the **Authenticators** page, you'll be given an overview of all the current active authenticators:

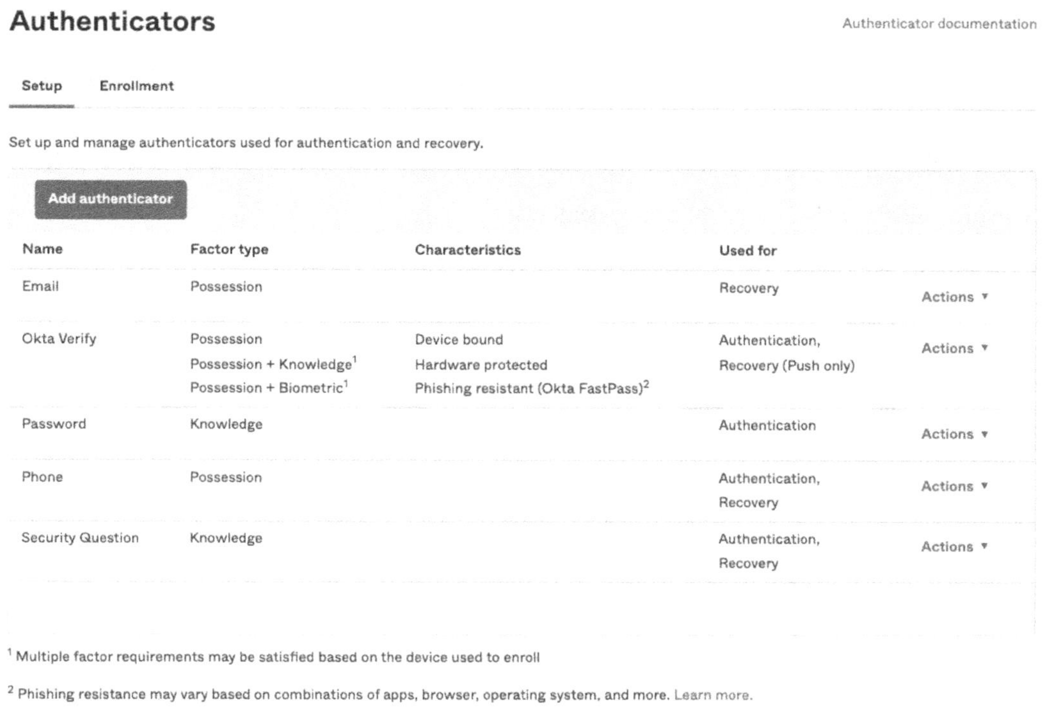

Authenticators

Authenticator documentation

Setup   Enrollment

Set up and manage authenticators used for authentication and recovery.

Add authenticator

Name	Factor type	Characteristics	Used for	
Email	Possession		Recovery	Actions ▾
Okta Verify	Possession Possession + Knowledge[1] Possession + Biometric[1]	Device bound Hardware protected Phishing resistant (Okta FastPass)[2]	Authentication, Recovery (Push only)	Actions ▾
Password	Knowledge		Authentication	Actions ▾
Phone	Possession		Authentication, Recovery	Actions ▾
Security Question	Knowledge		Authentication, Recovery	Actions ▾

[1] Multiple factor requirements may be satisfied based on the device used to enroll

[2] Phishing resistance may vary based on combinations of apps, browser, operating system, and more. Learn more.

Figure 4.1 – Default authenticators in Okta

Some of these authenticators are turned on by default when the Okta org is created by Okta. In this window, a quick overview is given of the **Factor type**, **Characteristics**, **Used for** scenarios, as well as **Actions** that can be taken when applicable.

In some cases, an authenticator can be used just for self-service recovery or used with authentication. Security questions and email authenticators are good examples of this.

Under the **Factor type** column, you can see what types that authenticator can fulfill. This is helpful to understand how strong or strict it is, and what might be required to make sure the security is up to par.

For example, **Okta Verify** is an authenticator that is capable of fulfilling all factor types with a single authenticator. This means that you, as an admin, can use it, without having the users be frustrated with multiple authenticators, but still fulfill your factor type requirements.

Let's go over the different types of authenticators available for each factor type.

Knowledge factors

Knowledge factors are the authenticators you need to memorize. The first is your password, which needs to abide by the password requirements set up in Okta. The password authenticator has its own policy rules. When you click on the **Actions** function and select **Edit**, you will be presented with a new page that allows you to set up password policies. This is done in the same way as with the global session policies, as we went over in *Chapter 3*.

Here, the same type of priority is utilized; users will go through these policies until their conditions are met.

A default, undeletable policy is preset to make sure the org is accessible with a default password policy.

A password policy consists of the following elements:

- **Add Policy**: In this section, you can give the policy a name, description, and assigned group, as shown here:

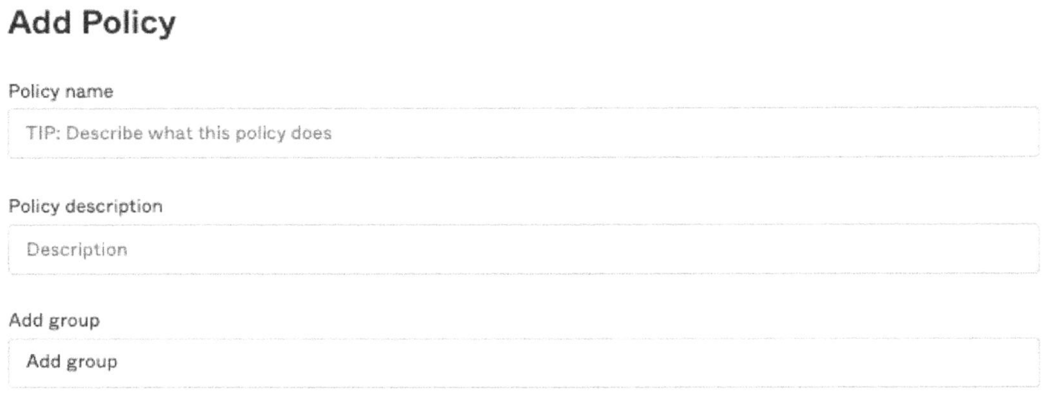

Add Policy

Policy name

> TIP: Describe what this policy does

Policy description

> Description

Add group

> Add group

Figure 4.2 – The Add Policy section

- **Authentication Providers**: In this field, you can choose from **Okta**, **LDAP**, or **Active Directory**:

Figure 4.3 – The Authentication Providers section

- **Password Settings**: In this field, you can determine the complexity and password strength settings:

Password Settings

Minimum length   8   characters

Complexity requirements   ☑ Lower case letter

                                                         ☑ Upper case letter

                                                         ☑ Number (0-9)

                                                         ☐ Symbol (e.g., !@#$%^&*)

                                                         ☑ Does not contain part of username

                                                         ☐ Does not contain first name

                                                         ☐ Does not contain last name

Common password check ⓘ   ☑ Restrict use of common passwords

Figure 4.4 – The Password Settings section

- **Password age**: These settings allow you to determine the duration and management of password changes when their lifetime is nearing its end or has been exceeded:

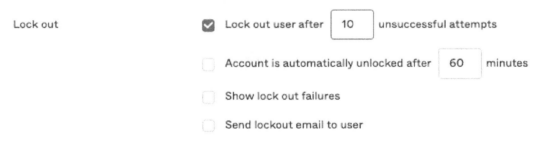

Figure 4.5 – Password age management

- **Lock out**: This section allows you to determine when a lock-out should happen and whether the user needs to be notified of issues:

Figure 4.6 – Lock out settings

When you save the password policy settings, you will be able to add rules to the policy. These rules determine in what scenarios the policy will be triggered, such as IP zones, geographical zones, and more. After saving, you will be presented with a window where you can create your first rule in the new policy.

The first part will be a section where you can define and name the rule, as shown in *Figure 4.7*:

Add Rule

Rule name

TIP: Describe what this rule does

Exclude users

Exclude users

Figure 4.7 – The Add Rule section

Secondly, any zones will be considered if they're set in this section:

IF User's IP is

Anywhere

Manage configuration for Networks

Figure 4.8 – Rule zone setup

Then, you can define the options a user is allowed to perform as part of self-service actions:

THEN Users can perform self-service ●   ✓ Password change (from account settings)
                                            ✓ Password reset
                                            ✓ Unlock account

Figure 4.9 – Self-service settings

Lastly, the **Recovery authenticators** section is available to determine whether any other authenticators are required to start any self-service process. This will help you strengthen these actions as you can add or change the type of authenticator and initiator for recovery:

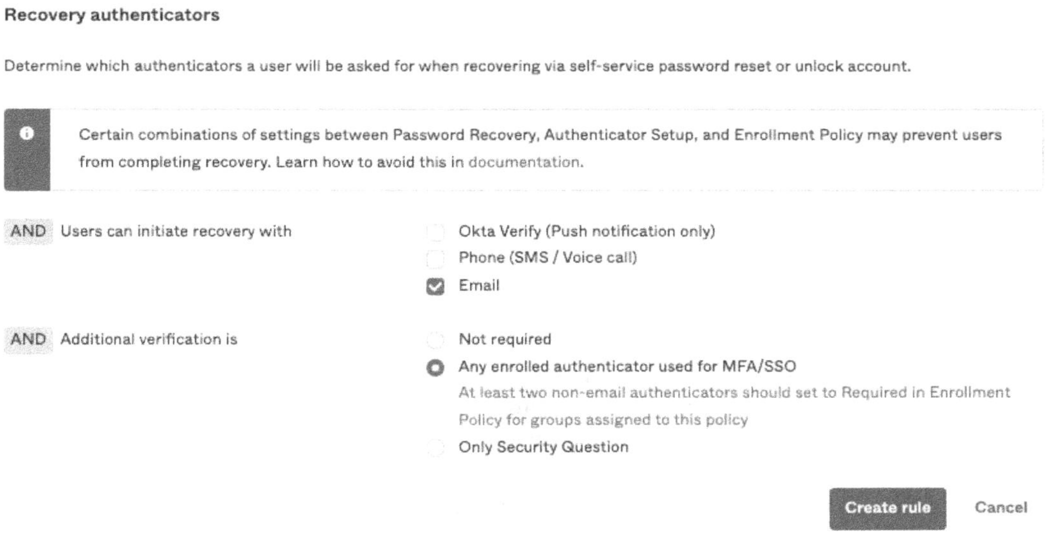

Recovery authenticators

Determine which authenticators a user will be asked for when recovering via self-service password reset or unlock account.

> ● Certain combinations of settings between Password Recovery, Authenticator Setup, and Enrollment Policy may prevent users from completing recovery. Learn how to avoid this in documentation.

AND Users can initiate recovery with   Okta Verify (Push notification only)
                                           Phone (SMS / Voice call)
                                        ✓ Email

AND Additional verification is   Not required
                                        ● Any enrolled authenticator used for MFA/SSO
                                           At least two non-email authenticators should set to Required in Enrollment
                                           Policy for groups assigned to this policy
                                           Only Security Question

                                                            Create rule   Cancel

Figure 4.10 – The Recovery authenticators section

When you click **Create rule**, the policy will be ready and available to be used in your setup. If you have no other policies, this first policy will be your top policy in the list. If you do have multiple policies, any new policy will be set to position 2 of the priority list. Here, with the help of drag and drop, you can move the policies so that they're in the right order.

If you ever need to edit or delete a policy, you can select the policy from the list and click on one of the options shown in the following screenshot:

Figure 4.11 – Policy actions

If you want to add more rules within a policy, priority can be set for them here. You can, for example, add specific zone rules and set their priority to make sure the policy acts correctly.

The rule section will show a summary of what it does:

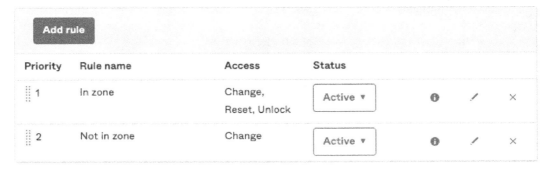

Figure 4.12 – Order of rules

> **Note**
>
> At the time of writing (June 2023), the **Password policy** section has a note explaining that password policies will be considered alongside enrollment policies. We will discuss enrollment policies later in this chapter. The most important aspect to understand is that when the rule of a policy requires other authenticators, of which the user is not enrolled, or not even capable of enrolling based on their conditions for the enrollment policy, they will still be asked to enroll to fulfill the requirement of the password policy.

Now that we have discussed how to set up one of the most common authenticators, let's look at a second knowledge authenticator.

A security question is used as a knowledge factor too. By enabling the security question authenticator for your end users, a window will appear, asking whether you only want the authenticator to be used for recovery flows, such as password reset, or also for authentication:

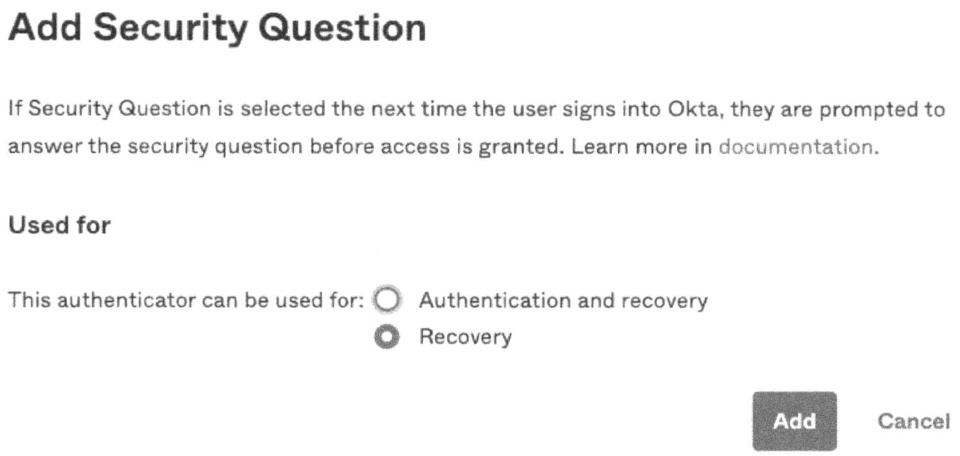

Add Security Question

If Security Question is selected the next time the user signs into Okta, they are prompted to answer the security question before access is granted. Learn more in documentation.

Used for

This authenticator can be used for: ○ Authentication and recovery
⦿ Recovery

Add   Cancel

Figure 4.13 – The option to use a security question as an authenticator

When you select **Authentication and recovery**, users will receive a notification saying **Extra verification is required for your account** if their behavior requires them to enroll into the authenticator. When end users enroll, they are required to follow these steps:

1. Click the **security question authenticator** setup button.
2. Choose a security question and enter the answer.

This security question has just a few limitations:

- The answer needs to be a minimum of four characters long
- The answer cannot be the user's username or password
- The answer cannot contain parts of the question

With these limitations, you can expect that this type of factor isn't the strongest one available. But perhaps in certain situations, it is a good way to allow users to log in with limited access.

The next category in line is possession factors.

Possession factors

Possession factors – that is, authentication by something you possess (something you have) – include the following:

- Okta Verify
- Google Authenticator
- Phone authenticator
- Email as a factor
- Third-party authenticators such as Duo, RSA tokens, and YubiKeys

Let's look at these one by one.

Okta Verify

Okta Verify is an application developed by Okta. It can be used either with a **one-time password** (**OTP**) or with a push option. Additionally, it can be set up to require biometric security. This is the reason why the Okta Verify authenticator can fulfill all factor types and requirements in one go. With its simple OTP option, the user opens the application, sees a rotating six-digit code, and enters it in their browser for verification:

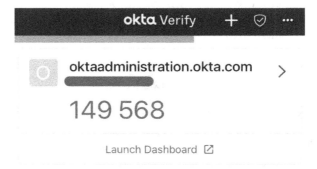

Figure 4.14 – Okta Verify with a six-digit code

Okta Verify can also be used as a regular OTP application for alternative codes from other applications. This allows the user to have one app that can do multiple things.

With the push functionality, the user receives a push notification on their device and must accept it by clicking **Yes, It's Me**:

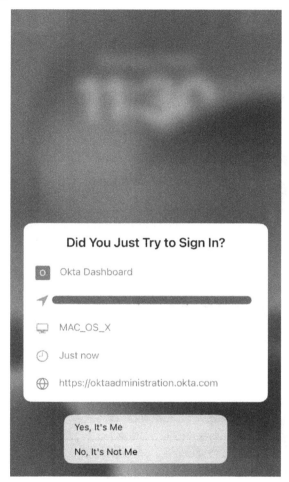

Figure 4.15 – Okta Verify push notification

Okta has also introduced a number challenge as an additional security measure. This requires the user to select a presented number on the screen in the Okta Verify app or directly in the push notification:

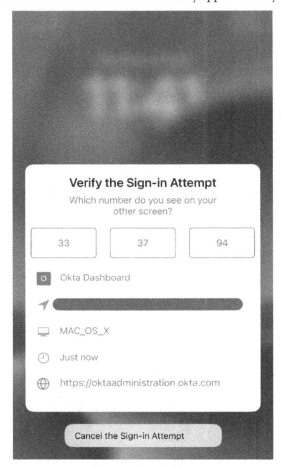

Figure 4.16 – Okta Verify push notification with a number challenge

With recent upgrades, Okta has extended its Okta Verify functionality, adding a device-bound option. This is called **FastPass**. FastPass is a way to allow passwordless entry to Okta and applications using an on-device-registered application and is used in global and authentication policies:

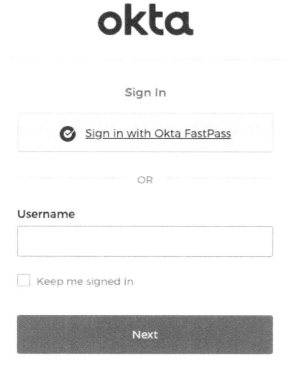

Figure 4.17 – The Sign in with Okta FastPass button on the login screen

Enrolling yourself into Okta Verify on a mobile device is fairly simple. It is required for the user to download the Okta Verify application from any known app store for mobile devices. Once the user has the app, they can set up enrollment by authenticating with Okta Verify on a separate device, after which FastPass will activate and enroll itself and verify whether biometrics are required. This makes the authenticator device-bound:

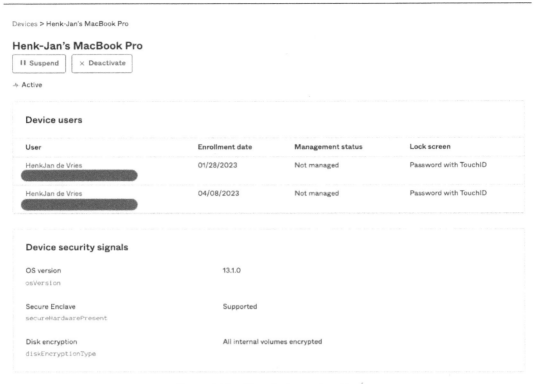

Figure 4.18 – Okta device registration

If the requirement for user verification is turned on, the user will have to enroll in Okta Verify with a device that supports a form of biometric security.

Now that we have discussed the Okta Verify app for mobile devices, we will learn more about Okta's newest addition to the app, which is the FastPass function for machines that use Okta Verify on a laptop.

Okta Verify for FastPass

At the time of writing, Okta Verify for FastPass is available for Windows and macOS devices. It can be installed by the user during enrollment or pushed via a **mobile device management** (**MDM**) service. The actual setup and enrollment will always require the user.

There are three steps you need to follow to set up FastPass:

1. Configure a global session policy.
2. Enable Okta FastPass.
3. Configure a specific authentication policy for FastPass.

Once you've done this, you must make sure users are enrolled in the latest version of Okta Verify, or that they enroll. We covered *Step 1* in *Chapter 3*. Let's take a closer look at the other two steps.

Enabling Okta FastPass

To enable Okta FastPass, navigate to **Security | Authenticators**, as we did earlier in this chapter. For FastPass, Okta Verify is used, so to enable it, click **Action** at the end of the row of Okta Verify and click **Edit**.

There are two settings to consider here. Under **Verification options**, you need to check **Okta FastPass** for users to verify with. Under **Okta FastPass**, you can choose **Show the "Sign in with Okta FastPass" button**. If you don't, users will automatically be authenticated with FastPass after they are enrolled. If you do check it, users can authenticate by clicking the button if the silent flow fails. The best practice here is to start with this unchecked for a slower rollout:

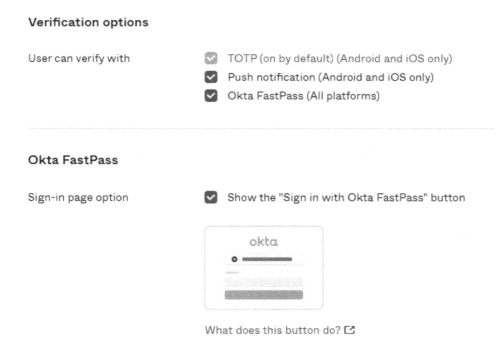

Figure 4.19 – Settings for Okta FastPass enablement

Below these two settings, you can select whether this should be the **Preferred** sign-in option or **Required** by clicking the dropdown. **Preferred** is the default and works for users even though they don't have biometrics. If you select **Required** and users don't have devices that support biometrics, the enrollment will fail:

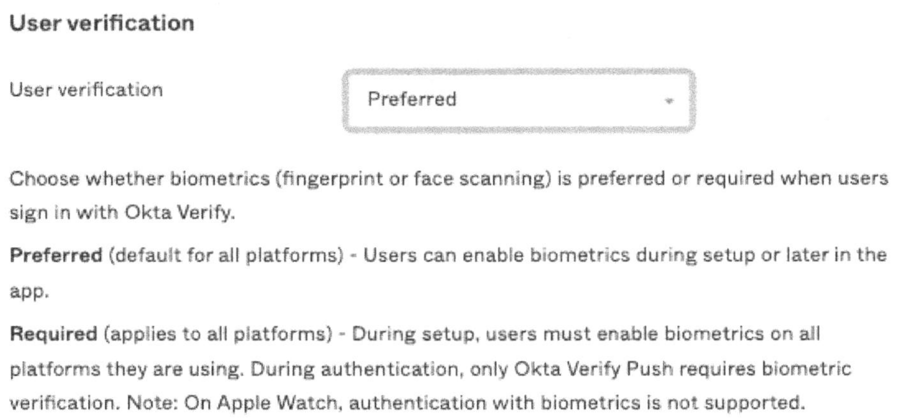

User verification

User verification

| Preferred ▾ |

Choose whether biometrics (fingerprint or face scanning) is preferred or required when users sign in with Okta Verify.

Preferred (default for all platforms) - Users can enable biometrics during setup or later in the app.

Required (applies to all platforms) - During setup, users must enable biometrics on all platforms they are using. During authentication, only Okta Verify Push requires biometric verification. Note: On Apple Watch, authentication with biometrics is not supported.

Figure 4.20 – Settings for Okta Verify User verification

After that, click **Save**.

The last step is that we have to have a specific **Authentication** policy for FastPass. Follow the instructions that we went through in *Chapter 3*, *Using Single Sign-On for a Great End User Experience*. You can add multiple rules in the same policy, where the top rule should be the most restrictive. An example of this could be that the first rule is for users to authenticate on trusted and registered devices that are compliant and can authenticate seamlessly with FastPass. The second could be for registered but unmanaged devices where users also need to authenticate with another authenticator. The last rule would deny all attempts that didn't meet the conditions of rules one and two.

Excellent – you have now set up authenticators and created policies and rules for your users to authenticate safely to Okta.

Now, let's look at the alternative possession authenticators Okta has to offer.

Google Authenticator

Google Authenticator is an application developed by Google that has the same function as Okta Verify OTP. To use it, the end user needs to open the Google Authenticator app and use the six-digit OTP to authenticate to get into Okta.

> **Information**
>
> Even though this authenticator is branded with Google, you are not required to use Google Authenticator. This OTP is standard and can be used with any digital OTP application. Scanning the QR code with your application of choice will generate the six-digit code, just like the Google Authenticator app.

To enroll, a user will need to be prompted by Okta. The steps to take are as follows:

1. Select the mobile OS type.
2. Scan the QR code with the app.
3. Input the generated OTP code to verify it worked.

And done! Now, the user has an alternative authenticator to use when required.

> **Tip**
>
> Some MFA options are available in the SSO licenses. It's possible to set MFA both when signing in to Okta and when signing into applications. Different levels of security and authenticators can be set for different logins. As an example, if Okta Verify is determined as safe enough to log in to Okta, a biometric type might be added as an authenticator to log in as an administrator to the Okta admin console or a business-critical system.

Phone authentication

Most people have experienced the *phone authenticator*, where some sort of code is sent via SMS or a phone call. As an administrator, this is a typical authenticator to enable since end users are used to it and most people have a phone that can receive SMS or phone calls. What would enrollment look like for your end users? If the user is required to enroll into the phone authenticator during login application access, they will be asked to enroll:

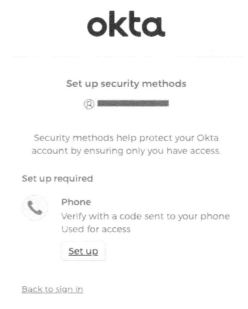

Figure 4.21 – Phone screen for enrollment to the phone authenticator

End users will receive a notification saying **Set up required**. End users will need to follow these steps:

1. Click **Setup**.

2. Select the country the number is registered in.

3. Enter their phone number.

4. Confirm by entering the security code that was sent to that phone number.

After that, you're done!

> **Tip**
>
> Even though phones are easy for your end users to handle and enroll in, it's not as secure as many people think. If this will be an active authenticator in your organization, you should consider alternative authenticators to utilize. If the phone is lost or replaced, having extra authenticators to use to log in to Okta diminishes disruption for the end user.

To set up the phone authenticator, you must simply enable it in the **Security | Authenticators** section. Here, you can also determine whether the phone authenticator is solely used as a self-service recovery option or also for MFA. This allows you to be more granular with the functionality and usage of the authenticator type.

Email as an authenticator

Email as an authenticator is exactly what it sounds like – end users will receive the OTP via email, and they need to enter it on the login screen. If this authenticator is set as required, the user's primary email will automatically be used to send the OTP. The lifetime of the emailed OTP is set to five minutes. It can be increased by increments of 5 minutes up to 30 minutes. Just like the security question, email as an authenticator can be considered a weak choice and should not be used as a primary authenticator. This authenticator can also be set to just a self-service authenticator or both MFA and self-service. This can be set in the same editing window as the selection for the lifetime:

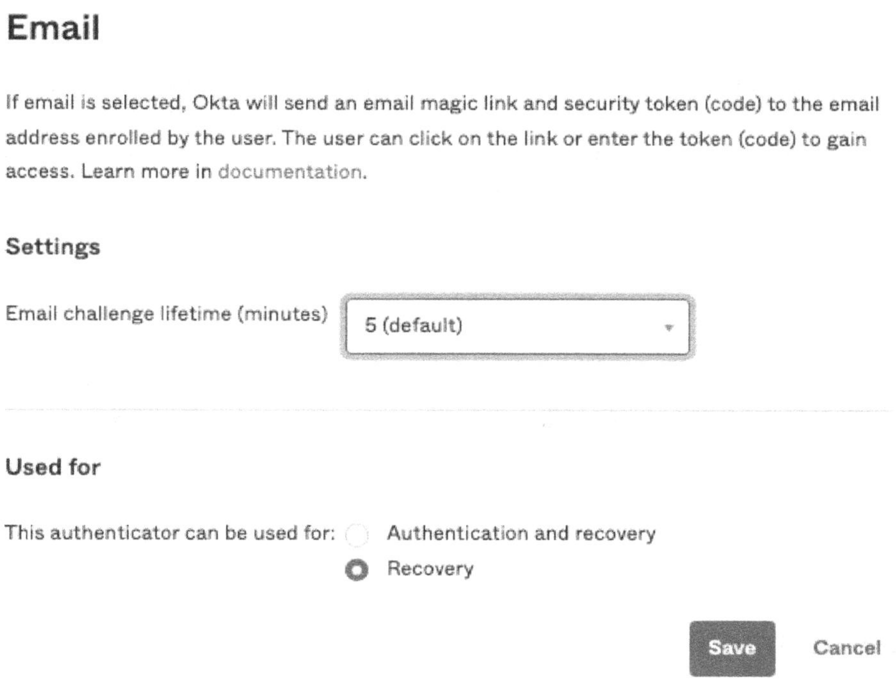

Email

If email is selected, Okta will send an email magic link and security token (code) to the email address enrolled by the user. The user can click on the link or enter the token (code) to gain access. Learn more in documentation.

Settings

Email challenge lifetime (minutes) | 5 (default)   ▼ |

Used for

This authenticator can be used for: ○ Authentication and recovery
                                       ● Recovery

| Save | Cancel

Figure 4.22 – Settings for email as an authenticator

Third-party authenticators such as Duo, RSA tokens, and YubiKeys

Okta supports an array of third-party authenticators, such as an **RSA token**, **Symantec VIP**, and **Duo Security**. These are set up differently, but with easy-to-follow instructions when enrolling the authenticators. For instance, a certificate is needed for setting up Symantec VIP. With the RSA hardware dongle, it's possible to use an on-premises agent from Okta to enable on-premises MFA. The Okta agent then acts as a **Remote Authentication Dial-In User Service** (**RADIUS**) client and communicates with your RADIUS-enabled MFA server.

YubiKeys have a wide range of options and functionality, where they also use **Fast IDentity Online 2.0** (**FIDO2**). FIDO is a web API that uses cryptographic keys that are unique for every website. The authentication tokens cannot be compromised, and the private keys never leave the end user's device. This eliminates all forms of password theft, as well as reduces the risk of phishing and replay attacks.

Biometric factors

Biometric factors include WebAuthn FIDO2 (such as Windows Hello and Apple Touch ID). This is the most advanced and secure MFA option. End users with a MacBook with Touch ID or a Windows laptop with Windows Hello can simply identify themselves with their fingerprint on the reader or face scan. After the end user has enrolled with their machine to the Okta service, they will be prompted to authenticate with their biometrics upon logging in.

Regarding any authenticator a user needs to enroll in, they will be prompted to do so based on the enrollment setup. Depending on the type of authenticator, instructions are given to make sure the user enrolls successfully.

With FastPass, this has taken an even more secure posture, where the device is registered against the user. Okta will not allow the user to switch to a device PIN or password if the biometrics fail, which is the case with **WebAuthn** options.

With that, we have learned what types of authenticators and factor types Okta supports and how they are set up by the end users. Now, let's look at how to set them up from the admin panel and manage them from there. First, we'll discuss the basic features.

MFA enrollment

Before we can do anything, we must enable the different kinds of authenticators that we want to allow our end users to be able to enroll in. Navigate to **Security | Authenticators**. On the first tab, you will choose which authenticators you want to be available. Remember, any authenticators you enable aren't mandatory to all end users and are not active until end users enroll themselves in them. You can have your end users enroll in them by using a combination of global session policies, enrollment policies, and authentication policies. We will be able to create policies and assign them to different groups or users in the same way as we did for sign-on in *Chapter 3, Using Single Sign-On for a Great End User Experience. Figure 4.23* shows the authenticators that are available when you click **Add Authenticator**:

Add Authenticator

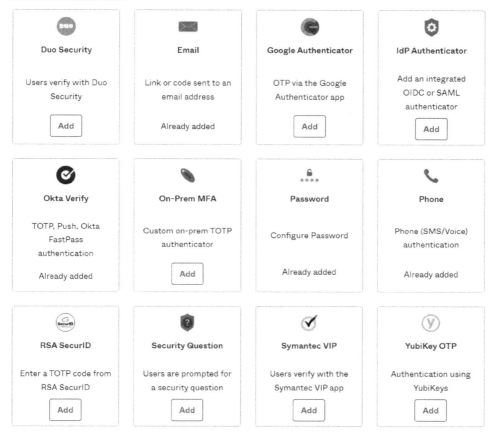

Figure 4.23 – Authenticators that are available to add and information on which are already enabled

Click **Add** under any of the authenticators you want to enable. You will be able to read some information about the authenticator and then click **Add** to enable it. For some authenticators, you have to add more information, such as security keys or certificates. Each type has instructions and is easy to enable.

When it comes to what authenticators to enable for your organization, there are some conditions to take into consideration. Security is, of course, very important. Authenticators such as hard tokens with FIDO2 are the strongest across different risk levels, but they are not the easiest to deploy among end users. In some organizations, employees don't receive a corporate phone, don't have a phone, or simply aren't allowed to use one during work. Setting up an authenticator such as **Voice Call Authentication** can be a problem in such scenarios.

After the authenticators you want to use are enabled, you can set how end users can enroll in them. There is always a default policy available. Navigate to the **Enrollment** tab, then click **Add a policy**:

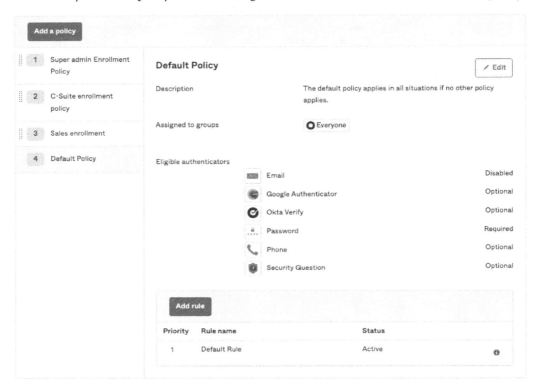

Figure 4.24 – The hierarchy for enrollment policies

When clicking the **Add a policy** button, you can add an additional enrollment policy.

> **Tip**
> Keeping your organization's structure in mind, you can set up policies to enforce enough security as per the requirements. Assigning department groups allows you to fine-grain access with accompanying authenticators based on requirements and level of access, all while combining different factors.

Setting up an authenticator is easy; you just have to enter the following details:

- **Policy name**: Give the policy a name that is easy to understand.
- **Policy description**: Give it a description.

- **Assign to Groups**: Add what groups should be assigned to the policy. When you start typing, you will see a list of available groups matching what you have written. These groups can be of any type: Okta, application, directory, and more.

The last step is to select **Optional**, **Required**, or **Disabled** for the available authenticators. With the best practices tip preceding this, you would enter **Optional** or **Required** on only one authenticator and **Disabled** on the rest. Finish off by selecting **Create Policy**. Once you've done this, it's time to create a **rule** for the policy. This rule states under what conditions the policy will take place. Here is how to set it up:

1. **Rule Name**: Give the rule a clear name.

2. **Exclude Users**: If any users in the assigned groups should be excluded from this rule, you can subtract them here.

After that, it's the usual **IF**, **AND**, and **THEN** statements:

1. **IF User's IP is**: Select **Anywhere**, **In zone**, or **Not in zone** from the dropdown. How to set up zones will be explained later in this chapter.

2. **THEN Enrollment is**: Select from **Denied** or **Allow** if the required authenticator is missing.

Click **Create Rule**. As you can see, you can add multiple rules to a single policy so that you have granular management of your users. You can activate and deactivate rules as you see fit; you can also edit them after creation if needed.

So, with all these sections and steps, we are ready; we have set up basic MFA for your organization. Now, let's take a look at the additional features that come with Adaptive MFA.

Contextual access management

> **Important note**
>
> Some functionalities explained in this chapter – for instance, contextual access, dynamic zones, and behavior detection – are only available with licenses for Adaptive MFA and Adaptive SSO products.

With Okta's contextual access, it becomes possible to use different technologies and combine them into a more complete picture of the user's situation and requirements. Instead of assigning roles or groups to corresponding policies, Okta can act much more fluidly with a multitude of security vectors that are accessible and known by Okta during authentication activity.

By allowing this context to be used, Okta decides in a much more fine-grained way what to do and how to allow the user to sign in to Okta or the required application(s). Okta can build a risk assessment based on a stack of vectors, such as location, device posture, type of request, timing, and so on. From this, together with group assignments and roles, Okta can either ease or restrict access.

It is required that these requests are quickly assessed and automatically assigned to the user for that specific instance. Any delays can result in a different risk assessment because of changed conditions in any of the vectors used.

Part of the adaptive elements is that users are notified about these decisions and changes. If the risk goes up during the process, users are informed that additional authenticators are required. If a login attempt seems suspicious, send an email to the user to allow them to assess the incident and notify Okta administrators if it seems necessary.

Allowing self-service resets not only relieves the IT and support staff from manually helping users but also allows the users themselves to better understand and have control over the situation. They can affect what happens and bring their own risk down by repeating conditions to ensure lower risk scores.

Think of a user always going to the office; their risk assessment can be set to low because of the following vectors:

- The **wide area network (WAN)** address of the office is added to a zone
- The user logs in regularly around the same time and on the same days
- The user is using the same device, which is enrolled on their MDM, or they are using FastPass to log in
- The user is using the same OS and browser, and the device is sending device posture information

Perhaps in this scenario, you would allow the user to access all applications, with a lower threshold for MFA.

But say this user wants to do the same work but with these vectors changed in the following ways:

- The user is hopping from Wi-Fi to mobile data, thus changing IP addresses constantly
- They're doing so while being based in different time zones, or at different hours of the day
- The user is using their own devices, such as an iPad, an Android mobile, and a self-owned laptop
- They are using different OSs and browsers

The risk assessment will evaluate the situation to be riskier and will prompt the user to identify themselves using more secure authenticators, and perhaps even deny access to some or all business-critical applications.

This way, the assessment is done using a lot of different elements. The role of the user within the organization and the assignment to different groups can help create these policies and methods. Prompting the user to change passwords because their risk assessment became much higher, enrolling new authenticators, and receiving notifications allows them to go through this process completely self-managed and in control. They could decide not to do it at that point and allow Okta to restrict their workspace for the time being. Once they comply with more secure requirements by enrolling into authenticators, they can continue to work with all their required applications.

Eventually, Okta wants to make sure security doesn't get in the way of productivity. By allowing the user to do their own assessment, they are in control of the situation. Users can decide whether they think it's required to fall in line with the restrictions, or whether they are going to forgo them and work using a more restricted workplace.

Implementing these context-aware policies requires an understanding of the different situations and needs a user-focused approach.

At the beginning of this book, we spoke about the zero-trust approach, using Okta's contextual access management, which allows you to move on to higher levels of zero trust. This doesn't mean that implementing contextual access management means you tick off the box to be in the zero-trust model and you can raise the flag. It means you are changing your focus from an organizational perimeter to a user-centric perimeter.

Now, let's see how signals from your device can help increase security postures.

Device security signals

Okta has extra device signal options that will allow you, as an administrator, to add more context to your policy building. Using the Okta Verify app (either on mobile or on the desktop with FastPass), the device's posture is sent to Okta. The application will register a device under the user's account and highlight specific details. But it can also send over signals regarding the device's posture. These signals can be used in authentication policies. First, device profile information can be used to add context – think of the OS's type or whether the device is managed or registered. Secondly, even without an MDM solution, Okta can use Windows Security Center on a Windows device to understand its posture utilizing Okta Verify. Signals such as **AntiVirus**, **FireWall**, **securityCenterService**, and more can be used as context in the authentication policy.

If you also utilize a product such as **CrowdStrike**, Okta can integrate with that and use its signals to add more context to authentication policies. At the time of writing, only CrowdStrike is integrated, but additional vendors are expected to be added in the future.

> Tip
>
> To understand these signals and how to set them up in authentication policies, Expression Language is required. Go to the Okta device profile page to learn more about Expression Language and the signals different sources send to Okta: `https://developer.okta.com/docs/reference/okta-expression-language-in-identity-engine/#okta-device-profile`.

Additionally, you can add device assurance policies to the authentication policies to fine-tune the security risk. Device assurance policies are meant to be used as sets of checks for security-related device attributes. Okta will activate the option for device assurance in an authentication policy if the device is at least registered via the Okta Verify application. At that point, you can add the device assurance policy or policies. In *Chapter 3, Using Single Sign-On for a Great End User Experience*, we explained how to set up the basics of the authentication policy. Here, we will explain how to create and add the device assurance policy.

The **Device Assurance Policies** menu can be found under the **Security** menu in the Okta admin console. Once you are there, you will find two sections:

- The main policy section, which will look similar to what's shown in *Figure 4.25*:

Figure 4.25 – Adding a policy for device assurance policies

- A **User help** section, which you can use to determine how to support a user when access is denied because of the device assurance policy:

Figure 4.26 – The User help section

The last section gives you the option to determine whether Okta will present a standard help page or if you want to add a custom link to a help page for users.

Let's add a policy. Click on **Add a policy** in the top section. A new pop-up window will open where you can determine the name of the policy and the OS type it is applied to:

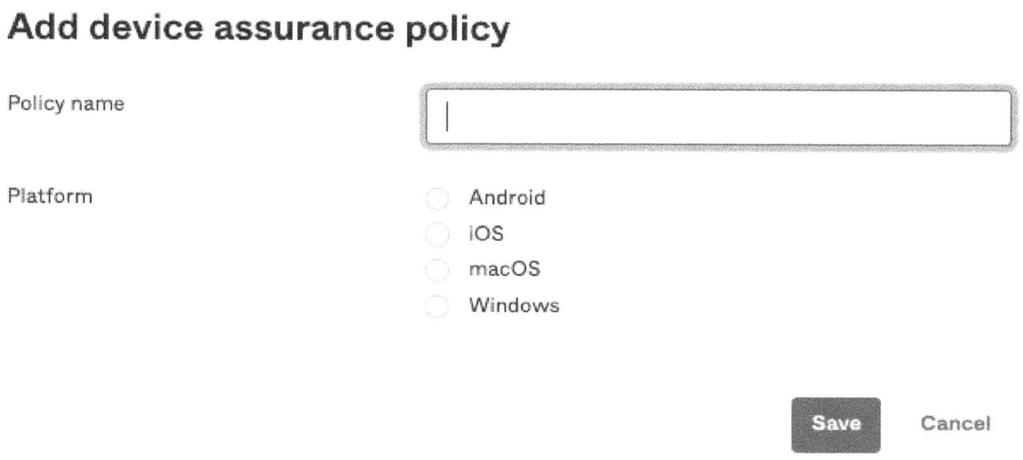

Add device assurance policy

Policy name

Platform
- Android
- iOS
- macOS
- Windows

[Save]   Cancel

Figure 4.27 – Add device assurance policy

When you select any of the platform types, a bottom section will open and allow you to determine the settings that apply to that platform type.

These settings are straightforward; we will explain these settings using the iOS and Windows options.

Once you select **iOS**, you will be presented with the following settings:

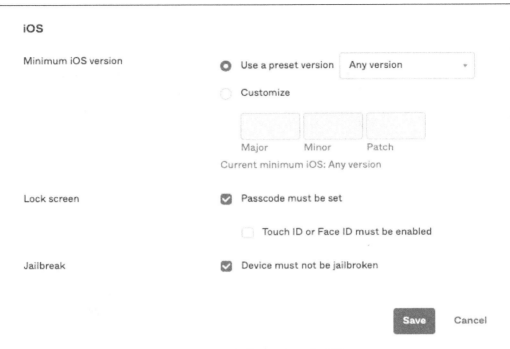

Figure 4.28 – Policy settings for iOS

Here, you can set the following options:

- **Minimum iOS version**: Either select a standard version or customize and specifically determine a version using the **Major**, **Minor**, and **Patch** versions

- **Lock screen**: This setting will determine whether at a bare minimum, the passcode is set or not, and additionally requires Touch ID or Face ID

- **Jailbreak**: This will determine whether access to the device is allowed or not when the device is jailbroken

For Windows, the settings are similar but there are nuances. This is what this section looks like:

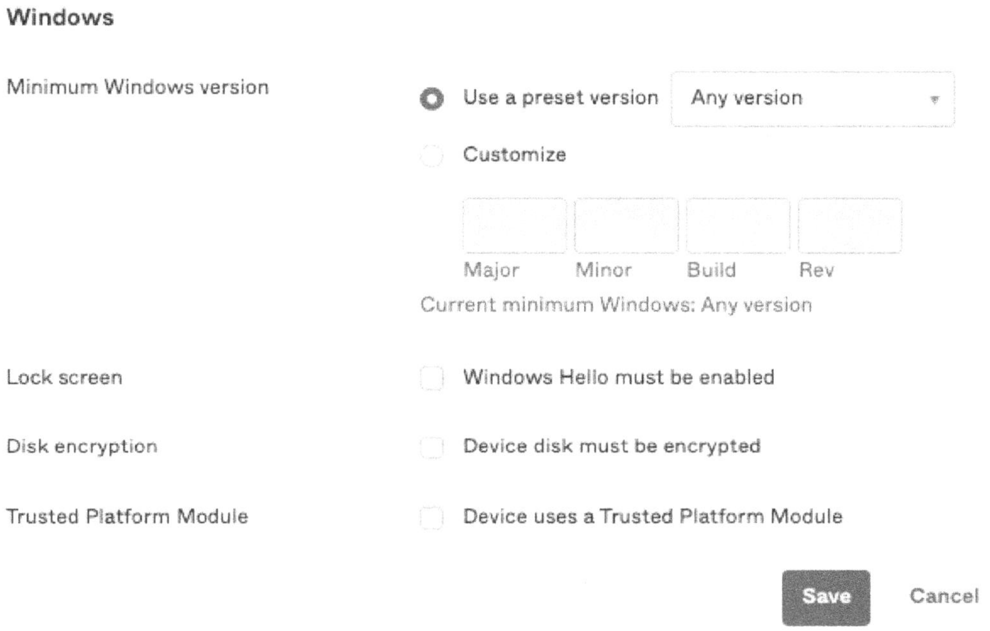

Windows

Minimum Windows version

◉ Use a preset version   Any version ▾

○ Customize

Major   Minor   Build   Rev
Current minimum Windows: Any version

Lock screen   ☐ Windows Hello must be enabled

Disk encryption   ☐ Device disk must be encrypted

Trusted Platform Module   ☐ Device uses a Trusted Platform Module

Save   Cancel

Figure 4.29 – Policy settings for Windows

You also have options to set here:

- **Minimum Windows version**: Here, you can either select a standard OS version or specify one using the **Customize** option
- **Lock screen**: This will require Windows Hello to be enabled and used for accessing the device
- **Disk encryption**: Selecting this option will make disk encryption mandatory to allow access
- **Trusted Platform Module**: Here, you can specify whether using a TPM will be required

The combination of these settings will give you a device assurance policy that can be added to the authentication policy.

So, let's take a look at that specifically. Once you have created your authentication policy, under any rule you have added, click on **Action | Edit**. Scroll down to the **AND Device state is** setting. If you select **Registered**, a new setting will appear, where you can select one or more device assurance policies:

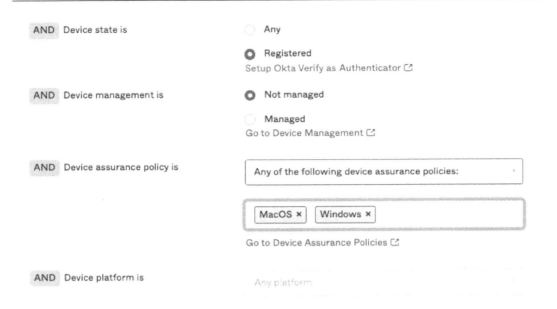

Figure 4.30 – Settings for the authentication policy

The **Device assurance policy is** setting will give you the option to select the policies you want to add. If you select a policy, you will see that the next setting, **Device platform is**, will become unavailable. This is due to conflicting settings if both were to be available.

And there you go – you now understand device signals, device posture, and device assurances. Now, let's look at even more device security by integrating Okta with an MDM solution.

Integrating with MDM

Okta allows MDM solutions to integrate with Okta to exchange possible information on the user and device. This adds a more consolidated security experience around a user and its access. Okta offers integrations with **Microsoft Endpoint Manager** (**MEM**) (formerly known as **Intune**), **Jamf**, or a custom CA.

We will discuss the high-level requirements and features of the MDM integrations.

When you go to the **Security | Device integrations** section, you will find a section where you can set up MDM integrations. First, you have the opportunity to integrate with existing endpoint security systems. By clicking on **Add platform**, you can start the process of adding one.

This will give you the choice to select a platform – either **iOS**, **Android**, or **Desktop (Windows and macOS only)**:

Device Integrations

Endpoint management   Certificate authority   Endpoint security

Add device management platform

1 ——————————— 2
Select platform   Configure management attestation

Select platform

Select platform   ◉ iOS
○ Android
○ Desktop (Windows and macOS only)

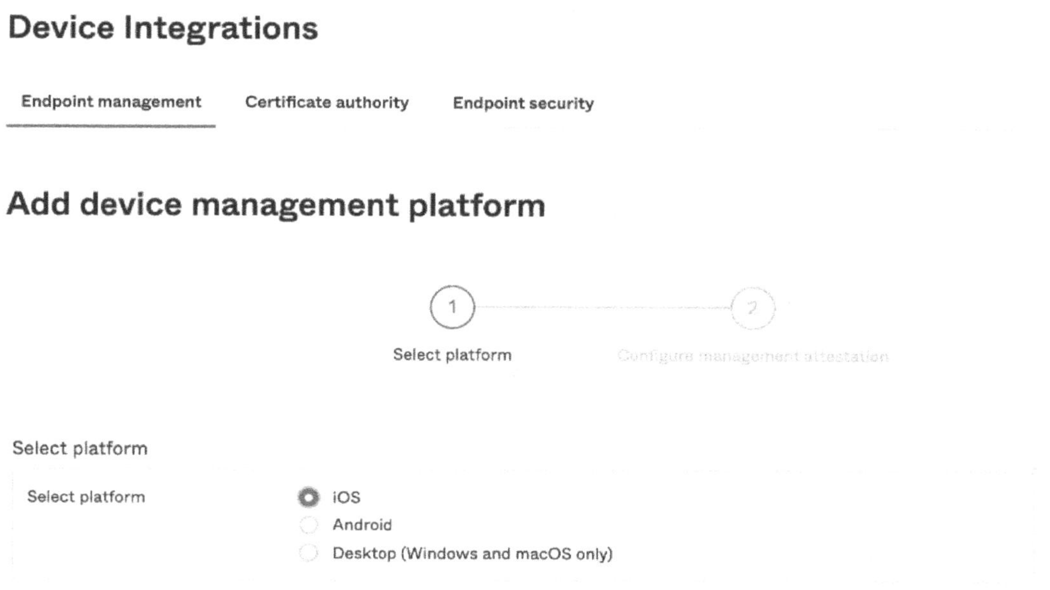

Figure 4.31 – Endpoint management settings

If we select **Desktop (Windows and macOS only)** and click **Next**, we will be presented with the next window, where we can configure management attestation.

If we want to set up MEM, this means we need to select **Dynamic SCEP URL** and then **Microsoft Intune (delegated SCEP)**:

> Note
>
> **Simple Certificate Enrollment Protocol (SCEP)** is a way for devices such as computers and phones to get digital certificates, which are like digital ID cards that let them securely connect to networks and services. MEM can add these certificates to enrolled devices to ensure security and identification.

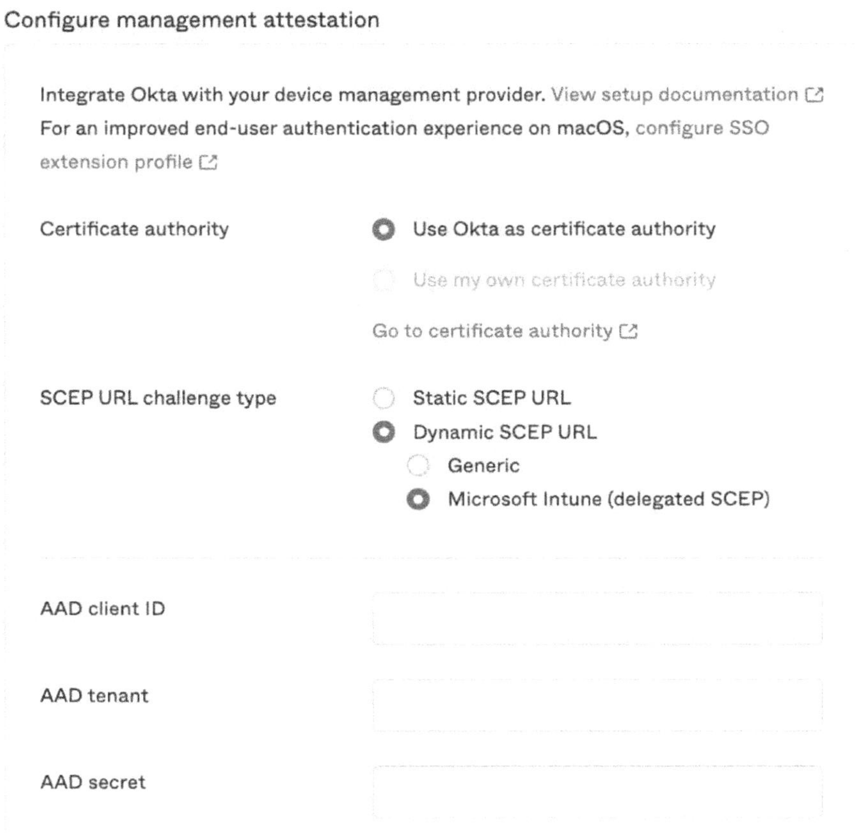

Configure management attestation

Integrate Okta with your device management provider. View setup documentation ⤴
For an improved end-user authentication experience on macOS, configure SSO
extension profile ⤴

Certificate authority	⦿ Use Okta as certificate authority
	○ Use my own certificate authority
	Go to certificate authority ⤴
SCEP URL challenge type	○ Static SCEP URL
	⦿ Dynamic SCEP URL
	○ Generic
	⦿ Microsoft Intune (delegated SCEP)
AAD client ID	
AAD tenant	
AAD secret	

Figure 4.32 – Configure management attestation

By following the documentation for the setup, you can eventually pass the **AAD Client ID**, **AAD tenant**, and **AAD secret** properties.

After that, click **Save**; the integration will be set. This is just a part of the required setup. To allow the device management to be utilized by Okta, the following is required:

- Okta Verify must be installed on the machine and registered by the user to their profile in Okta
- The user profile must be associated with the MDM solution
- The user must have authenticated at least once with FastPass

This will make sure the SCEP certificate will be picked up by Okta Verify and that the information is passed along to Okta.

> **Note**
>
> For other MDM solutions, Okta has detailed information available to help you set that up: `https://help.okta.com/oie/en-us/Content/Topics/identity-engine/devices/managed-main.htm`.

In the second tab of the **Device Integrations** menu, you will find Okta's own **certificate authority (CA)**. You can add your own if you want to, but it will require understanding, resources, and upkeep, which can quickly become costly. Using Okta's CA allows you to outsource this to Okta:

Figure 4.33 – View of Okta's CA

The CA certificate can be uploaded to an MDM (**Jamf Pro** or **VMware Workspace ONE**) so that it can be integrated with their solution with Okta. You can also add the static SCEP URL as the endpoint that the MDM solution can call upon.

For details on how to set this up, please go to `https://help.okta.com/oie/en-us/Content/Topics/identity-engine/devices/configure-ca-main.htm`.

Okta also allows other vendors to integrate and use their signals as part of the assessment. By having third-party MDM tools manage the device, you can generate a trusted certificate exchange with Okta. This device trust can then be used in application sign-on rules as an extra vector. This allows you to add to the security by using your Okta global session and authentication policies to assess the user's situation.

Beyond that, with the help of device trust, you can use custom SAML attributes to inform the application about the status of the device and have the application itself use that status for more granular limitations. This is called device context for limited access.

For device context – for limited access as well as dynamic authentication context – the **service provider (SP)** must be able to consume these extra values during authentication. Based on this, the SP acts upon the values to do its own risk assessment and guide the user according to its policies that have been set up for the different risk levels. This can require certain licenses or other add-ons to be set up. Salesforce is one example that can consume and use this input to set its policies and determine whether the user is allowed to change values, read information, or perform any other task, based on the outcome.

So, now that we have understood the concept of Okta's contextual access, let's dive deeper into the different types of context vectors that are used in these processes.

Setting up network zones

Network zones within Okta are used through all policies. The usage of network zones is quite simple to explain, whether you are in a zone or not. The network zone is a security perimeter that's used as a restricted access layer. A network zone can be a single IP address, one or more IP ranges, or geolocations. You can have multiple networks to be used in different ways. You can also categorize network zones as blocklists, flipping the idea of being safe in a zone to not allowing access at all from that zone.

Depending on your situation, consider the following:

- You can have static zones, such as IP ranges, WAN addresses, and proxies, or dynamic zones, such as proxies, country zones, or Tor anonymizers.
- When creating rules for sign-in policies, while using notifications for VPN and incorporating **Integrated Windows Authentication (IWA)**, network zones can be used for more granularity.
- When a zone definition is changed, this will automatically update policies and rules. A maximum of 100 zones can be configured.
- Each zone can contain up to 150 gateway IPs and 150 proxy IPs. This excludes IP blocklist zones.
- Similarly, IP blacklist zones can contain up to 1,000 gateways per zone and up to 25,000 per org.

Setting up zones is straightforward; you can find the settings for network zones under **Security | Networks**. You can create and specify all your network zones right here:

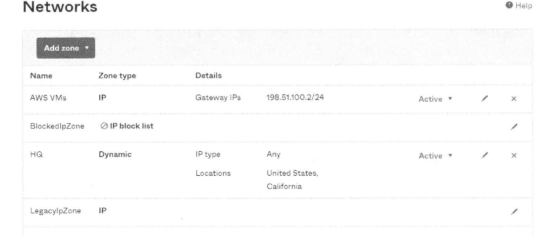

Figure 4.34 – Networks overview

When you start creating your list, you will always start with two network zones that cannot be deleted: LegacyIpZone and BlockedIpZone. These are defaults within Okta.

> **Tip**
> When a new Okta org is created, these zones are created with it. As they aren't that descriptive, it might be wise to rename them so that it's clearer how you want to use them in your policies.

Setting up an IP zone

Any additional network zones can be added by using the **Add zone** button.

The dropdown that appears will give you the choice to set up either an IP zone with ranges of IPs or a dynamic zone:

Figure 4.35 – Adding an IP zone

If we choose **IP Zone**, we will be presented with the following options:

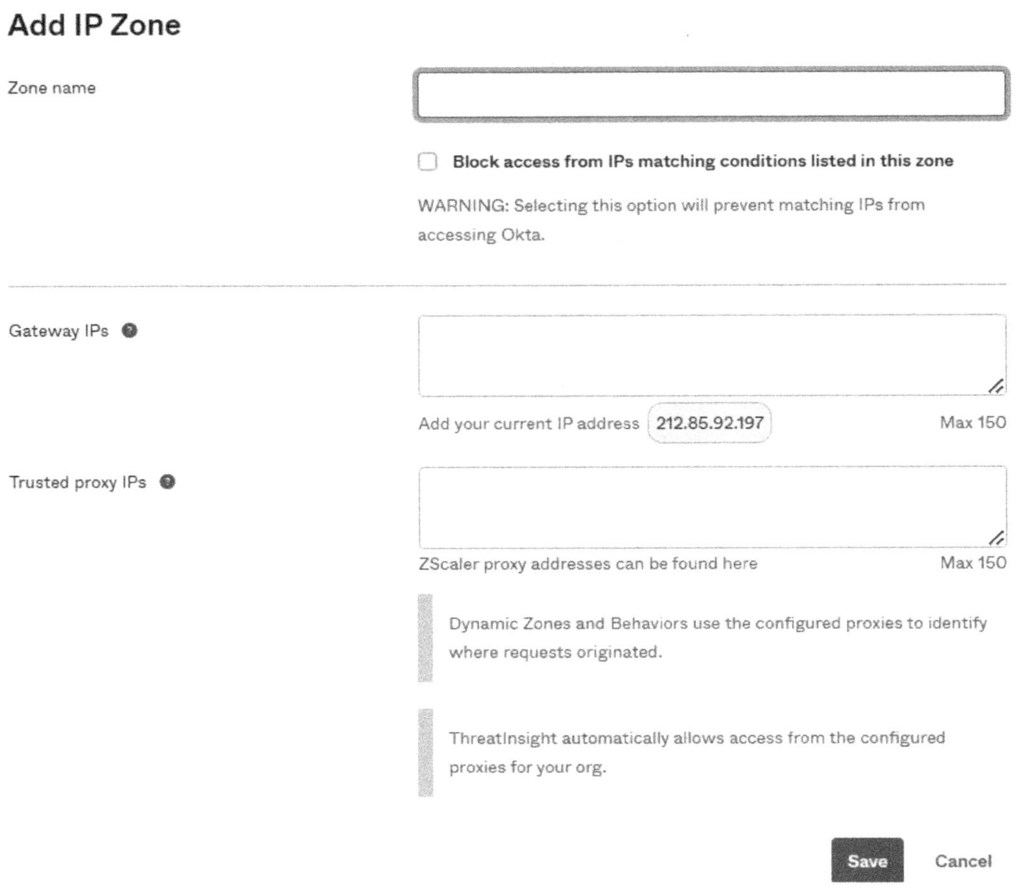

Add IP Zone

Zone name

Block access from IPs matching conditions listed in this zone

WARNING: Selecting this option will prevent matching IPs from accessing Okta.

Gateway IPs ❓

Add your current IP address 212.85.92.197   Max 150

Trusted proxy IPs ❓

ZScaler proxy addresses can be found here   Max 150

Dynamic Zones and Behaviors use the configured proxies to identify where requests originated.

ThreatInsight automatically allows access from the configured proxies for your org.

Save   Cancel

Figure 4.36 – Add IP Zone

You can see the following fields in the preceding screenshot:

- **Zone name**: Give your zone a name; making it readable and explanatory is helpful

- A checkbox to turn this network zone into a blocklist, therefore blocking access entirely toward Okta

- **Gateway IPs**: These can either be single IP addresses, ranges of IP addresses separated by hyphens, or **Classless Inter-Domain Routing** (**CIDR**)-notated IP ranges – for example, `216.119.143.01`, `216.119.143.02-216.119.143.22`, or `216.119.143.01/24`

- **Trusted proxy IPs**: These can either be single addresses, addresses separated by commas, ranges with hyphens, or CIDR notation

By clicking **Save**, you will add the new zone to the network zone overview. After this, you can start using the zones immediately.

Setting a dynamic zone

Setting up a dynamic zone is similar to the IP zone, only we get the opportunity to add geo zones as perimeters. This allows for much more dynamic options regarding the usage of these zones in policies and so on.

Start by clicking the **Add zone** button and selecting **Dynamic Zone.**

The following window shows a slightly different setup. We are now presented with a few options:

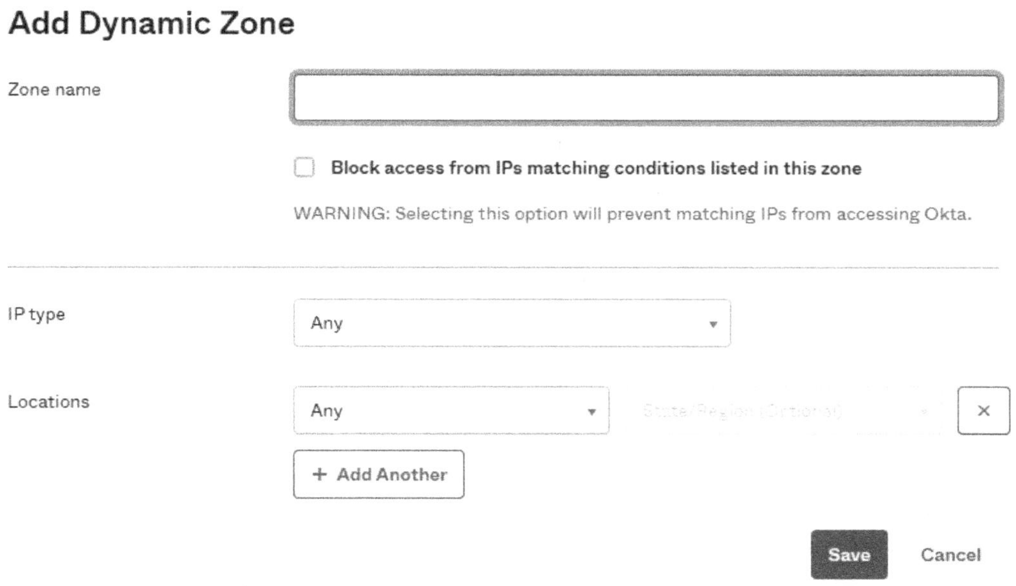

Add Dynamic Zone

Zone name	
	☐ **Block access from IPs matching conditions listed in this zone**
	WARNING: Selecting this option will prevent matching IPs from accessing Okta.
IP type	Any ▾
Locations	Any ▾ State/Region (Optional) ▾ ✕
	+ Add Another
	Save Cancel

Figure 4.37 – Setting up a dynamic zone

For **Zone name**, make sure the selected zones match the naming to avoid confusion in using the zone. Examples of this can be a country name, a specific office location, and so on.

Then, there is a checkbox to make this dynamic zone a blacklist.

After that, you have the choice to select an IP type:

- **Any**: To allow any type of IP
- **Any Proxy**: To allow any type of proxy
- **TorAnonymizer**: To filter untraceable IP addresses
- **Not a TorAnonymizer**: To exclude Tor Anonymizers from the zones

Lastly, we can add locations. This allows for a more geolocated approach:

1. First, you must select the country you want to include in the zone.

2. You can further filter it down into states or regions.

After you hit **Save**, the zone can be used in different areas. It can be really helpful to filter a region so that you can manage at a more granular level. Let's say the workforce in New York needs access to Salesforce, but outside of New York, no one should be allowed access. You can create a New York zone to achieve this.

Let's look at some other dynamic elements that Okta uses to further the granularity of options.

Behavior detection

Behavior detection is an important part of the zero-trust path with Okta. Understanding the user's context is key. Okta allows you, as an admin, to use parts of this context in different policies. By adding these vectors, Okta is capable of setting risk scores and using them to tighten or loosen the policies.

Behavior detection has two components: trackable behaviors and definable actions based on changes from the user.

Here are some examples of trackable behaviors:

- Signing in from a new location, such as a country, state, or city

- Signing in from a specified distance from a previous successful sign-in location

- Signing in from a device that is new for the user – for example, a different laptop or mobile workstation

- Signing in from an IP address that is new for the user – for example, a mobile hotspot, home IP, or public transport

- Signing in after an impossible journey, which means it's deemed impossible for a user to have traveled between two geographical locations between two successive sign-in attempts

Here are some examples of actions:

- Allow or deny access

- Require the user to verify with an additional authenticator

- Set the session lifetime

Under **Security | Behavior Detection**, we can see all the behaviors Okta created by default and add any more or change the defaults to our liking:

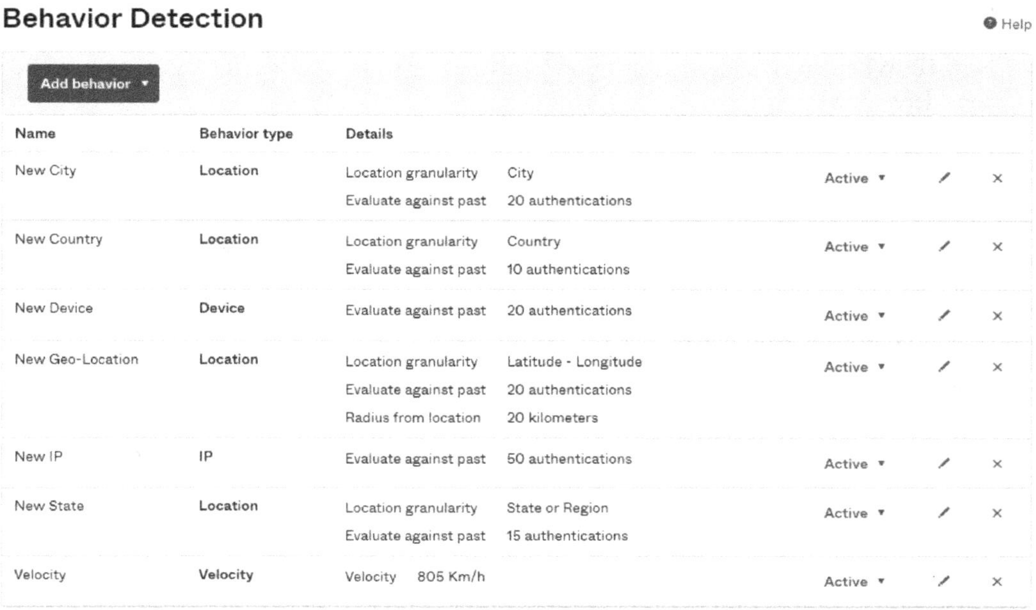

Behavior Detection

Add behavior ▼

Name	Behavior type	Details				
New City	Location	Location granularity Evaluate against past	City 20 authentications	Active ▼	/	×
New Country	Location	Location granularity Evaluate against past	Country 10 authentications	Active ▼	/	×
New Device	Device	Evaluate against past	20 authentications	Active ▼	/	×
New Geo-Location	Location	Location granularity Evaluate against past Radius from location	Latitude - Longitude 20 authentications 20 kilometers	Active ▼	/	×
New IP	IP	Evaluate against past	50 authentications	Active ▼	/	×
New State	Location	Location granularity Evaluate against past	State or Region 15 authentications	Active ▼	/	×
Velocity	Velocity	Velocity 805 Km/h		Active ▼	/	×

Figure 4.38 – Behavior Detection

Here, you can **add**, **edit**, **delete**, and **set** behaviors to **Inactive** or **Active**. Let's go through them and see how they are used or act in Okta.

We can group these behaviors into four different types.

First, let's see **Location**:

- **Country**: A country that hasn't been part of previous successful logins.
- **State**: A state that hasn't been part of previous successful logins.
- **City**: A city that hasn't been part of previous successful logins.
- **New Geo-Location**: You can specify a location within a specified radius from a previous successful login. Anything outside of that would be new behavior.

Next, we will learn about **Device**:

- **New Device**: A device new to the specific user that previously wasn't used for a successful login. If you switch browsers on a previously used device, that would be considered a new device, since it's client-based.

Next in line is **IP**:

- **New IP**: When an IP address hasn't previously been part of a successful login, it would be considered new

Lastly, let's learn about **Velocity**:

- **Velocity**: A measurement of velocity that's used to identify suspicious logins. Velocity is evaluated based on the distance and time that's elapsed between two subsequent user logins.

Each of these types allows more granularity and can be added individually or combined in a global session policy or authentication policy:

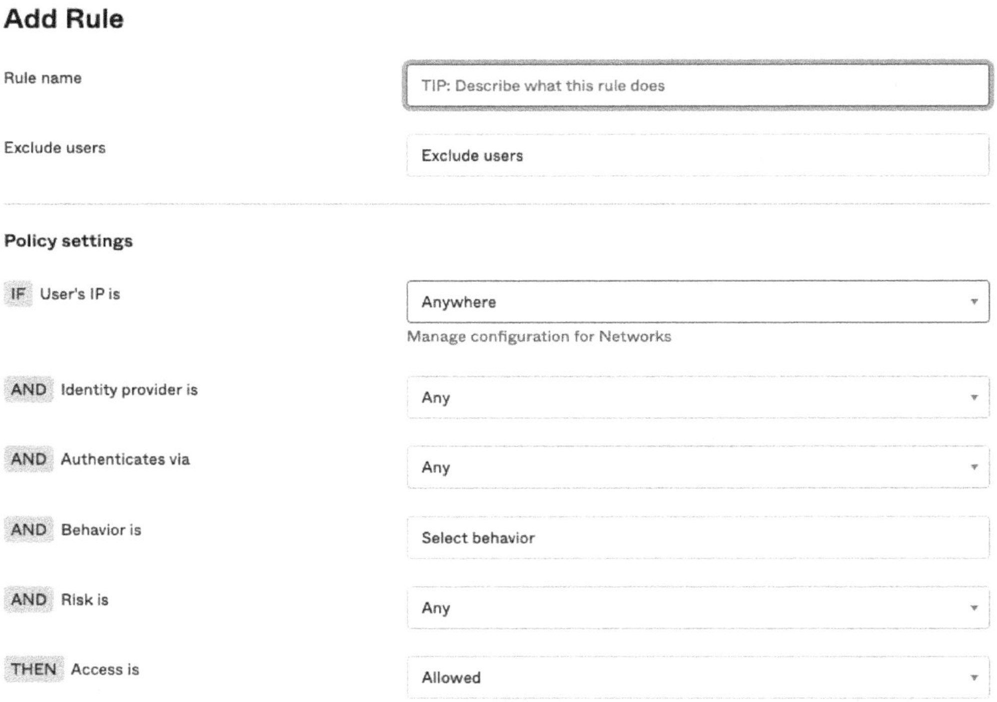

Add Rule

Rule name	TIP: Describe what this rule does
Exclude users	Exclude users

Policy settings

IF	User's IP is	Anywhere
		Manage configuration for Networks
AND	Identity provider is	Any
AND	Authenticates via	Any
AND	Behavior is	Select behavior
AND	Risk is	Any
THEN	Access is	Allowed

Figure 4.39 – Behavior detection elements added to a policy rule

By adding this to a policy, you can add layers to the steps of the risk assessment. Let's say we have sales teams on the move. They might go from town to town. Adding the state and city behavior to the sign-on policy allows us to validate previous logins. New states and towns will be checked against the given amount in the behavior. If Okta then determines the risk as **High**, the user will fall into that rule of the policy.

We can create multiple rules per policy, setting the risk level to **Any**, **High**, **Medium**, or **Low**. Based on those conditions, we can have the user go through different sign-on flows.

As with any other policy, these work in a hierarchy, and the user will be vetted against them from top to bottom. Therefore, it is wise to start with the highest risk or strongest rule at the top and end with the weakest rule at the bottom.

By using rules within policies, you allow Okta to work for you and no longer force the users into one set of strict or loose policies and rules. You allow yourself to create more elaborate sign-on policies, which prevents the overhead of creating one for every scenario.

All of this is saved in the end user's profile. If for whatever reason it is necessary to clear this out, you can go to the user's profile and reset their entire behavior profile:

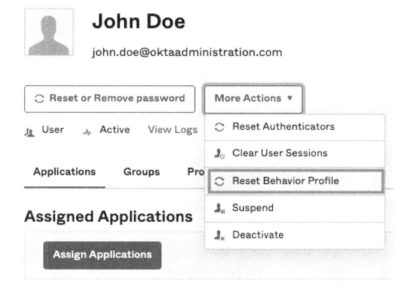

Figure 4.40 – Resetting the user's behavior profile

This will make sure the user will start recreating their profile with new information.

We covered a lot of ground within Okta's contextual access options, such as using external systems as additional vectors for risk assessment and working with different zones. Then, we talked about setting up policies with rules and additional behaviors to complete the grand scope of policy-making.

Now, let's have a look at the experience of enrolling in MFA for an end user.

Enrolling end users in MFA

Previously, we looked at how enrollment with different authenticators works, but let's take a closer look at it from an end user perspective. We'll learn this with the help of an example: an end user enrolling in Okta Verify. After a new MFA policy is rolled out, end users will be prompted to enroll in one or multiple authenticators on their next sign-on or when that authenticator is required. Let's look at how it would work when the user clicks **Setup for Okta Verify**:

In the first step, the end user will select what device they are using, and then be informed to download the Okta Verify application from the device's app store. Afterward, with the downloaded app, the user can scan the QR code to connect and register:

Figure 4.41 – Okta Verify download and QR scan step to enroll

Once the code has been scanned, the user is asked to turn on and use biometric options if the device supports fingerprint or facial recognition, for example.

Once the setup is done, the user will be sent back to the authenticator page. Here, they might need to enroll additional authenticators to complete enrollment entirely, if the policy requires the user to do so. If they are not required to enroll in more, they can select to finish the setup and proceed to log in to Okta.

Now that we've enrolled an authenticator, let's take a look at how to reset one.

Resetting authenticators

There can be situations where users need to reset their authenticators, as follows:

- The end user has a new device and needs to recreate an active Okta Verify or Google Authenticator account

- Something isn't working with the end user's authenticator – for instance, they are stuck in a loop, or the OTP code isn't working

> **Tip**
> Make sure your end users enroll in at least two authenticators on setup. This should preferably be on two different devices or platforms (for example, Okta Verify and SMS, or a MacBook's Touch ID and Google Authenticator). That way, they can reset one of them while using the other.

As an administrator, you can always help your end users reset their authenticators. Navigate to **Directory | People** and, under **More Actions**, click **Reset Authenticators**:

Figure 4.42 – Resetting the user's authenticators

But users can also help themselves. If an authenticator reset is planned, such as changing their device, they can go to **Settings** and scroll down to **Extra Verification**:

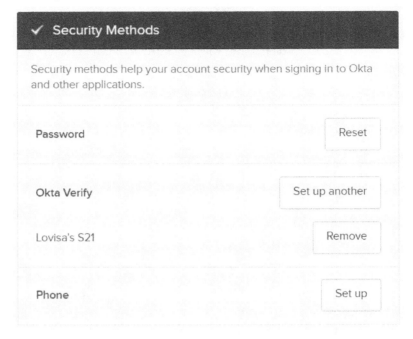

Figure 4.43 – Enrolled authenticators, and the ability to reset or remove them

For instance, with Okta Verify, the end user can remove **Okta Verify** from this menu and re-enroll from this page, or let it happen at the next required authentication moment.

We now understand Okta from an end user's perspective. It will benefit the administrators if end users learn how to enroll and reset authenticators. Next, we'll look at using MFA with a VPN.

Securing a VPN with MFA

VPNs have been one of the standard ways to connect securely to applications and data behind organizational perimeters. As VPNs evolve, so do options to secure them. The credentials to log in can be compromised, and having additional security allows outside threats to be thwarted and secures what is usually most critical and sensitive behind the VPN.

Different VPN software and vendors deliver different types of integrations. Some might allow SSO to be set up, while others might use directories such as **Active Directory** or LDAP, and perhaps even RADIUS. In any of these methods, you can set Okta's login credentials to be the only set of credentials the user has and add MFA to the login process.

As we spoke about earlier in this chapter, we can utilize at least two categories in securing access: *something we know* and *something we have*, and perhaps even *something we are*.

Depending on the type of VPN software running, the client of the user might be able to visually allow the user to choose an authenticator type:

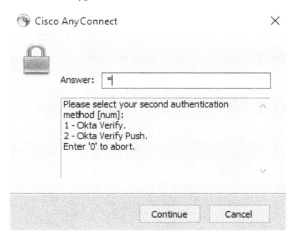

Figure 4.44 – Requesting for authenticator selection

As shown in the preceding screenshot, the user will be prompted to choose an authenticator, and the window will then either switch to a window to input an OTP or simply await confirmation from Okta based on the Okta Verify push response. The software might even use modern authentication and allow a browser login to be used. This can fully incorporate Okta's login flow.

In other cases, the VPN software might not allow this to happen, and the user will have to input the password and string an authenticator OTP to it in the password field. If it's allowed to use Okta Verify push notification, Okta will directly push the request and the user can verify it. During this process, the VPN authentication request will pause until Okta fully verifies the user's login and then allows the process to continue.

Of course, sometimes, you must make the best of the situation, and the user might need additional authenticators. This can be hard to manage, but with Okta's adaptive multifactor functionality, you have the full array of options ready to be used, and as an admin, you can make sure that the least amount of friction is used to deliver the highest possible security.

Setting up these rules depends on the VPN software. Some can be set up with authentication policies, while others might require global session policies to be used.

Summary

In this chapter, we learned everything we need to know about using different kinds of authenticators and setting up policies for them, both for signing in and for accessing applications. We also deep-dived into Okta's features around contextual MFA, where your authentication and global session policies can be adaptive. You now understand how to set up zones and how to use them in different ways. Lastly, we looked at the possibility of using MFA for VPNs and similar solutions.

In the next chapter, we will look into Okta's **lifecycle management (LCM)** features. We will discuss the basics of LCM and its powerful features, such as provisioning and HR-as-a-source.

5

Automating Using Lifecycle Management

In this chapter, we will look at how we can use some of the knowledge we gained in previous chapters for a complete user lifecycle. We will look at how we can use integrations for user provisioning, such as setting up a **Human Resources Information System** (**HRIS**) as a sourcing service. We will also dive deeper into editing a user's profile, for instance, with expression language.

For the groups we learned about in *Chapter 2, Working with Universal Directory*, we'll now learn how to use automation to get them to work for us.

By automating the on- and offboarding flows, we not only save time for new hires, HR, administrators, and system owners – we also increase accuracy, but most importantly, security. This is done by making sure tasks aren't skipped or forgotten by using automation.

These are some of the skills you will learn:

- Automating user provisioning
- Provisioning rich profiles
- Setting up group rules
- Setting up self-service options

Automating user provisioning

In *Chapters 2, 3*, and *4*, we discussed topics that describe individual elements of the user provisioning process. In this chapter, groups, directory integrations, application provisioning, and so on will all come together for complete onboarding and offboarding. Let's look at how we can put it all together.

As we mentioned in *Chapter 3, Using Single Sign-On for a Great End User Experience*, there are different kinds of integrations available in the **Okta Integration Network** (**OIN**), and many of the applications have **Systems for Cross-Domain Identity Management** (**SCIM**) possibilities. SCIM is an open standard for managing user identity information. With SCIM, there is a defined schema and a REST API for **Create, Read, Update, and Delete (CRUD)** operations. To put it more simply, SCIM is a protocol for storing user information in a way that identity data can easily be shared with multiple applications.

Let's look at it with an example. If an end user quits and an administrator deactivates their account in Okta, the **Active** user attribute is set to false, and the attribute is also updated in any SCIM-connected applications.

This is a possible **lifecycle management (LCM)** flow for applications that support CRUD operations. When a new user is created with certain attributes, a new account can be created in downstream applications that have a SCIM or other integration that supports the *create* operation. You can discern this by looking at the capabilities of the integrations. Navigate to **Applications** | **Applications** | **Add Application** and select the application you will integrate. In the **Overview** section, you will see the application's capabilities:

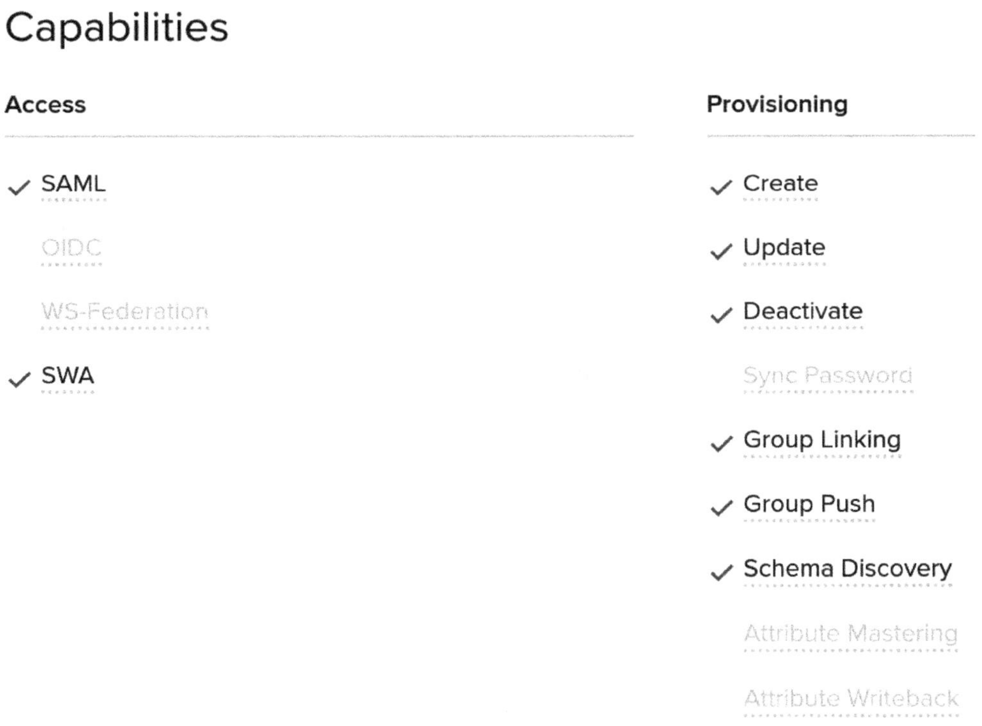

Capabilities

Access

✓ SAML

OIDC

WS-Federation

✓ SWA

Provisioning

✓ Create

✓ Update

✓ Deactivate

Sync Password

✓ Group Linking

✓ Group Push

✓ Schema Discovery

Attribute Mastering

Attribute Writeback

Figure 5.1 – Examples of the capabilities of an application

Using group rules allows you to automate the account assignment of users to applications.

For instance, if a user changes department, the *update* operation can deprovision a user from an application, if that application isn't assigned to the user's new department. That way, you stay updated and secure, and this can pass any audit coming your way.

As the last step, if a user is deactivated in Okta, they can also be deactivated in downstream applications if they support the *deactivation* operation. This way, you can be certain that users have no access to data after they have left the organization.

First, let's take a look at how we provision users.

Provisioning users

Setting up applications with provisioning capabilities can be pretty straightforward. We have looked at some of these features before in different chapters, but let's see how the full provisioning process would look for an application to get an overview. Once the app has been added, as we did in *Chapter 3, Using Single Sign-On for a Great End User Experience*, go to the **Provisioning** tab and start the integration. Okta will guide you through this; it can be different for each application. In general, Okta mainly uses a service account to gain access to the application and its resources. Once the integration is set up, the service account will leverage SCIM or other means to manage the users. The side panel may have some or all of the options, such as **To App**, **To Okta**, and **Integration**, which could look like this:

Settings

To App

To Okta

Integration

Figure 5.2 – Provisioning settings

In the **Integration** tab, you can see information on how Okta and the application connect. As every application has a different requirement, it is beyond the scope of this book to go over all of them. These integrations usually use an API key but also might require a service admin who can authorize certain scopes of the application. We go over APIs, authorization, and scopes in *Chapter 8, API Access Management*. Let's go over the **To App** and **To Okta** options now.

In the **To App** section, you can set up how Okta can manage different options for the users in the application. By simply enabling the **Create Users**, **Update User Attributes**, **Deactivate Users**, and **Sync Password** options, you enable Okta to start managing the identities in the application:

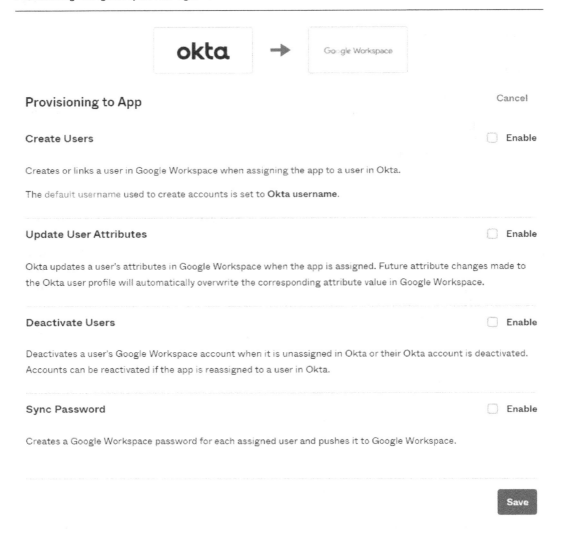

Figure 5.3 – To App settings

These options are not very hard to understand but they can have an impact on how you want to manage your users with Okta:

- **Create Users**: Use this if you want to automate the creation of users from Okta to the app. If the application has different sources that create users and Okta only needs to manage the users after they have been created, that might be a reason not to activate this feature.

- **Update User Attributes**: This allows Okta to sync anything that changes on the user's profile through profile mapping into the user's profile in the integrated application.

- **Deactivate Users**: This makes sure the user's state is synced with Okta. If that is not the desired state for that application, leave the **Deactivate Users** checkmark box unchecked.

- **Sync Password**: This allows Okta to update the password in the app by either syncing a random password or the Okta password into the app after the user's password in Okta has been updated. Unchecking it will lead to passwords not being synchronized and might be good enough if SSO is set up. Depending on the scenario and strategy, one of the options will probably fit your needs.

Some applications might have extra options. For instance, the content management application box provides some extra options for managing data once a user gets offboarded:

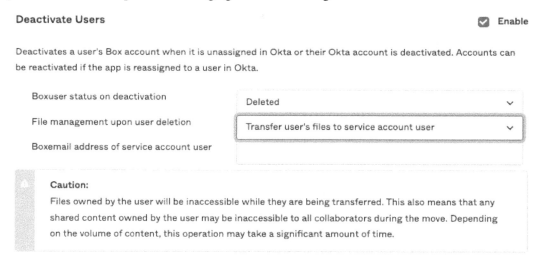

Figure 5.4 – Box options for content management after deactivation

These options are very specific to the application and aren't commonly used across all applications supporting provisioning.

In the **To Okta** settings, we can set up different elements concerning importing data into Okta and how to handle that. Let's go over the different settings:

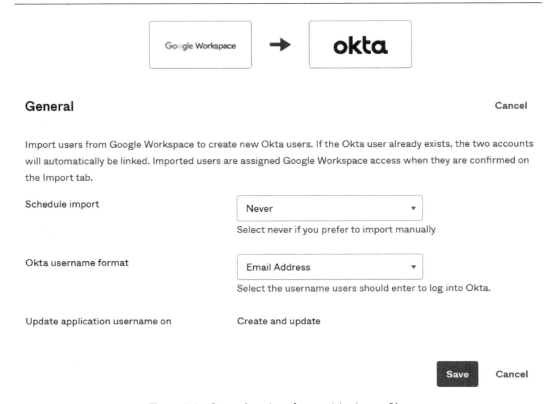

Figure 5.5 – General settings for provisioning to Okta

Here's what these settings mean:

- **Schedule import**: After you click **Edit**, you can choose in which periodic time frame you want the integration to scan for new users. For every import it does, it will also check for groups and update that information too. A scheduled import can be done as often as every hour or as rarely as every 2 days, but this depends on the app's capabilities. If you set it to **Never**, it will only import manually, which you can do on the **Import** tab of the application.

- **Okta username format**: The imported users might need to have a username set and the next option allows you to choose which imported value is set as the Okta username. You can either go for **Email Address** or pick **Custom** and use **Expression Language** to create your structure for the username based on the attributes available to you from the application and Okta. The setting looks like this:

Figure 5.6 – Custom username options for newly imported users

- **Update application username on**: Click **Save** and the periodic import and name convention will be applied to all new users coming in from that specific application.

On the next section of settings on the same page, you can determine what to do with these imported users:

User Creation & Matching   Cancel

Imported user is an exact match to Okta user if	○ Okta username format matches ● Email matches ○ The following attribute matches: firstName ○ The following combination of attributes matches: Okta username format or Email
Allow partial matches	☐ Partial match on first and last name
Confirm matched users	☐ Auto-confirm exact matches ☐ Auto-confirm partial matches
Confirm new users	☐ Auto-confirm new users ☐ Auto-activate new users

Save   Cancel

Figure 5.7 – User Creation & Matching

Just as we discussed in *Chapter 2, Working with Universal Directory*, these settings are similar in setup. In that chapter, it was concerning the directory setup. Here, we can set similar settings for applications. In this **User Creation & Matching** section, you can set how imported users are checked against possible existing users in Okta and how Okta needs to confirm and activate these users.

Under the **Imported user is an exact match to Okta user if** setting, you can choose from the following options:

- **Okta username format matches**: This setting checks whether the username in the app matches an existing Okta username

- **Email matches**: Selecting this option checks whether an email address matches the user's Okta email address

- **The following attribute matches**: By choosing this option, you can select an attribute you want to match on – for example, `firstName`, `title`, or `phoneNumber`

- **The following combination of attributes matches**: This is similar to the previous option but allows you to choose pre-set attribute combinations, such as **Okta Username format or Email** or **Email and Name**

> **Important note**
>
> Be cautious with using attributes that might have values that are similar to other users. It can allow users to be overwritten or misused.

All these options make sure Okta won't import the user as a new user if there is a match. Having multiple users with unconnected identities has consequences for the user experience. Think of importing a user from Google Workspace with user profile values that don't match with its equivalent in Slack. The user might be automatically activated by both import methods and all of a sudden have two accounts in Okta. Preventing that is the main reason to match users.

The next option is to allow partial matches. By turning that on, Okta will also check on matches with the first and last name. It can be that usernames, email addresses, and other attributes are different. Depending on how the mapping is set up, this can have an impact on the user's login credentials. Be cautious with this option – it can unexpectedly change the user experience and have an impact on what IT needs to do to remedy the problems.

After this, Okta wants to know how to act if matches are found. The first selection is for whether users can be auto-confirmed if an exact match or partial match is found. By ticking any of those boxes, Okta will import the user and connect the identities. Active users will get access to the app through Okta, and the identity in the app will be managed based on what you set up in the **To App** tab.

Lastly, Okta would like to know what to do with newfound users. The two options are as follows:

- Auto-confirming will import the new user into Okta, but will not activate the imported users. You might have good reasons to do that at a different time or after managing the identity manually or with other services.

- Auto-activating will immediately activate the user and send an activation email to them. This is the fastest way to import new users into Okta from another source.

You can also manually import users if required. By going to the **Import** tab, you will be presented with an **Import** button. Clicking on that will start an import job. Depending on the application, this can either go quickly or rather slowly. It depends on how the APIs are integrated.

The following screenshot shows an empty **Import** tab:

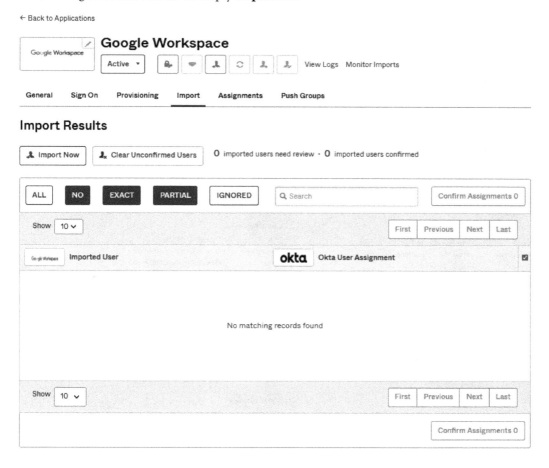

Figure 5.8 – Manually importing users from the Import tab

> **Important note**
> The **Import** tab is always available, even if provisioning isn't set up. In that case, you can import a CSV file that will import the users into the application's **Import** tab, allowing you to manually match users in the app with their Okta counterparts.

Once you have run an import, users will start coming in and have different statuses.

If you have set up any auto-confirmations or auto-activations, users following your matches will be auto-confirmed and perhaps auto-activated. If not, you can do that from the **Import** window.

This is what an **Import** tab filled with newly imported users looks like:

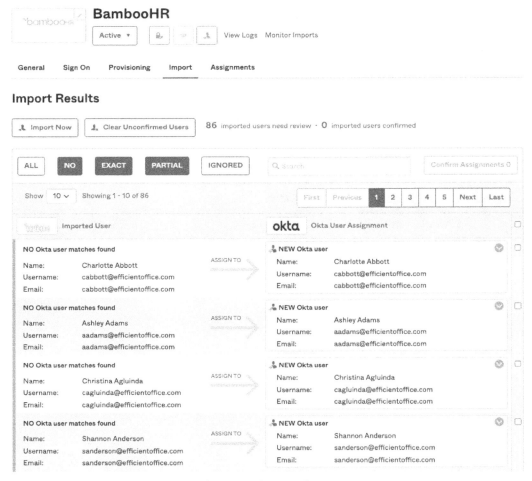

Figure 5.9 – Imported users

On the left, you will see the imported users with their application information, showing their **Name**, **Username**, and **Email** values.

On the right, you can see whether Okta found a match based on any of the previously mentioned attributes.

On each of the imported users, you can choose what to do with them by clicking the small round arrow. This will show the different options:

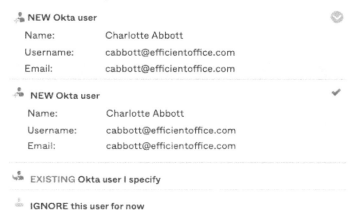

NEW Okta user

Name: Charlotte Abbott
Username: cabbott@efficientoffice.com
Email: cabbott@efficientoffice.com

NEW Okta user

Name: Charlotte Abbott
Username: cabbott@efficientoffice.com
Email: cabbott@efficientoffice.com

EXISTING Okta user I specify

IGNORE this user for now

Figure 5.10 – Import options

Let's look at all the options:

- **EXACT**: An exact match is found by Okta with an existing Okta user based on the matching rules you defined in the **User Creation & Matching** section.

- **NEW**: Create a new Okta user with the information found in the application.

- **EXISTING**: Match the user that was found against an existing user we search and specify within the **Import** window.

- **IGNORE**: No action will be taken on the found user. The import for this user will be ignored and the user will be added to the **IGNORED** filter in the **Import** window.

Perhaps you want the user to have an alternative account in Okta. In that case, creating a new user is the best way to go. Matching the user against an Okta user we specify is often used if the user is partially matched or has different email or username attributes. Ignoring the user will not confirm or activate the user. This is often done for service accounts that are also imported or guest users that do not need to be added to Okta.

Once you have checked the matches Okta made and are ready, you can select the users you want to confirm by ticking the checkbox next to their names.

If you have a large import, you can change the page view to show more users, and ticking the checkbox at the top will tick all checkboxes on the page shown. If you go to the next page, you can bulk-select all the users you want to confirm.

The **Confirm assignments** buttons at the top and bottom of the page will show the number of users you have selected in any option. When you click on it, it will ask you if you also want to activate the users. Depending on your import strategy, this might be a welcome option, or perhaps you want to wait until the activation date or need to do more on the user accounts before activating, such as importing and matching them from another source to complete the users' data.

Here, we can see a **Confirm Imported User Assignments** window ready to import, but not activate, the users:

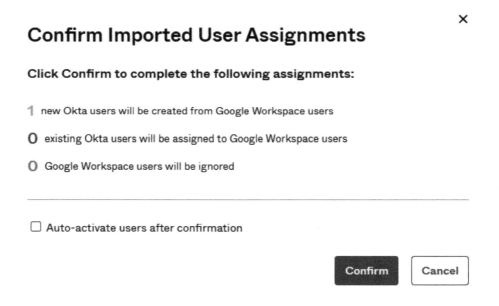

Figure 5.11 – The Confirm Imported User Assignments window

Once you have clicked **Confirm**, the selected users will disappear from the list. The ones you have ignored will be added to the **IGNORED** filter in the **Import** tab; the rest will be in your directory, ready to be managed from this point on.

In this case, we have set up an integration to be able to provision users to an application and import new users from it. This is a great way to manage and consolidate your users in the different applications you might have. But this can be made even more automated with an HR system to source users. Let's take a look at that.

Sourcing users

An employee's journey within a company usually starts and ends with the HR department. They are in charge of the hiring process and collect critical information about a new hire, such as contact information, the role they are going to fill, the department they are part of, the location they will be working at, and their start date. This is typically information that IT admins want, to maintain a correct user directory and make sure employees have the right access at the right time. Using your HR system as a source can allow you to manage all this from top to bottom with integrations.

Some HR systems have an existing integration in OIN, such as Workday, BambooHR, Namely, UltiPro, and SuccessFactors. These different systems have different capabilities. Some have deep integrations with possibilities such as group push, while some are more basic, with just attribute sync as a possibility.

If you are using an HR system without an available integration, there are still ways you can use it as a master: API calls or CSV mastering.

> **Important note**
> Using Okta's REST APIs, you can simulate typical integration actions using any program or scripting language that is capable of submitting web-based API requests and processing the results. One such alternative is Okta Workflows, which we will go through more in the next chapter.

If your HR system can export a CSV file, you can use that as a master in Okta. Let's look at how to set that up in Okta. Navigate to **Directory | Directory Integrations**, click **Add Directory**, and choose **Add CSV Directory**. In the **General** settings, for the initial setup, you only have to give your directory a name. Click **Done**. After that, you will do the rest of the setup.

The menu options look like this:

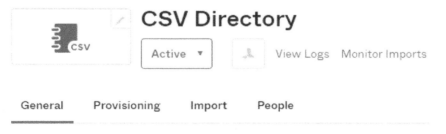

Figure 5.12 – Settings for CSV Directory

In the **General** tab, you only provide basic settings, such as describing the directory. If you use different CSV directories for different types of users (such as one for employees, one for contractors, and one for partners), you can describe that here.

The **Provisioning** tab is where the magic happens. To process the data in the CSV file, you have a lightweight agent at your disposal. You can install this agent on a Linux or Windows server. These are the prerequisites:

- The **On-Premises Provisioning** (**OPP**) agent needs to be installed on Linux (CentOS or RHEL) or Microsoft Windows Server (x86/x64) and sits behind a firewall

- The OPP agent version must be 1.03.00 or higher

- The CSV file must have a `.csv` extension and be saved to a folder on-premises

- Your CSV file must be in `UTF-8` format

- The OPP agent needs read permissions for the CSV file

- All active users must be present for every CSV import

- All required attributes must be present for every CSV import

- All attributes and headers must be formatted properly

These are the settings in the **Provisioning** tab under **Integration**:

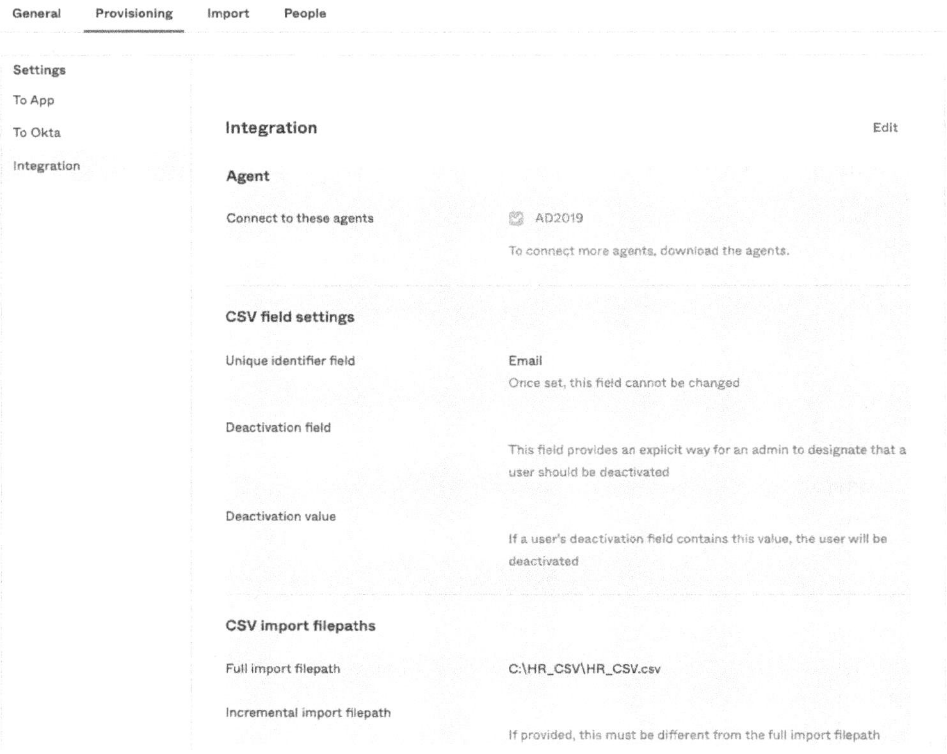

Figure 5.13 – Overview of the CSV Directory Integration page

Here's what each of these settings is used for:

- **Connect to these agents**: This will show all running agents. Ticked boxes will be the selected agents that this integration will be used to sync with.

- **Unique identifier field**: This is the attribute from your CSV file that will be used as a unique identifier. Remember that this should be the attribute name, not the display name – for example, `userID`.

- **Deactivation field**: The deactivation field in the CSV file can be used to determine whether the user needs to be deactivated. By setting the field name here, Okta will check and act if the value is given for that user. Think of having a field named **Status**.

- **Deactivation value**: This setting has the value on which Okta must trigger a deactivation, such as a value of `Deactivated`.

- **Full import file path**: The full file path to the CSV file – for example, `Windows: C:\Users\Administrator\Desktop\csv\test.csv` or `Linux: /opt/Okta ProvisioningAgent/csv/test.csv`.

- **Incremental import file path**: This is optional and can be used if you also have incremental updates. This file path needs to be different than the full import file path.

With that, we're done with the **Provisioning** tab. Next are the **Import** and **People** tabs. They work similarly for CSV directories as for other directories, such as the AD integration we looked at in *Chapter 2, Working with Universal Directory*. The settings for **EXACT** and **PARTIAL** matches in **Import** are set as described previously in this chapter, in the *Provisioning users* section. The **People** tab shows imported users from this directory.

Now, let's take a look at how an HR system can source your users, and how that is set up.

For HR systems with pre-built integrations in the OIN, there are different kinds of settings for each, which are guided through the setup. Let's look at how this works for **BambooHR**, a popular HR application. Start by navigating to **Applications | Applications** and click **Add Application**. Search for `BambooHR` and click to start the setup. In the **General** settings, you get to set up the following:

1. **Application label**: The name of the app seen by end users.

2. **Subdomain**: Enter your domain name. So, if you usually log in with `http://acme.bamboohr.com/` (this is an example URL), enter `acme`.

3. **Application visibility**: Checkboxes for whether the application is to be visible or not.

4. **Browser plugin auto-submit**: A selection to automatically log in users when they land on the login page.

For this specific application, you can select SWA or SAML 2.0. If you also want to set up SSO for your users, the best end user experience will be with SAML. Since we went through how to set up applications for SSO in *Chapter 3, Using Single Sign-On for a Great End User Experience*, you can now just select **SWA**. What we want to achieve is to get to the **Provisioning** tab in the application setup.

> **Important note**
> You don't have to set up SSO for your end users within applications to be able to use the provisioning features.

Once you've set up the application and gone through the integration steps to allow provisioning to happen, you can now switch on your HR application as a source. Go to the **Provisioning** tab and select **To Okta**. Scroll down to **Profile & Lifecycle Sourcing**. You have to enable the **Allow BambooHR to source Okta users** checkbox in this section. Click **Edit** to check it. When you do, you get some additional options:

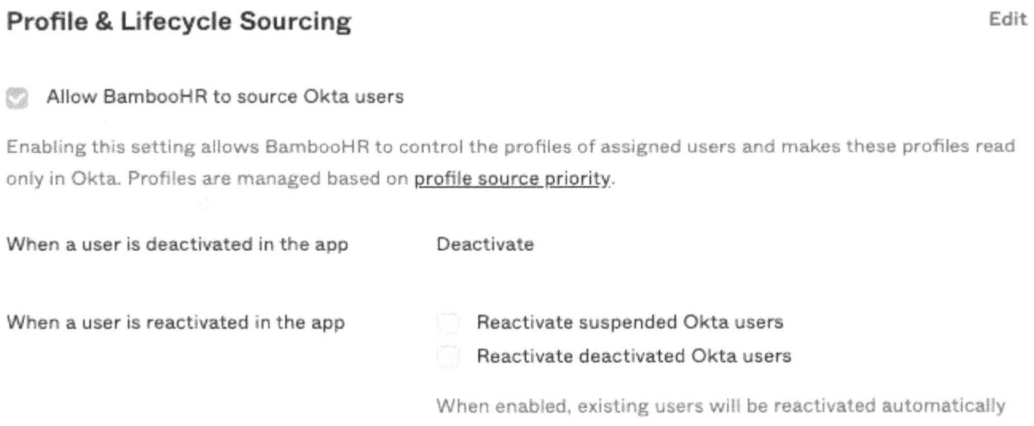

Profile & Lifecycle Sourcing   Edit

☑ Allow BambooHR to source Okta users

Enabling this setting allows BambooHR to control the profiles of assigned users and makes these profiles read only in Okta. Profiles are managed based on **profile source priority**.

When a user is deactivated in the app   Deactivate

When a user is reactivated in the app   ☐ Reactivate suspended Okta users
                                               ☐ Reactivate deactivated Okta users

                                               When enabled, existing users will be reactivated automatically

Figure 5.14 – Options for provisioning

For a typical provisioning setup, you would want the default setting set to **Deactivate**, meaning a user is deactivated in Okta when they are deactivated in BambooHR. You can also select the following options if the user is deactivated in the app:

- **Do nothing**: This will not change the account's status in Okta at all

- **Suspend**: This will suspend the account in Okta, but not deactivate it, to prevent any other deactivations in other applications

The next setting depends on what you choose for the first option. If you select to deactivate a user in Okta, you might also want to set it to activate them if they are activated again in BambooHR.

Now, we need to import the users from BambooHR to connect their identities against any already existing accounts in Okta or import new users. Once you have done that, on the **Import** tab, you will see that all users that have been connected or imported will show a reference on their profile stating that they are mastered by BambooHR.

You will also see that you are no longer able to edit any attributes on the user directly, and it will state that the user is sourced by your HR.

So far, we have talked about provisioning users and setting up sourcing from different sources. Now, let's look at how we can go even deeper using Okta's options to further enrich user profiles.

Provisioning rich profiles

The capabilities in Okta to enrich user profiles within provisioning are big. One example of a feature that will help you is **Okta Expression Language**. It is based on **Spring Expression Language (SpEL)**, with which you can transform and query objects at runtime. With Expression Language, you can make changes to attributes and reference them before storing them on the Okta user, or before sending them to an application for authentication or provisioning. There is a lot of information on this topic, and going through all of it is outside the scope of this book. What we will do, however, is look at the most commonly used categories and examples of them. If you have any other needs within your organization, you can find more information here: `https://developer.okta.com/docs/reference/okta-expression-language/`. To be able to look into these topics, we need some basic knowledge. All users have an Okta profile, independent of how the user is sourced. In addition to that, all users have an application user profile for each application they are assigned to.

Before we look at exactly what we can do within Expression Language, we'll look into profile mapping. We've touched upon it in *Chapter 2, Working with Universal Directory*, for directories, but let's look closer at it for applications. If you have a directory integrated or an application with provisioning capabilities, you can map attributes from them to the user stored in Okta. This is called **attribute mapping**. Let's look at what this looks like in an application such as Google Workspace.

Keeping track of attributes with attribute mapping

Navigate to **Applications** and find your application – in this case, Google Workspace. Click on the **Provisioning** tab. In the menu to the left, you can select whether you want to set mapping to or from the application. You can do both. If you, for instance, select **To Okta** and scroll down, you will see the Okta attribute mapping at the end. You will see a list of mapped attributes. This looks the same whether you pick **To Okta** or **To App**:

Google Workspace Attribute Mappings

Select a(n) Google Workspace attribute to set its value based on values stored in Okta.

Attribute	Attribute Type	Value	Apply on		
Username userName	Personal	Configured in Sign On settings			
First name nameGivenName	Personal	user.firstName	Create	✏	✕
Last name nameFamilyName	Personal	user.lastName	Create	✏	✕

Figure 5.15 – Example of attribute mapping

In this example, we can see that **Username** is based on **Sign On Settings** and that the **First name** attribute for this application's user profile is picked up from the application. If you want to make changes to this, you can click the pen icon to the right. By doing so, you can select attribute values:

- **Same value for all users**
- **Expression**
- Map from *application*, for example, your Google Workspace profile

This last selection is what was used for our preceding example. By selecting this, you get a list of the available attributes to match. You will also get to set when you want to apply your mapping – that is, on **Create** or **Create and Update**.

If we go back to the list of attributes, we can also click the button at the bottom to see all **Unmapped Attributes**. For instance, from an application such as Workplace by Facebook, we might want to get the ProfileURL attribute, and then push that attribute to a second application. You might also want to look into the **Profile Editor** section of your application, and for that, you have a convenient link.

Under the first section of the **Provisioning** tab at the bottom of the page, you can find the different mappings, and also the quick link to the normal mappings:

Google Workspace Attribute Mappings

Select a(n) Google Workspace attribute to set its value based on values stored in Okta.

Attribute	Attribute Type	Value	Apply on		
Username userName	Personal	Configured in Sign On settings			
First name nameGivenName	Personal	user.firstName	Create	✏	✕
Last name nameFamilyName	Personal	user.lastName	Create	✏	✕
Primary phone phonesWorkValue	Personal	user.primaryPhone	Create	✏	✕
Mobile phone phonesWorkMobileValue	Personal	user.mobilePhone	Create	✏	✕

Figure 5.16 – The Google Workspace Attribute Mappings section

With **Profile Editor**, you can, for instance, set that a specific attribute is sourced by a different source, such as an application with provisioning capabilities. Find that attribute in the **Profile Editor** list, then click the **i** icon to the right:

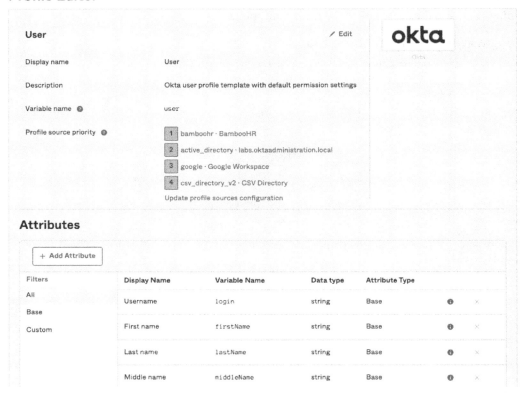

Figure 5.17 – Profile Editor overview

If you select **Source priority**, you can set a different source for this specific attribute. You can also set up a custom attribute:

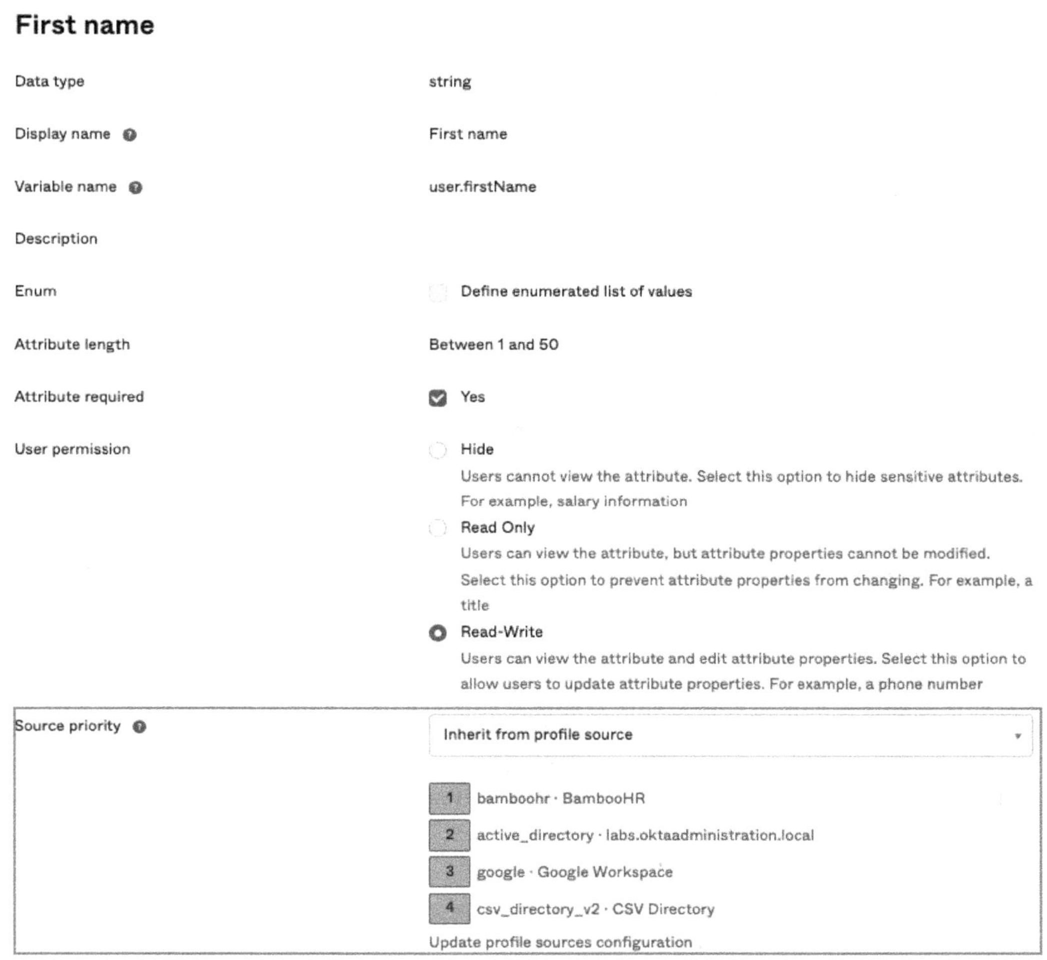

First name

Data type	string
Display name ❓	First name
Variable name ❓	user.firstName
Description	
Enum	⬜ Define enumerated list of values
Attribute length	Between 1 and 50
Attribute required	☑ Yes
User permission	⬜ Hide

Users cannot view the attribute. Select this option to hide sensitive attributes. For example, salary information

⬜ Read Only

Users can view the attribute, but attribute properties cannot be modified. Select this option to prevent attribute properties from changing. For example, a title

🔘 Read-Write

Users can view the attribute and edit attribute properties. Select this option to allow users to update attribute properties. For example, a phone number

Source priority ❓

Inherit from profile source   ▼

1   bamboohr · BambooHR

2   active_directory · labs.oktaadministration.local

3   google · Google Workspace

4   csv_directory_v2 · CSV Directory

Update profile sources configuration

Figure 5.18 – Okta attribute – Source priority

For both of these, see *Chapter 2, Working with Universal Directory*. If you want to populate that attribute with parts of other attributes or reference another attribute, you will need to use Expression Language. So, let's jump into that!

Attribute magic with Okta Expression Language

As mentioned earlier, there are different categories of Okta Expression Language operations. We will look into the following:

- Referencing user attributes
- Referencing application and organization attributes
- Functions

So, where will these expressions be placed? For instance, if you create a new attribute, you will be able to map and populate it with expressions. Navigate to **Directory | Profile Editor** and select the application or directory where your new attribute will be available. If we continue with the preceding example of Google Workspace, you will click **Mappings** next to **Google Workspace** in the list.

So, what can you enter there? Let's look at *referencing user attributes* first:

- If you are in an application mapping, such as Google Workspace, and you want to reference the Okta user, you can use the `user.$attribute`, where `$attribute` would be replaced with the actual attribute name – for example, `user.firstName`.
- If you want to reference an attribute from an application user profile instead, you can use `$appuser.$attribute`.
- For an example where you might want to pull in an attribute from the Zendesk application user profile to the Google Workspace application user profile, you would use `Zendesk.firstName` in the Google Workspace **Profile Editor** mapping.

In the same way, we can use *Reference Application and Organization* attributes:

- For instance, if you want to use an application's domain name, you can use `$app.$attribute`, which would give you `zendesk_app.companySubDomain`.
- To reference the Okta organization in an application mapping, you would use `org.$attribute` and would get, for example, `Org.subdomain`.

These two categories are quite straightforward and there are more kinds available. Refer to the preceding link for more examples. A more intricate category is to transform attributes with functions. These would typically be used when you want to, for instance, remove one part of an attribute or combine two different attributes, to create a new one. There are many functions, so let's look at some of them. With `String`, you can change up attributes in multiple ways:

- The first one is `String.join`.

  An example of this would be `String.join("", "This", "is", "a", "test")`, which would output `Thisisatest`. If you want that with spaces instead, you can use `String.append`.

- A useful kind of string function is to get output from what is before or after a character. This could, for instance, be `String.substringBefore`. This is good to use with an @ character if you want to use the unique name from an email and remove the domain name. `String.substringBefore("john.doe@acme.com", "@")` would give `john.doe` as output.

- It's also possible to reference standards such as the numeric standards or country and state codes. `Iso3166Convert.toAlpha3(string)` could be used to transform a numeric country code into a text country code – for example, `Iso3166Convert.toAlpha3("840")` turns `840` into USA according to ISO 3166. This can be useful if one application outputs it in one format and it's needed by another application in another format.

These mappings will be used in the profile mapping dialogue box. You can select whether you want to do the mapping from the application to Okta or the other way around. What mappings are in place is indicated with a yellow arrow – see *Figure 5.19*. If you enter a new expression mapping, you can test it out by searching for a user in the **Preview** box at the bottom. When you're done, click **Save Mappings**:

Google Workspace User Profile Mappings

| Google Workspace to Okta User | Okta User to Google Workspace |

Google Workspace User Profile appuser			okta	Okta User User Profile user	
Username is set by Google Workspace				login	string
appuser.nameGivenName	▾	→ ▾		firstName	string
appuser.nameFamilyName	▾	→ ▾		lastName	string
Choose an attribute or enter an expression...	▾	-/→ ▾		middleName	string
Choose an attribute or enter an expression...	▾	-/→ ▾		honorificPrefix	string
Choose an attribute or enter an expression...	▾	-/→ ▾		honorificSuffix	string
appuser.userName	▾	→ ▾		email	email
appuser.organizationsWorkTitle	▾	→ ▾		title	string

Figure 5.19 – Example of Expression Language mappings for an application

Now that you've saved your mappings, you're done with this part. Many more examples of Expression Language can be found at the link referenced in the *Provisioning rich profiles* section of this chapter. Now, let's move on to how you can do automation with and for your groups.

Setting up group rules

Group automation, or group rules, can be considered the best way to simplify administrators' work with Okta. Anything that requires setup and maintenance and is repetitive work can be automated with Okta's group rules.

Setting up group rules allows you to manage your workforce in bulk including the following:

- The user directory
- Application provisioning and **single sign-on** (**SSO**) assignments
- Security policy assignments
- Directory and application group pushes

Because of the 360-degree view of a user in Okta and its assigned groups, administrators can easily deliver quick setup, automation, remediation, and application management when using Okta groups. By allowing users to come in from different sources and have their groups be added to Okta too, you can make sure the users are correctly assigned and managed by using Okta's group rules.

The strength lies in the simple options for the multitude of functions to be used in these group rules. Sometimes, a simple assignment based on a profile attribute value can be enough to assign a user to a specific group or multiple groups:

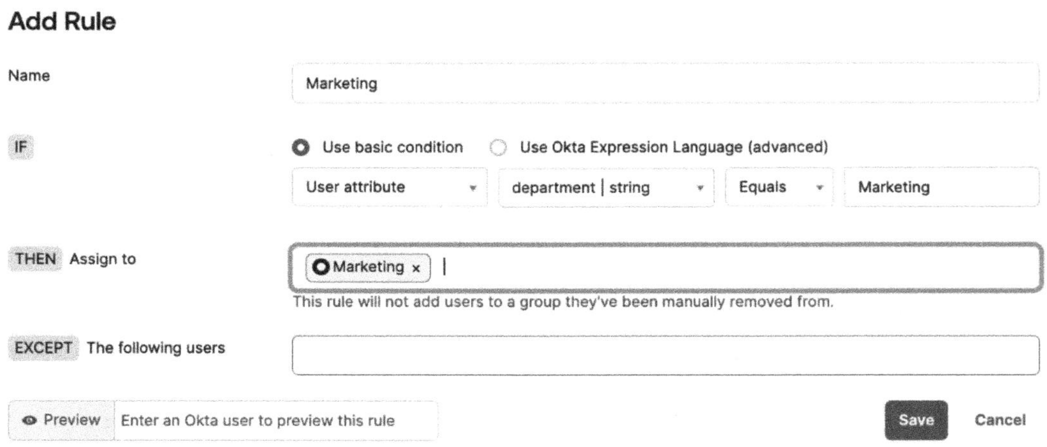

Add Rule

Name					
	Marketing				

IF	● Use basic condition ○ Use Okta Expression Language (advanced)			
	User attribute ▾	department | string ▾	Equals ▾	Marketing

THEN	Assign to	○ Marketing × |

This rule will not add users to a group they've been manually removed from.

EXCEPT	The following users	

◉ Preview	Enter an Okta user to preview this rule	**Save** Cancel

Figure 5.20 – Group assignment based on an attribute value

As shown here, a simple attribute value will assign the user to the selected group. This can be straightforward and easy to use for organization structures who are using the department attribute to assign users to their corresponding department groups.

Sometimes, it's because you want users to be added to a group based on another group assignment:

Add Rule

Name	Global Sales
IF	● Use basic condition ○ Use Okta Expression Language (advanced)
	Group membership ▾ includes any of the following
	○ Sales ×
THEN Assign to	○ Global Sales × |
	This rule will not add users to a group they've been manually removed from.
EXCEPT The following users	
● Preview Enter an Okta user to preview this rule	Save Cancel

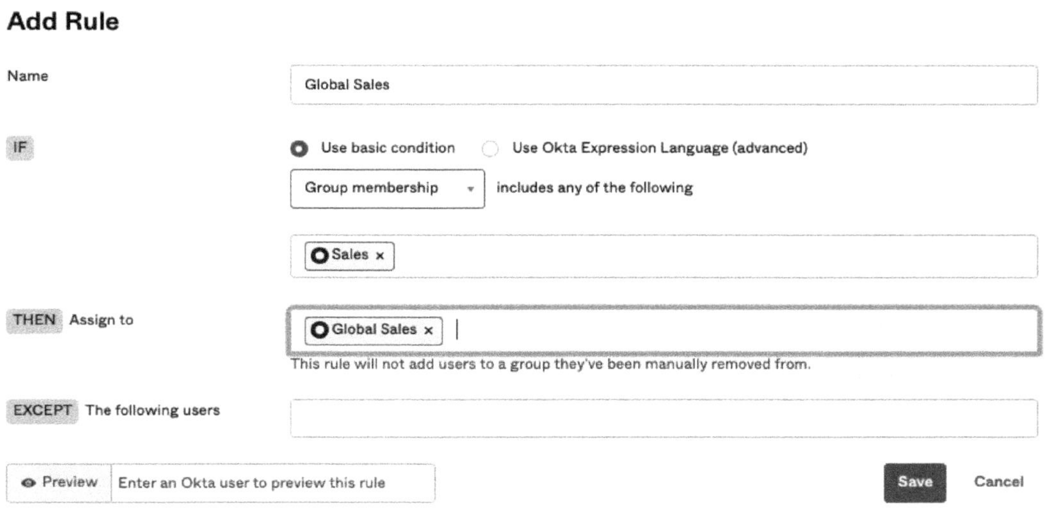

Figure 5.21 – Group assignment based on another group assignment

Perhaps you have a granular setup and want to bring in users from other groups based on their assignments. So, in this case, we assign users to the generic **Global Sales** group if they are part of a more specific sales group.

Sometimes, you might want to use application or directory groups to assign the user to other groups. Let's say an **Active Directory** (**AD**) group allows automation to assign other pushed AD groups to a user:

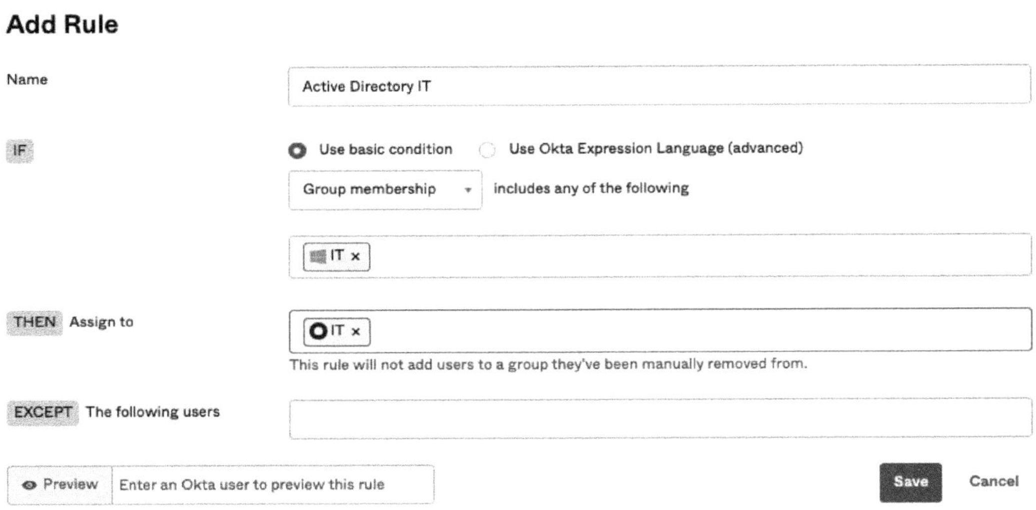

Add Rule

Name

Active Directory IT

IF

⦿ Use basic condition   ◯ Use Okta Expression Language (advanced)

Group membership   ▾   includes any of the following

▦ IT ×

THEN Assign to

◉ IT ×

This rule will not add users to a group they've been manually removed from.

EXCEPT The following users

👁 Preview   Enter an Okta user to preview this rule   **Save**   Cancel

Figure 5.22 – Group assignment rule based on AD group membership

Sometimes, the group assignment can be a bit stricter and require more rule values before being assigned. In that case, Okta allows you to use Expression Language to set up larger and stricter rules:

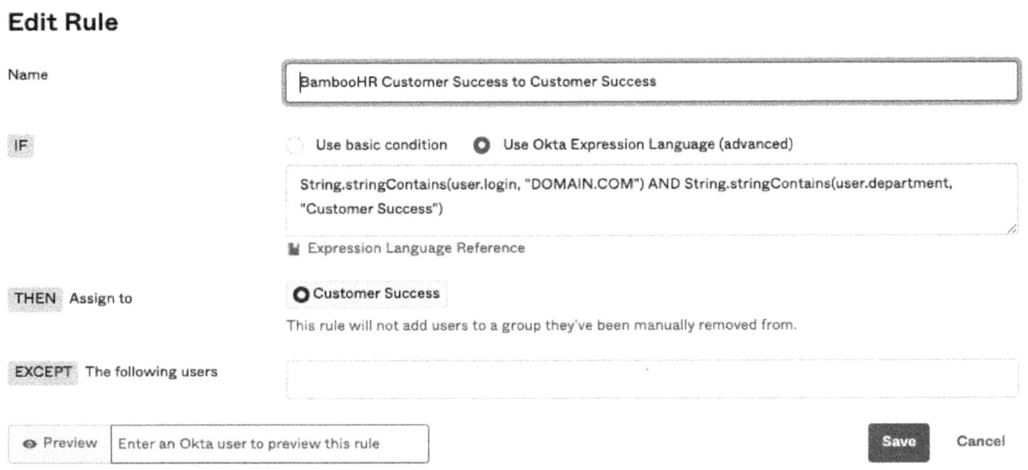

Edit Rule

Name

BambooHR Customer Success to Customer Success

IF

◯ Use basic condition   ⦿ Use Okta Expression Language (advanced)

String.stringContains(user.login, "DOMAIN.COM") AND String.stringContains(user.department, "Customer Success")

📖 Expression Language Reference

THEN Assign to

◉ Customer Success

This rule will not add users to a group they've been manually removed from.

EXCEPT The following users

👁 Preview   Enter an Okta user to preview this rule   **Save**   Cancel

Figure 5.23 – Group assignment rule based on Expression Language

Using Expression Language, you can filter and tunnel the users you are looking for before you assign them to the correct group. In this case, a specific domain and department value will assign the user to the **Customer Success** group.

It can also be that certain circumstances allow the user to be added to a group because of policy changes. For example, perhaps offboarding requires the user to move over to SMS during their grace period. Using a group to assign the user to a policy that needs them to enroll in SMS and grant access to Okta with only SMS as a factor would look like this:

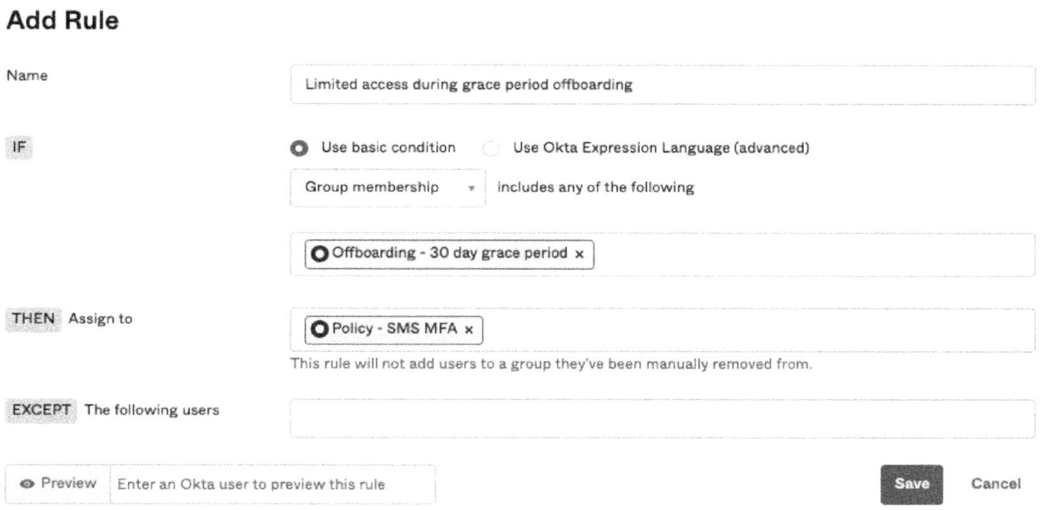

Add Rule

Name	Limited access during grace period offboarding
IF	● Use basic condition ○ Use Okta Expression Language (advanced)
	Group membership ▾ | includes any of the following
	○ Offboarding - 30 day grace period ×
THEN Assign to	○ Policy - SMS MFA ×
	This rule will not add users to a group they've been manually removed from.
EXCEPT The following users	
◉ Preview	Enter an Okta user to preview this rule **Save** Cancel

Figure 5.24 – Group assignment to a group for policy enrollment

While you might allow offboarded users to keep access to certain applications, you want to make sure they are accessing your systems securely. Perhaps they now need to use their own device and have problems with installing apps. Enrolling them in SMS might be less secure, but it's still better than no security at all.

Let's say you allow users to have specific access to licenses that are group-managed. Sometimes, it's wise to have these options as profile attributes and use them to assign the user to the license with the help of a group:

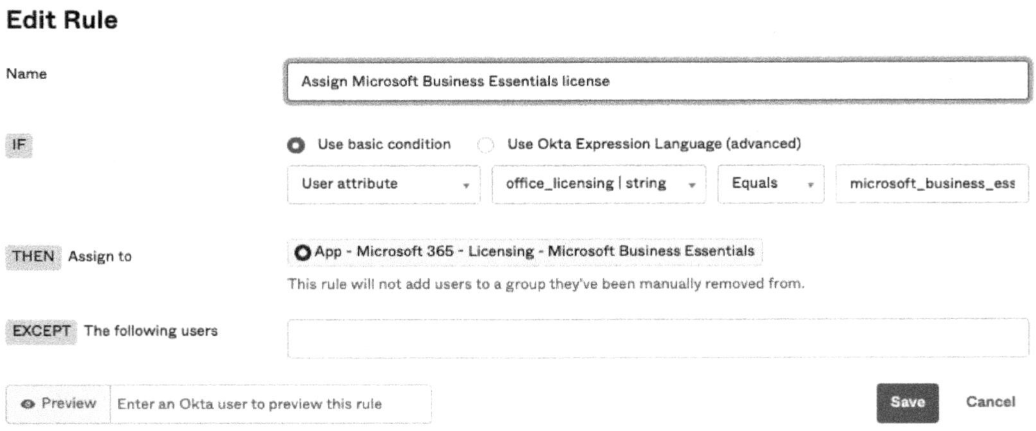

Edit Rule

Name		Assign Microsoft Business Essentials license		

IF   ● Use basic condition   ○ Use Okta Expression Language (advanced)

User attribute ▾	office_licensing	string ▾	Equals ▾	microsoft_business_ess

THEN   Assign to   ● App - Microsoft 365 - Licensing - Microsoft Business Essentials

This rule will not add users to a group they've been manually removed from.

EXCEPT   The following users

◉ Preview   Enter an Okta user to preview this rule   **Save**   Cancel

Figure 5.25 – Group assignment rule for license management

Adding the different types of profile attributes can help you further automate this process. Sometimes, it requires input from HR; sometimes, IT needs to do it. In this case, a drop-down choice field on the user profile allows the user to be assigned to the Microsoft Business Essentials group, which will provision the user into Microsoft services with that specific license.

All these and many more rules can easily be set up in the Okta **Group Rules** section. There might be situations where you need to be more efficient or you simply like your work to be coded. In that case, Okta allows all of this and more to be managed by its APIs, where you can use the same functionality to create, update, (de)activate, or delete any or all of these rules.

> **Important note**
>
> As the options are very broad, and the documentation on APIs is very extensive, it won't be possible to go into detail on this topic. To find out more about group rule APIs, please visit Okta's extensive developer API resource site: https://developer.okta.com/docs/reference/api/groups/#group-rule-operations.

Whenever the value changes for the user (for example, the user moves from the Sales to the Marketing team), and the rules pick up the change, the user will get reassigned to the marketing group and unassigned from the sales group. This allows lean management and no need to add custom management to unassign users. Okta will be able to understand the impact and change accordingly.

On a user's profile, it is clear to see in what way groups are assigned to the user by looking at the descriptive text. Any group assigned with rules is shown with a clickable link to the rule itself:

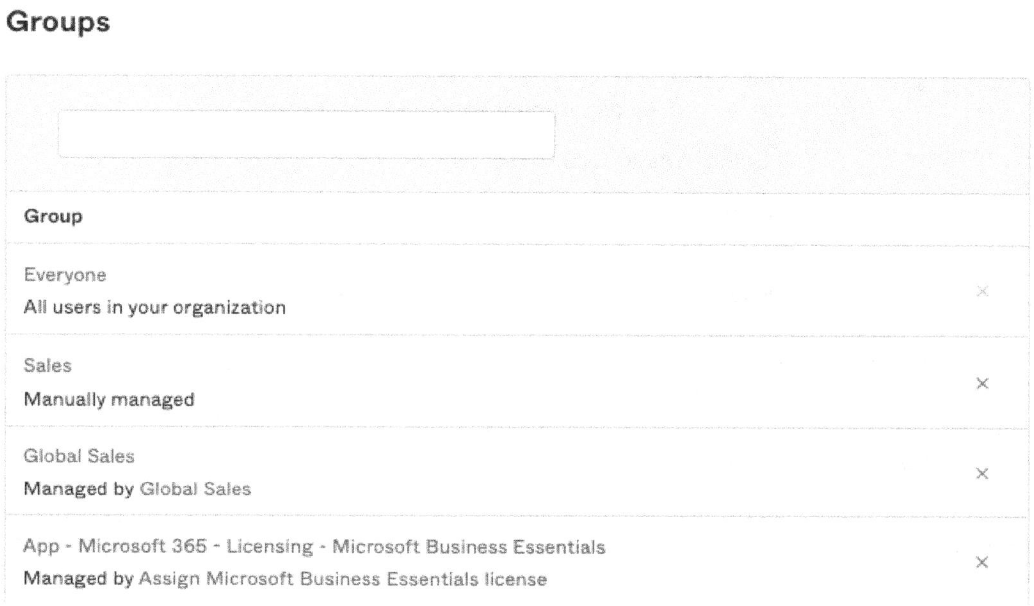

Groups

Figure 5.26 – Group rules shown in the Groups section of a user's profile

As discussed in *Chapter 3, Using Single Sign-On for a Great End User Experience*, usually, there is an order to how policies are presented. In the case of group rules, this doesn't apply. These do not need to be, and technically cannot be, differently ordered to allow them to work properly.

Group rules can act upon changes made by other group rules. This means that one group rule can trigger other group rules because of group (re-)assignment. These cascading rules can have performance issues and it's considered best practice to try to combine them into one rule.

A user may get assigned to a group based on the condition of the rule, even if they shouldn't be, because of logic that isn't configurable in the rules. In that case, you can exclude a user's assignment through a couple of methods:

- Exclude the user in the rule
- Remove the user from the group

This exclusion could look like this:

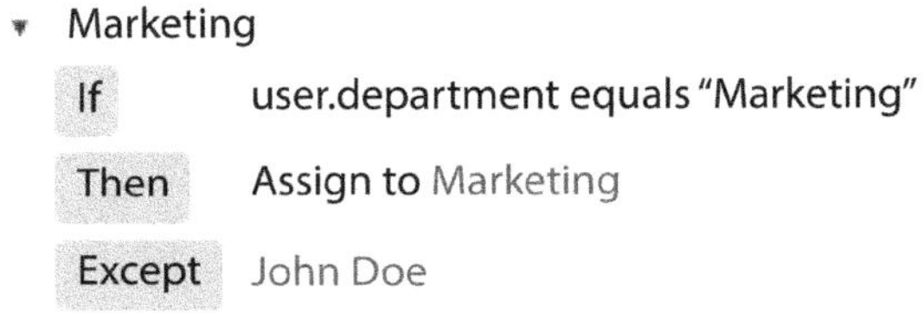

▼ Marketing

If	user.department equals "Marketing"
Then	**Assign to** Marketing
Except	John Doe

Figure 5.27 – Group rule with an excluded user

The actions shown in the preceding screenshot make sure the users aren't assigned to the group. If the user needs to be re-assigned to the group after being excluded by a rule, you can remove the user from the **EXCEPT** list in the rule. Re-activating the rule will re-evaluate the user and add them back to the group based on the group rule.

Sometimes, group rules can have uncalculated results that can have a worse outcome than you would have predicted. Especially in the case where groups are used for provisioning, it's wise to keep in mind what certain changes can do to application assignments.

Group rules truly help automate most of your tasks, allowing user creation, management, and application assignment. They are also used for policy management and therefore can have multiple tasks to do. And while the setup is fairly simple, they can have a positive influence on any IT employee's daily routine, but can also have a large impact and need to be handled with caution and thoroughness.

In the next section, we will go over how users can request access to applications that might not be captured within automation rules so that their management is more manual.

Setting up self-service options

Users have their personal dashboards to see and manage their applications. For applications integrated with SAML or OIDC, they would be automatically signed in when clicking on any of them. For SWA applications, where admins have set that end users will enter their own credentials, they will be prompted to do so the first time they click on an icon. Once they are logged in, Okta will ask whether the login was successful. If the answer is yes, the credentials will be stored. If not, the end user will be able to try again.

The end users can re-arrange their applications by simply clicking and dragging. To find applications quickly, you can arrange applications in different sections or simply use the search bar at the top of the page.

With the **Add Applications** feature in the dashboard for end users, they can add private applications or corporate-owned applications if this is enabled. Navigate to **Applications | Self Service** in the admin console. In the topmost section, you can see the available options of requestable applications, and your current selections that have been enabled:

- **Allow users to add org-managed apps**
- **Allow users to add personal apps**
- **Allow users to email "Technical Contact" to request an app**

Below, you can see what applications you have configured for users to request.

If you have org-managed applications that you don't want to provision for all users from the start but would like to offer them if users need an application, you can turn on the feature to allow users to add them.

By going to **Applications | Self Service**, you can choose to turn on the **Allow users to add org-managed apps** feature:

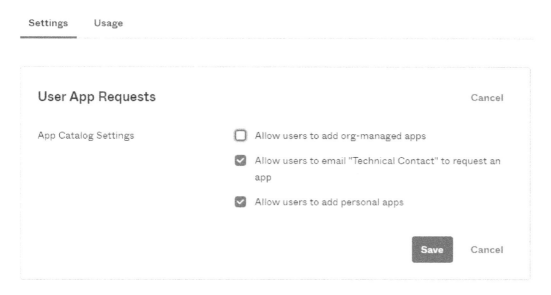

Figure 5.28 – Options to enable users to request an application

To enable an application to be self-assigned by a user, navigate to **Application | Application** and select the app you want to configure. In the **Assignments** tab, you'll find **Self-service** to the right. Click **Edit** and change **Allow users to request app** to **Yes**. If you want to set an approval flow, you can also change **Approval** to **Required**. If left on the default setting, **Not Required**, the application can be assigned by the user without any approval being needed:

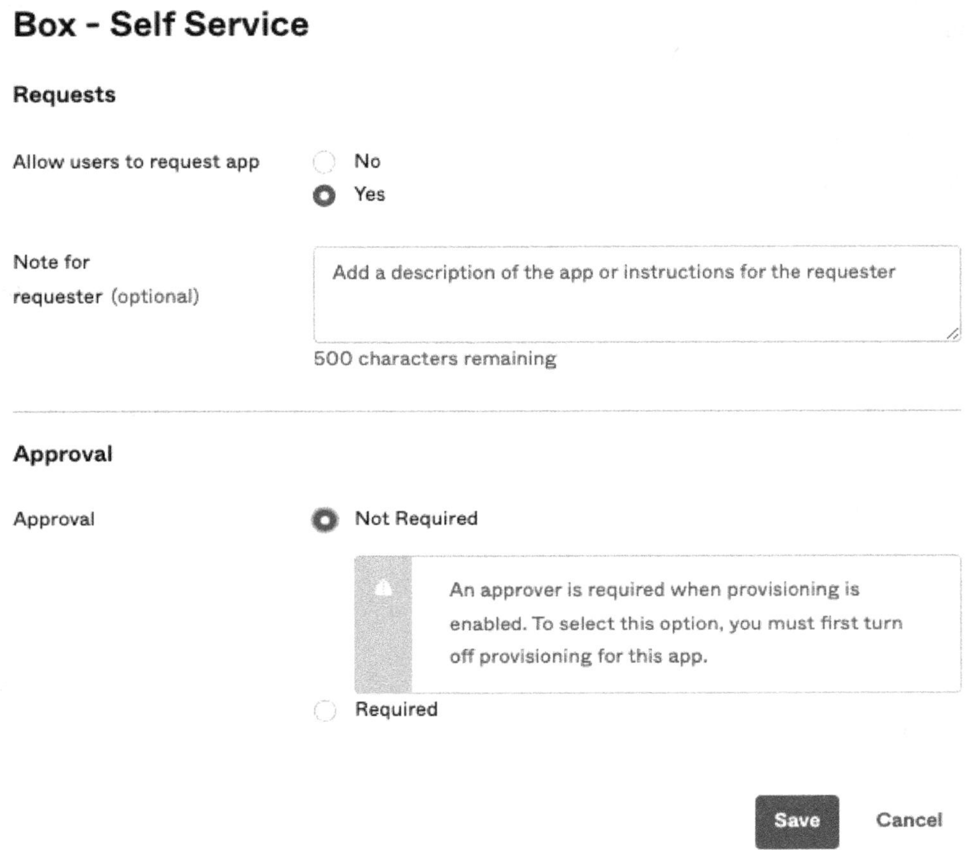

Box - Self Service

Requests

Allow users to request app   ○ No

○ Yes

Note for
requester (optional)

> Add a description of the app or instructions for the requester

500 characters remaining

Approval

Approval   ● Not Required

> ⚠ An approver is required when provisioning is enabled. To select this option, you must first turn off provisioning for this app.

○ Required

Save   Cancel

Figure 5.29 – Options to enable users to request an application

You can assign the approval of the request to one or multiple users, or one or more groups. For groups, one single group can't contain more than 100 members when it comes to approvals. Everyone in the group gets a notification of the request but only one has to approve it. By assigning it to more than one, you can create a chain of approval. This chain of approval is limited to 10 layers and approvers can only be part of the chain once. Approvers will be given entitlements: **Hidden**, **Read**, or **Write**. These are used to set what approvers can do on the requester's account. You should always aim for the least-privilege approach, but some applications require attributes for provisioning. If so, set an approver to have **Write** access. If you want to change the order of approvers, you can easily just drag and drop the users or groups. If the application doesn't support automatic provisioning, you can use the last step of an approval chain as the provisioning. Make sure the last approver is an administrator able to provision the account and give access.

The last step is to set the settings for notifications as well as a time frame for approvers:

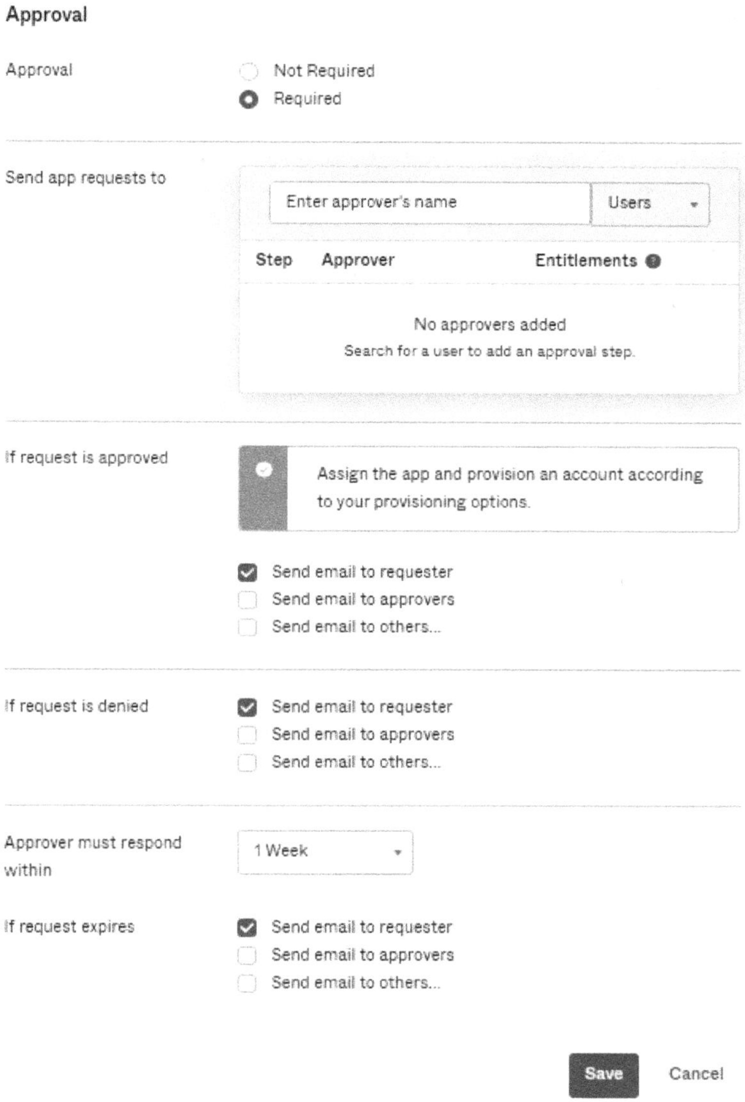

Approval

| Approval | ○ Not Required |
| | ● Required |

Send app requests to

| Enter approver's name | Users ▾ |

| Step | Approver | Entitlements ❶ |

No approvers added
Search for a user to add an approval step.

If request is approved

● Assign the app and provision an account according to your provisioning options.

☑ Send email to requester
☐ Send email to approvers
☐ Send email to others...

If request is denied

☑ Send email to requester
☐ Send email to approvers
☐ Send email to others...

Approver must respond within

| 1 Week ▾ |

If request expires

☑ Send email to requester
☐ Send email to approvers
☐ Send email to others...

[Save]   Cancel

Figure 5.30 – Options for notifications in the approval flow

If you didn't check the box to allow users to request applications at the beginning, you will be prompted to do so when clicking **Save**. Otherwise, you are now done!

Summary

In this chapter, we pieced together things we learned in previous chapters, and with that looked at how a complete user provisioning lifecycle can work. We looked at how using your HR system as a source brings extra power to your IT resources and reduces friction between HR and IT. We also went through how you can work with mapping from different applications and directories, as well as introducing referencing and changing attributes with Expression Language. Further, we looked at the capabilities within group automations, specifically for provisioning flows. With this knowledge, you will be able to start your provisioning setup with ease. Secondly, you have gained knowledge about how to use Oktas automation to help your IT operations.

In the next chapter, we will look into the Okta GUI and how you can customize the end user experience so that it fits your company profile and culture.

6

Customizing Your Okta GUI

So far, we have focused a lot on the **Administrator** panel and all the features that make Okta a leader in its field, but none of Okta's capabilities would matter if the user experience wasn't just as good. We will now look a little more at the user experience and what we as admins can do to change it. To start, we will look at the different features end users have. After that, we'll go into how we can customize the user dashboard, with a logo and colors. We will go through what different administrator settings there are to configure the dashboard. While looking at the admin settings, we will also see how to modify what is sent from Okta, such as emails and SMS messages. Lastly, we will investigate how you can customize the login page and how to manage and host a custom login widget on your own login page.

Utilizing your own branding will make your end users feel right at home and adapt better. It will also help new employees to get into your company culture directly from the start.

The following topics are covered in this chapter:

- Understanding the basics of end user functionality
- Customizations and the branding of your Okta
- The Okta plugin settings

Understanding the basics of end user functionality

Before we can change any settings for end users to optimize their experience, we must understand what their interface looks like and what we can change. As mentioned before, when an end user logs in to the dashboard, they see all available applications. By default, they have a tab called **Work**, where they can add their own tabs and organize their applications.

On the end user dashboard, users can modify how apps are shown, add their own applications, and manage any credentials within the apps that are set up as **Secure Web Authentication** (**SWA**) applications.

Let's go over the different sections on the dashboard:

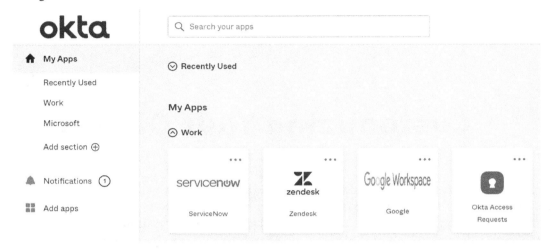

Figure 6.1 – The end user dashboard

The left column is where users can find the different sections they have and quick links to the **App catalog** (found under the **Add apps** option) and **Notifications** sections. In the search bar at the top, users can easily search for an application. On the right of the window, you have a drop-down menu under your username with **Settings**, **Preferences**, **Recent Activity**, and **Sign Out** and when you are an administrator, you will find the button to take you to the **Administrators** portal, as shown in *Figure 6.2*.

It will look like this:

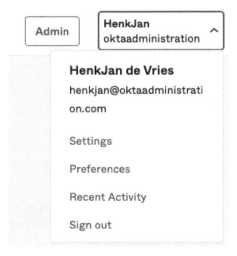

Figure 6.2 – The new end user menu in the sidebar

In the **Settings** menu, end users will find a lot of information. These are the sections:

- **Personal Information**
- **Display Language**
- **Security Method**

In the first section, users can modify their personal information and review any information that you, as an administrator, allow them to alter. Other attributes might be set to read-only. If a user clicks **Edit**, they can change the fields that are editable. At certain times, users might be required to re-authenticate to change any settings. This is a security feature you can change in the administrator console. It can only be set to 5 or 15 minutes.

In *Chapter 4*, *Increasing Security with Adaptive Multifactor Authentication*, we learned how to update your MFA enrollments, which is covered in the following part of the **Settings** page:

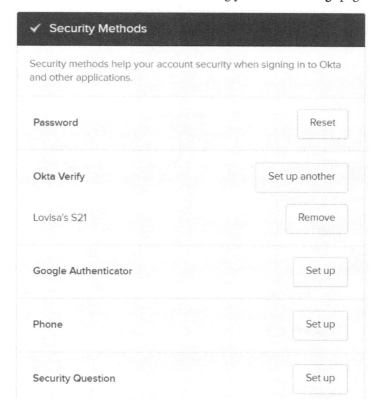

Figure 6.3 – The security method options

Depending on how your global, authentication, and enrollment policies are set up, this section will show the available factors that a user can enroll in that apply to them. If and when the user would like to enroll in more of the same (e.g., both Okta FastPass and Okta Verify for the iPhone), they can do that here. If you use passwords and security questions as part of your sign-in or recovery settings, they can also be enrolled in or changed in this section.

In the next section, the end user can update the display language. Changing to a different language will also change the language for SMS and email, if these have been configured. Currently, Okta supports 27 different languages – to see a list of supported languages, refer to `https://help.okta.com/en/prod/Content/Topics/Reference/ref-supported-languages.htm`.

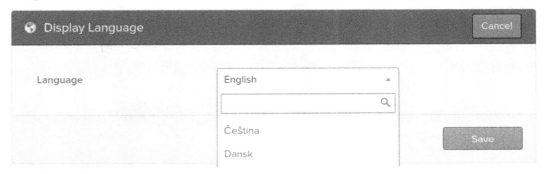

Figure 6.4 – The Display Language settings

In the same menu as where you find **Settings**, you will also find the **Preferences** section. Here, your end users can customize their experience of the end user dashboard. They can toggle on the use of the **Recently used** section. This will provide a section at the top of the dashboard with the most common applications they used most recently:

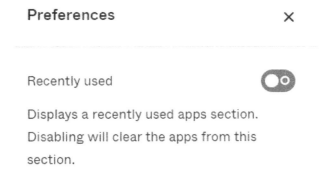

Figure 6.5 – The end user Preferences menu – Recently used

Secondly, they can choose whether they want to see their apps in a grid or list view:

Layout

Change how apps are displayed for your current browser.

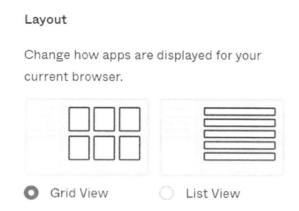

○ Grid View   ○ List View

Figure 6.6 – The end user Preferences menu – the dashboard layout

Lastly, they can set how long they want messages to appear on the screen, with **5 seconds** being the default. If you click the **Preview** button, you get to see an example of a pop-up message and the time it will stay visible:

Pop up messages timer

Customize how long pop up messages stay visible on the screen.

| 5 seconds ⌄ | Preview |

Figure 6.7 – The end user Preferences menu – pop-up message timer

The last option on the menu, apart from **Sign out**, is **Recent Activity** to highlight unexpected behaviors. This will trigger a notification email to administrators. A report from an end user can be picked up via a system log event named `user.account.report_suspicious_activity_by_enduser`. This can be utilized in an Okta workflow or event hook. The outcome of such an automation can be, for instance, to automate what to do in this occurrence, such as suspend the user or ask for biometric authentication.

At the bottom of the dashboard, additional information is shown. The support element here can be turned off and on via **Customizations | Other | Display Options**. We will explain further later in this chapter:

Figure 6.8 – Okta dashboard footer elements

The **Request an app** feature allows a user to send a request for an app via a small window in the browser. This will send the request of that user to the admins enrolled in the tenant:

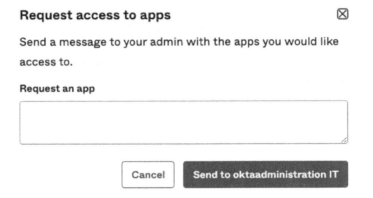

Figure 6.9 – The Okta dashboard Request access to apps pop-up window

Okay, that's all that end users can do and see from their side; let's look at what we as administrators can do to change the experience for end users.

Customizations and the branding of your Okta

A great way for you, as an admin, to make your users feel comfortable in Okta is to work with the visual settings. Let's see how that works.

In the **Admin** panel, navigate to **Customizations**. In the following section, we will explain the different menus of what can be customized. Following Okta's menu structure, we will explore the following menus:

- **Brands**: This contains all the elements to create and manage different brands
- **SMS**: Holds the settings to change SMS messages sent toward users
- **End-user dashboard layout**: Here, you can manage how the default end-user dashboard is presented to users
- **Other**: This contains a selection of additional settings regarding more general customizations

We will go over these in order, ensuring all elements are discussed.

Brands

Brands are a collection of visual options that will help you make the look and feel of your Okta align with your corporate requirements.

> **Note**
>
> The following features can be related to all brands, while some are specific to custom brands.

Each brand has the same settings you can work in:

- **Theme**: This contains generic theme settings you can alter for an Okta tenant
- **Pages**: Here, you can alter specific configurations to Okta pages that a user can encounter
- **Emails**: This contains all email templates that can be altered to your preference
- **Domains**: This is the section where you can manage a custom domain (for custom brands) or view the default settings of the default brand
- **Settings**: This is the place where extra settings can be changed for each brand individually

So, let's start at the beginning and explore the **Theme** section.

Theme

When clicking a brand, you always land on the **Theme** settings. Here, you can change the color scheme, upload a logo, and add a background for pages. These changes are applied to different pages that your end user interacts with:

Figure 6.10 – Theme settings

As you can see, you have full control of the experience, with hex color codes and the possibility to use logos, **Favicons**, and background pictures.

By selecting your own logo and clicking **Save**, you will replace the Okta logo in the top-left corner of the dashboard. Then, the top image in the login widget on the login page will be replaced. Lastly, the logo will also be visible in the Okta Verify app as a visualization. For best results, adhere to these recommendations:

- Use a .png file.
- Use a logo in landscape orientation with a 420*120 pixels size
- The file size must be less than 1 MB

Don't forget to click **Save** after you have modified your code and pictures.

Pages

The **Pages** menu gives you options to alter several settings that are applied to different pages within that brand. Within the **Pages** menu, we find three main sections:

- **Sign-in page**
- **End-User Dashboard**
- **Error pages**

You can see the sections here:

Figure 6.11 – The available branding categories

Let's investigate these sections.

By clicking **Configure** for the sign-in page, you get the option to choose from two different preset layout options that slightly differ. Alternatively, you can choose to use a browser code editor and create the HTML completely yourself:

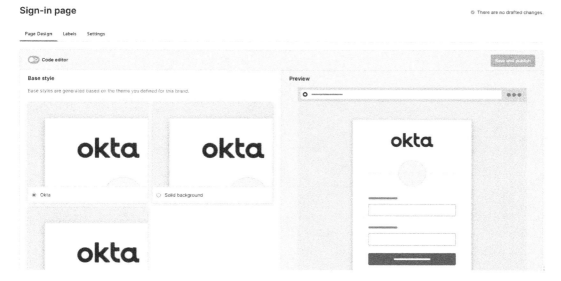

Figure 6.12 – The available base branding styles

> **Note**
>
> Using a code editor requires the setup and usage of a custom domain. We will discuss this in further detail later in this chapter.

In the second tab section, **Labels**, you can edit the labels of the different fields of the sign-in widget. This is helpful if you want them to be clearer for your users. Each of the sections has its own standard naming and an option to rename it with something to your liking:

Username & password fields

Username label   Username

Username info tip

Password label   Password

Password info tip

Password visibility toggle   Enabled

Figure 6.13 – An example of the Sign-in page | Labels section

In the last section of this page, we can select **Settings**. Here, you can select a widget version, if you are using a custom domain and custom widget. Otherwise, the standard widget will always follow the most recent version:

Figure 6.14 – The widget version settings

If you want to take the sign-in customization to the next level, you can also self-host an Okta widget on your own custom page. In this scenario, you can host the login on, for instance, your intranet, making it easy for your end users to log in from a page that they recognize.

To get this working, you need to install the widget.

> **Tip**
> There are a lot of code snippets available; you can visit this link for more information: `https://developer.okta.com/docs/guides/embedded-siw/main/`.

To install the widget, there are two options:

- Linking to the Okta **Custom Domain Name (CDN)**
- Local installation via npm

If you want to use the CDN, use this code in your HTML:

```
<!-- Latest CDN production Javascript and CSS -->
<script src="https://global.oktacdn.com/okta-signin-widget/4.1.4/js/
okta-sign-in.min.js"
        type="text/javascript"></script><link href="https://global.
oktacdn.com/okta-signin-widget/4.1.4/css/okta-sign-in.min.css"
        type="text/css" rel="stylesheet"/>
```

If you want to use npm, use this:

```
# Run this command in your project root folder.npm install @okta/okta-
signin-widget -save
```

For more information and the latest data, refer to the preceding *Tip* link.

After that, you will have to enable **Cross-Origin Resource Sharing, (CORS)** access. Since the widget needs to make cross-origin requests, you need to add your application's URL to the trusted origins of your Okta tenant. This is how you do that:

1. Navigate to **Security | API | Trusted Origins**.
2. Click **Add Origin**, and in the field, enter a name for the organization's origin.
3. For the origin URL, enter the base URL for the website you want to allow cross-origin requests from.
4. **CORS** needs to be selected as the **Type** option.

When you're done, click **Save**.

If you want to read more about CORS and Okta, you can visit this URL: https://developer. okta.com/docs/guides/enable-cors/main/.

After enabling CORS, you can start using the widget. Use this code to initialize it:

```
<
div id = "widget-container" > < /div> <
script >
    var signIn = new OktaSignIn({
        baseUrl: 'https://${yourOktaDomain}'
    });
signIn.renderEl({
        el: '#widget-container'
    },
```

```
        function success(res) {
            if (res.status === 'SUCCESS') {
                console.log('Do something with this sessionToken',
res.session.token);
            } else { // The user can be in another authentication
state that requires further action.
                // For more information about these states, see:
                //   https://github.com/okta/okta-signin-
widget#rendereloptions-success-error}
            }
        ); <
        /script>
```

The preceding link specifies different use cases and what code to use for them. For instance, if you want to use the widget to let your end users log in to the default dashboard, you would use this:

```
function success(res) {  if (res.status === 'SUCCESS') {    res.
session.setCookieAndRedirect('https://${yourOktaDomain}/app/
UserHome');  }}
```

Now, you know all the basics to host your own login widget.

If we go back to the **Brands | Brand | Pages** menu section, we can also select the following:

- **End-user Dashboard**
- **Error pages**

On each of these pages, configuration can be set for their corresponding settings. The basic branding styles can be set on each of them, allowing you to create a cohesive look and feel across all visualizations of Okta.

So, let's now move on to the next menu item, **Emails**.

Emails

The email section in each brand allows you to alter any email communication. These templates can be changed from a basic style perspective, by clicking on the right side of the email style editor.

This allows you to override the brand and add some customization. This is just a single change, from **Basic** to **Solid background**, but only if you have set that in the brand theme setting:

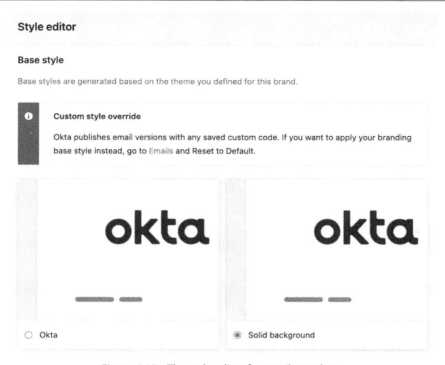

Figure 6.15 – The style editor for email templates

If we go back, we can also alter each individual email that Okta can send.

> **Note**
> Editing each individual email is a paid feature and is not always available.

If you click on any of the email template names, you are directed to a preview window of that email. You can click on <> **Code** to edit the email template in a browser-based HTML editor. You can also create custom language templates for each email template, to be fully in control of all the options. If you edit a template, the translated versions will not be automatically updated:

Figure 6.16 – The functionality to edit in the browser and select a language

For each of the templates and template language, you can send a test email. At the end of the row of the template, a **Send test email** button is available. Clicking this will generate a pop-up window like this:

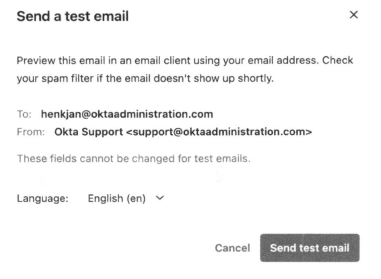

Figure 6.17 – Enter an email address to test the new template

Okay, now that we have seen how to change some basic and generic features for the Okta environment, let's add some real customization by setting up a domain and checking how we can add a custom email.

So, let's now move on to the next menu item, **Domains**.

Domains

On every brand (except for the default brand), we can add a custom domain. This can be useful if you don't want end users to know that you use Okta for application access. For instance, this can be interesting if you want to host an Okta login widget on your intranet. We will look into this later in this section. This custom URL needs to be set up on an Okta subdomain, and your main domain will remain as is. When you start, it will look like this:

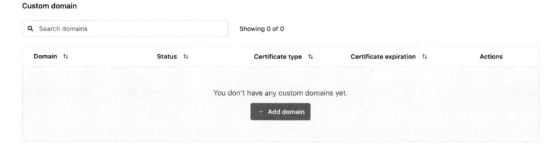

Figure 6.18 – Clicking the button to add a new domain

These are the steps to set up a custom domain:

1. First, you need a domain you own (as well as a subdomain, such as `login.example.com`), and you will need to be able to prove that you own it.

    After that, you will have to update the **Domain Name System** (**DNS**) records. You will receive information about the host and data from the setup wizard, which is then used in your domain registrar. Wait for the DNS registrar to update, and then go back to Okta to verify it.

2. After that, you need to accept Okta's certificate generation, or enter your own **Transport Layer Security**, (**TLS**) certificate, private key, and certificate chain if applicable. If you use Okta's solution, it is as easy as clicking. If you use your own certificate, you need to paste the **Privacy Enhanced Mail**, (**PEM**)-encoded certificate and public key in the assigned fields. Remember to use the `Begin` and `End` lines for each of them.

> **Note**
>
> Okta uses `Letsencrypt.org` as a service to create and manage SSL certificates for free. Even though it is a great way to secure your page to the highest standard, there might be reasons to use your own certificates.

The final step is to add an alias from your custom domain to the Okta subdomain by creating a **Canonical Name (CNAME)** record for your custom domain name. You do this in your domain registrar.

> **Important note**
>
> When you set up a custom domain, users are not rerouted from your main domain. You will have to tell users to start using the new custom domain name. If you have SAML or **Web Services Federation** (**WS-Fed**) applications, you might have to update them with the new domain if you want them to see the custom domain.

Once we have finished these steps and Okta has verified the domain, you will have a successfully added domain:

Custom domain

Domain ⇅	Status ⇅	Certificate type ⇅	Certificate expiration ⇅	Actions
login.oktaadministration.com ⧉	• Active	Okta-managed	Monday, January 15, 2024 7:57:26 PM GMT+1	Edit ⌄

Q Search domains — Showing 1 of 1 — + Add domain

Figure 6.19 – A list of all the added custom domains

If you want, you could add additional domains, if they belong to the same brand.

Also, in this section, you can set up a custom email domain.

By default, Okta sets a brand to default – `noreply@okta.com`. If you would rather have the address of your IT support, for instance, you can set it up by adding an email domain. This will open up a new window where you can set up your own email address. This only works when you create a brand, not in the default brand. You will start with a section looking like this:

Emails

Domain	Status	From address	Actions
okta.com Default	● Active	Okta <noreply@okta.com>	Add domain

Figure 6.20 – Adding an email to a domain

We start the process by clicking on **Add domain**.

> **Important note**
>
> This setting requires you to change DNS records and potentially add **Sender Policy Framework (SPF)** records. As these records differ according to the domain provider and within the systems allowed to send emails from your domain, we recommend following this guide from Okta to understand the requirements to make these changes: `https://help.okta.com/en/prod/Content/Topics/Settings/Settings_Configure_A_Custom_Email_Domain.htm`.

The following window will guide us through the setup. We first need to input the following values:

- **Email address**: This is the address you want Okta to send mail as
- **Name of email sender**: This is the name that a receiver sees when an email lands in their inbox

Add domain

A custom email domain presents a branded experience to your users. Messages appear to come from your custom email domain instead of noreply@okta.com.

Email address

Name of email sender

Please fill in this field.

Cancel   Next

Figure 6.21 – Setting up a custom domain

Once you click **Next**, a list of **TXT**, **CNAME**, and **DNS** values is presented to add to your domain registrar. After those are verified by Okta, emails will be sent from this new custom email domain. It will require Okta to verify these records in your DNS before it accepts the custom domain. If your registrar needs time to populate these records, Okta will allow you to come back later to verify those settings, once all the records have been populated to DNS servers.

> **Note**
>
> Visit your domain registrar to understand how to add DNS records, and verify the time needed to allow Okta to accept the custom records.

Once your custom domain has been accepted, you can go back and see your custom email domain ready for use:

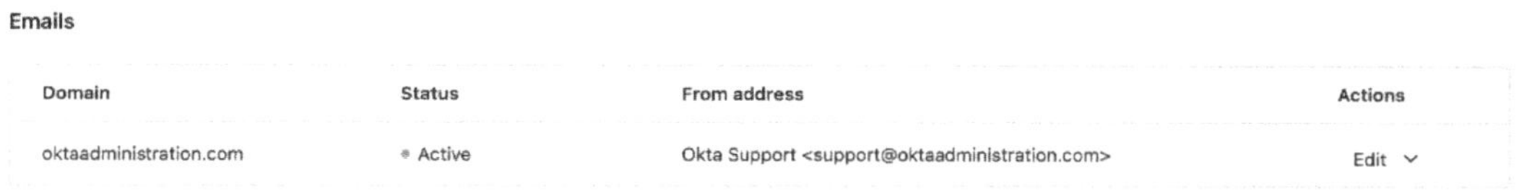

Emails

Domain	Status	From address	Actions
oktaadministration.com	● Active	Okta Support <support@oktaadministration.com>	Edit ⌄

Figure 6.22 – A custom email domain ready to be used

As you might have seen, for email domains, we can only add one, compared to main domains where you can add multiple.

Okay, let's move on to the last menu section, **Settings**. Here, a collection of different settings is editable and specific to the brand. Let's check it out.

Settings

In each brand, the **Settings** section contains additional options you can change for that brand specifically. Let's go over them one by one:

- **Brand name**: This is just a visual name change for the **Brands** section.
- **Sign-Out page**: In this section, you can determine where a user is taken to when they sign out of Okta.
- **Display language**: If you want the default display language to be something other than English for all of your end users, you can change it in the top-right section.
- **Loading Page Animation**: In this section, you can disable the animation Okta displays while redirecting users to applications. Instead, users will see a blank page. This can be useful if you have users with bad bandwidth, or if you really want to hide every element of Okta's branding.

- **Footer**: In the **Footer** menu, you can choose to edit two elements:

  - **Privacy policy**: This allows you to keep Okta's standard privacy policy, or link to one of your own

  - **Powered by Okta**: This is a footer branding from Okta that can be turned off to further obscure the usage of Okta to end users

Footer

You can customize the footer of your Okta pages by hiding this message or linking to your own privacy policy. Learn more.

Privacy policy

Configure your privacy policy link. You can reset to the Okta default policy at any time.

- ⊙ Okta privacy policy
- ○ Custom privacy policy

Powered by Okta

Configure whether Powered by Okta appears in any visible footers.

Show "Powered by Okta"

Figure 6.23 – The customizations available for the Footer menu in Okta

That brings us to the end of all options we can manage within **Brands**. Let's move on to the next section of the main **Customizations** menu, **SMS**.

SMS

For SMS, there is only one notification to edit. You can make changes to the message that end users receive for their SMS verification code – just remember to keep the message under 159 characters. To update the message, click the pencil icon under **Action**. Just as with email notifications, you can create your message in different languages:

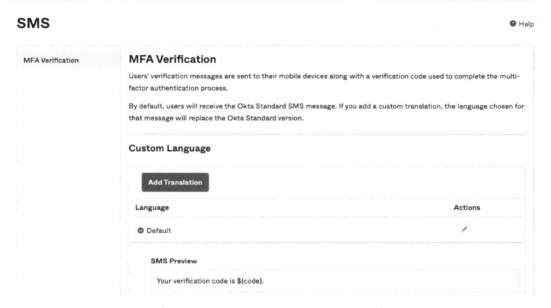

Figure 6.24 – The functionality to add alternative translations for email templates

You can also choose to add a translation to that message. Clicking the **Add Translation** button will give you the option to choose a language and the custom text message that will be sent. This translation will be used if a user chooses a specific language. If you do not use translations, Okta will always send the default SMS text.

Add Translation

Language

English (en)

Please select a language from the dropdown menu above

Your verification code is ${code}.

Please limit the SMS message length to 159 characters. (0 of 159 characters)

Add Translation   Cancel

Figure 6.25 – Adding additional translations for the SMS text

And that's it for SMS. The next main **Customizations** menu item is the **End-User Dashboard** layout.

The End-User Dashboard layout

In the **End-User Dashboard** layout, you can manage company-wide settings on how the dashboard works:

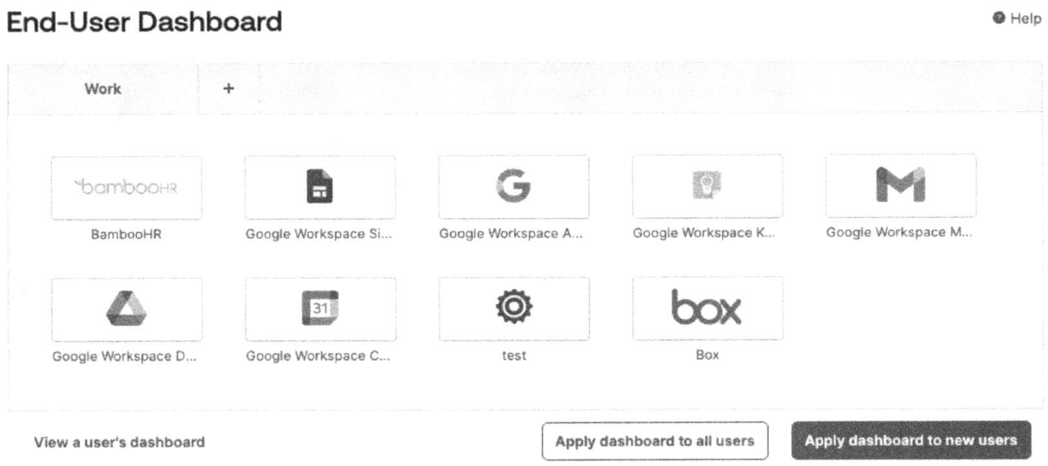

Figure 6.26 – Configuration of the dashboard

> **Note**
>
> Take note of the fact that the preview does not look like the actual dashboard. Okta is still showing the old layout. This menu might be updated at some point in the future.

Using the plus sign, you can create a new tab and assign that tab to all or only new users. After creating another tab, you can also click and drag applications to that tab. You can add up to four more tabs. The **Work** tab can be renamed by hovering over it and clicking the pencil icon.

> **Important note**
>
> If you choose to save your changes for all users, existing users will get a notification about the changes upon their next sign-in. Once applied, the user is free to rearrange their tabs and icons however they wish. The forced change will not reverse their settings.

All changes will overwrite any pre-existing dashboards arranged by individual users. This can be disruptive if used incorrectly, but it's helpful for new starters. As they cannot be set up to manage different departments or teams, make sure to keep your company-wide settings for tabs at a basic level, making it easy for end users to update them to fit their own needs afterward.

Under the last menu item of **Customizations**, **Other**, you will find more generic settings that will help you manage your Okta environment. Let's investigate these.

Other

This section has two columns of several settings. We will explain each of them, starting from the top left, moving down, and then back up to the top right.

In the **User Accounts** section, you can manage settings for how users can change their personal information and/or password information. If this information is managed by another application, you can write a message that will be shown to your end users on their settings page. If you click on the pen button, the following options will be shown in a pop-up window:

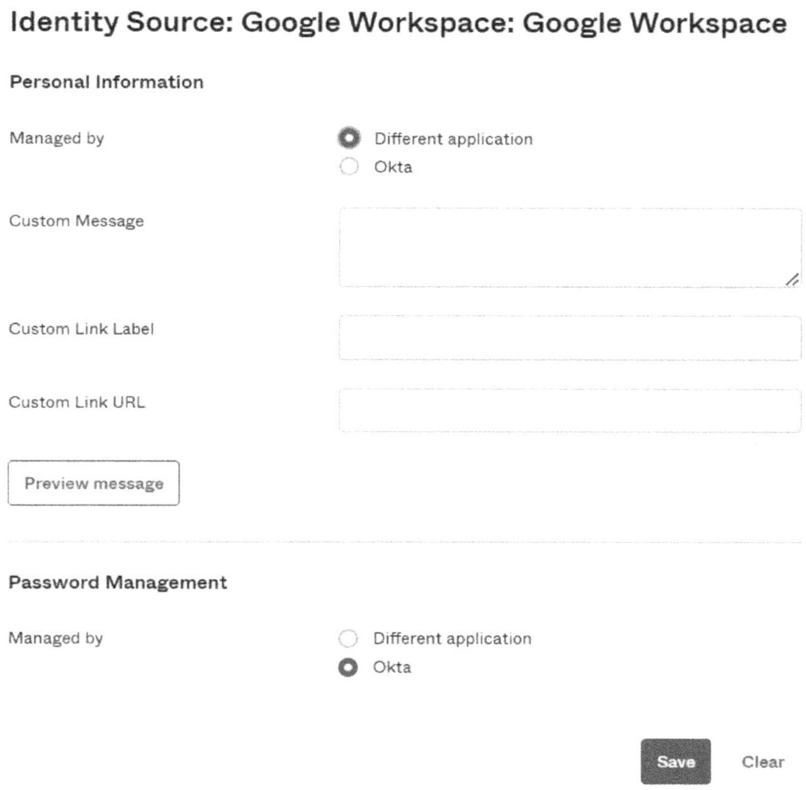

Identity Source: Google Workspace: Google Workspace

Personal Information

Managed by   ● Different application
                              ○ Okta

Custom Message

Custom Link Label

Custom Link URL

[Preview message]

Password Management

Managed by   ○ Different application
                              ● Okta

                                        [Save]   Clear

Figure 6.27 – Options for Personal Information

You can write a message to your end users about which application they should navigate to to update their information and supply a URL. This could, for instance, be an HR system. The same goes for password management.

In the next section, under **Optional User Account Fields**, you can enable or disable an end user's ability to update their secondary email:

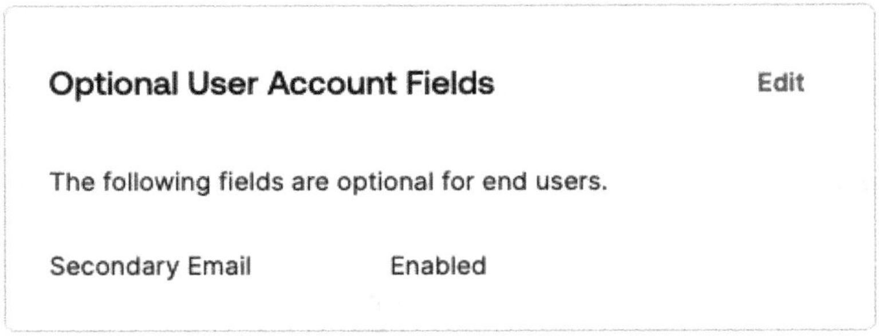

Optional User Account Fields   Edit

The following fields are optional for end users.

Secondary Email   Enabled

Figure 6.28 – Optional User Account Fields

In the next section, **Okta User Communication**, Okta can contact your end users to get information on their experience with Okta. If you don't want this, you can opt out of this communication for your tenant here:

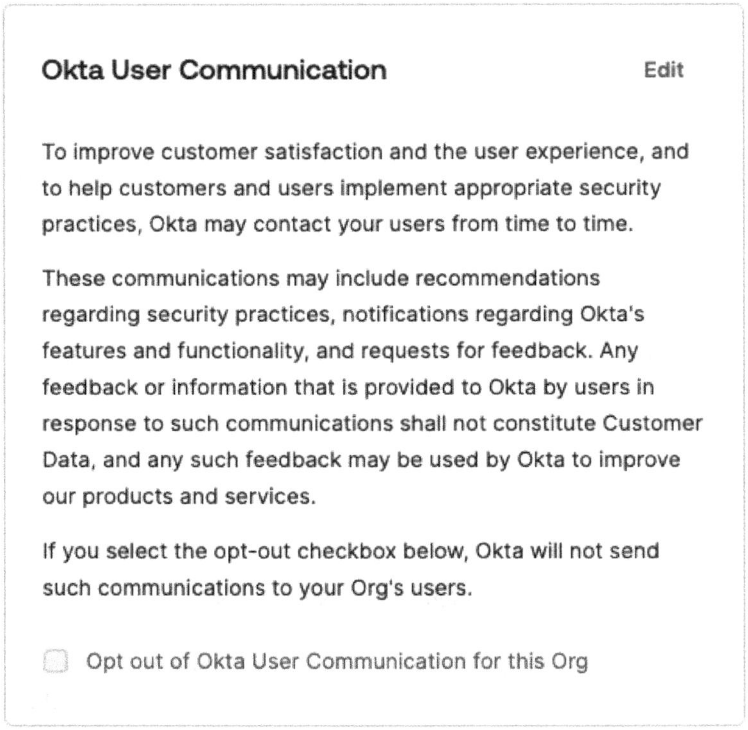

Okta User Communication   Edit

To improve customer satisfaction and the user experience, and to help customers and users implement appropriate security practices, Okta may contact your users from time to time.

These communications may include recommendations regarding security practices, notifications regarding Okta's features and functionality, and requests for feedback. Any feedback or information that is provided to Okta by users in response to such communications shall not constitute Customer Data, and any such feedback may be used by Okta to improve our products and services.

If you select the opt-out checkbox below, Okta will not send such communications to your Org's users.

☐ Opt out of Okta User Communication for this Org

Figure 6.29 – Okta User Communication

Moving forward in the available settings, **Deprovisioning Workflow** is next. Here, you can enable or disable deprovisioning tasks generated by lifecycle management actions on user accounts.

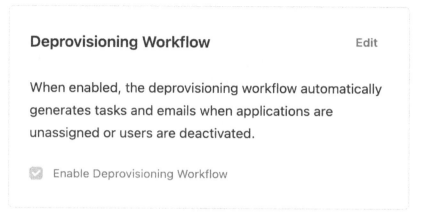

Figure 6.30 – Click Edit to enable the deprovisioning workflow

In the next section, **Just in Time Provisioning**, you can enable or disable **Just-in-time (JIT)** provisioning. This allows accounts to be automatically created if a user signs in for the first time using **Active Directory (AD)**-delegated authentication, desktop single sign-on, or inbound **Security Assertion Markup Language (SAML)**:

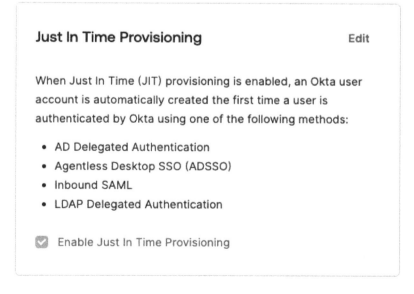

Figure 6.31 – Enabling JIT provisioning

> **Note**
> This setting is to allow global JIT. This can be used combined with app settings, as discussed in *Chapter 2, Working with Universal Directory*. This setting will not override individual settings on an app basis.

Next, you will see some **Okta Browser Plugin** settings. If your end users are not allowed to install plugins on their machines, you can enable centralized management for the plugin. With that, you can also select which groups you want to enable it for. The last configuration is to enable a warning if end users log in to an Okta organization other than your own. We will explore the use of the browser plugin in more detail a bit later:

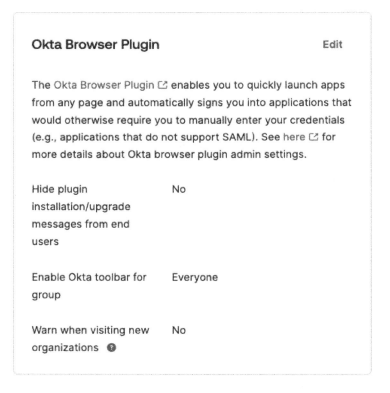

Figure 6.32 – The Okta Browser Plugin settings

If you need to embed Okta in an **IFrame**, you can do so in the next section. This allows you to incorporate Okta's **End-User Dashboard** into a frontend of your choosing. Think of an intranet, or other managed social environments that you control. Otherwise, Okta will not allow IFraming to prevent phishing or other takeover events from bad vectors:

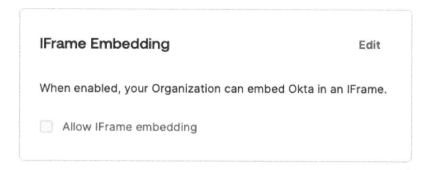

Figure 6.33 – IFrame Embedding

Lastly, on the left side of the page, you can adjust **Reauthentication Settings**. By default, users are required to reauthenticate after five minutes to change their user profile:

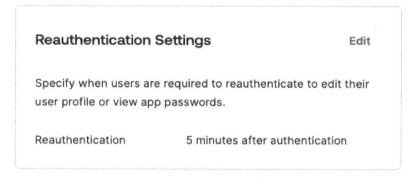

Figure 6.34 – Reauthentication Settings

This is the end of the left section of settings; let's go back and start on the right side.

If a user tries to access an application they are not assigned to, they will get an error message. If you want to redirect them to another URL instead of that erroneous URL, you can set that in the **Application Access Error Page** section:

Application Access Error Page   Edit

If your users attempt to access an application they are not
assigned, you can have them automatically redirected to a
custom URL. This may happen if a user tries to use an embed
link on a company website.

○ Use the default Okta error page
☐ Use a custom error page

Figure 6.35 – An access denied error message

When a user's conditions do not meet the requirements for access, an **Access denied error message**
window is displayed. You can change the default text and, optionally, add helpful links – for example,
to your IT support or support documentation.

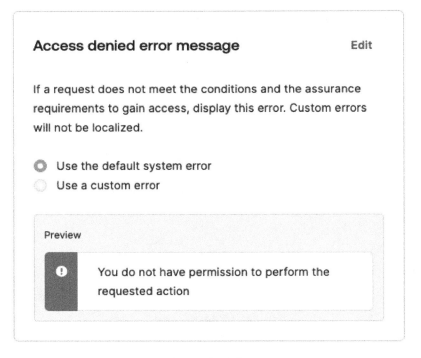

Figure 6.36 – Access denied error message

The following section is the global ability to allow end users to manage their **Recently Used Apps** option. We discussed this earlier in the chapter. Turning it off or on here will change the personal settings for the end users:

Recently Used Apps   Edit

When enabled, end users can show or hide a Recently Used Apps section from their settings. When disabled, the Recently Used Apps section and data will be cleared for all users. Learn more. ⧉

✅ Enable recently used apps

Figure 6.37 – Recently Used Apps

Lastly, we find the **Display Options** setting. Here, you can set the logo (Okta or your custom logo) in the top-left corner to redirect users somewhere – for example, your company website. You can also disable the home footer and onboarding screen for new users here:

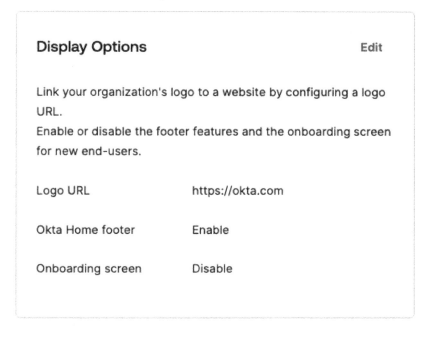

Display Options   Edit

Link your organization's logo to a website by configuring a logo URL.
Enable or disable the footer features and the onboarding screen for new end-users.

Logo URL   https://okta.com

Okta Home footer   Enable

Onboarding screen   Disable

Figure 6.38 – Display Options

And with that, we conclude our overview of the settings under the **Other** menu. This brings us to the final main section of this chapter, The *Okta plugin settings*.

The Okta plugin settings

The Okta plugin is a dashboard built into a browser extension. It allows you to navigate to any of your apps with ease, without having to go back to your Okta page.

One additional option is the account selector, which is for if you have more than one Okta session running with different tenants:

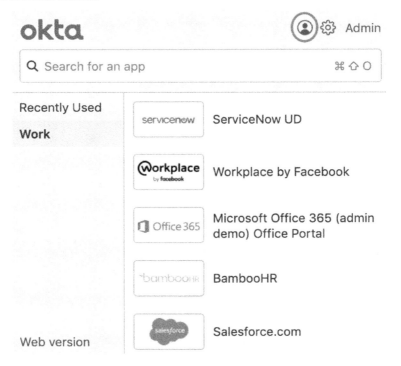

Figure 6.39 – The Okta plugin tenant selector

When you click on the cogwheel settings icon, you are brought to a new browser window. Here, you can find specific settings for the plugin:

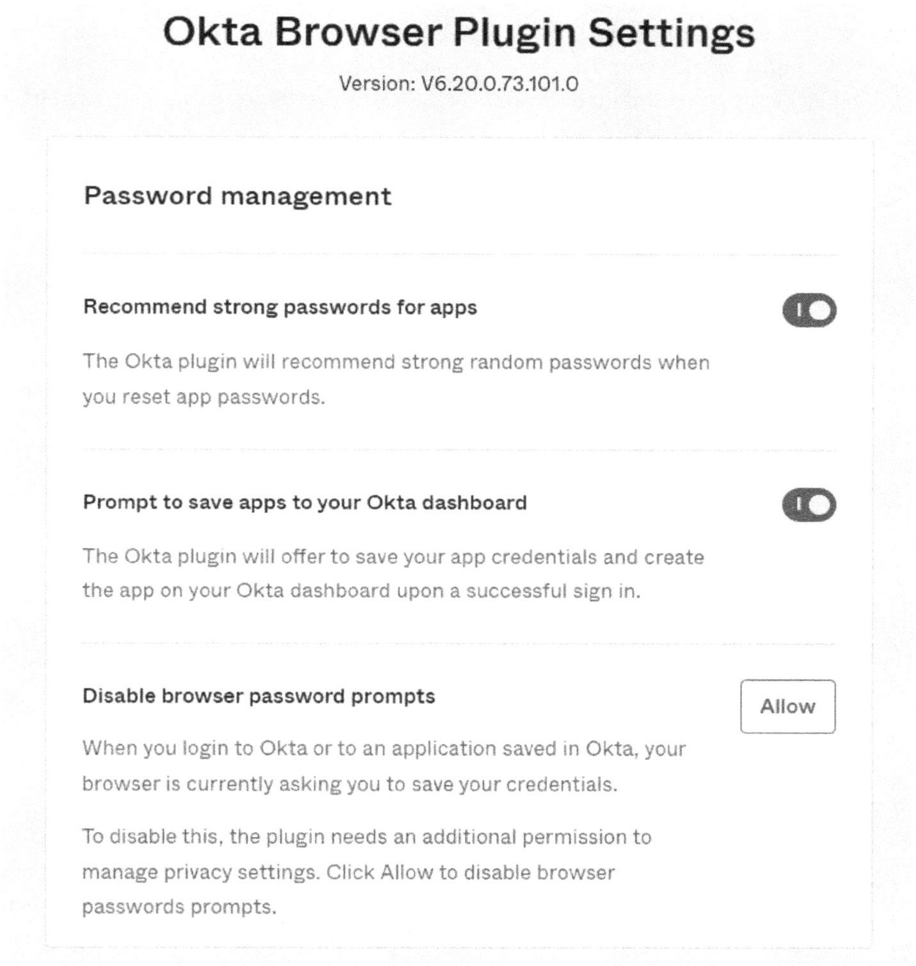

Okta Browser Plugin Settings

Version: V6.20.0.73.101.0

Password management

Recommend strong passwords for apps

The Okta plugin will recommend strong random passwords when you reset app passwords.

Prompt to save apps to your Okta dashboard

The Okta plugin will offer to save your app credentials and create the app on your Okta dashboard upon a successful sign in.

Disable browser password prompts

Allow

When you login to Okta or to an application saved in Okta, your browser is currently asking you to save your credentials.

To disable this, the plugin needs an additional permission to manage privacy settings. Click Allow to disable browser passwords prompts.

Figure 6.40 – The Okta plugin settings

With these settings, you can manage the following:

- Specifically, you can have the plugin prompt for strong passwords when it detects a password reset happening on a known application.
- The plugin will ask you to save new apps for end users if it's allowed to store new applications. This will pop up when the user logs in to a new application that Okta detects and determines to be new.
- You can prevent browser keychains from saving Okta login details, thereby ensuring that your secured and stored passwords for apps in Okta aren't leaked to unmanaged browser keychains.

In that same window, under **Advanced**, you have some extra settings for the plugin. First, you can turn on logging from the plugin to understand any issues with it. Secondly, you can reset the plugin entirely, deleting any issues there might be with the cookies and cache stored in the browser:

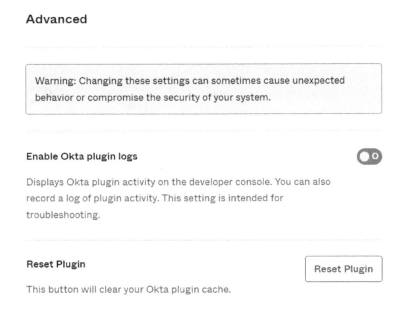

Figure 6.41 – The Okta plugin's Advanced section

The plugin is available for different browsers. Using the most recent version of the browser and plugin will give the best experience and the highest availability. It is recommended to make sure that users update their plugin. If you manage the plugin, you can update it in your **Mobile Device Management**, (**MDM**) update sequences too. Find out more information about the continuous development of the plugin here: `https://help.okta.com/en-us/content/topics/settings/version_histories/ver_history_browser_plugin.htm`.

Summary

In this chapter, we focused on end users and their experience with Okta. We have explored not only the default experience for end users but also the different ways in which we can change that experience. We looked at how we can make the sign-in page match your company profile. We also reviewed how we can configure the dashboard and the settings that end users can set themselves. To use Okta, we went over the Okta browser plugin and the settings we can manage for end users. For the more advanced reader, we also looked at how to configure a custom URL domain and the different settings we can use with that – for example, setting up a self-hosting login widget. Lastly, we updated the notification templates that are used to send users.

In the next chapter, we will look at some advanced possibilities in Okta and deep-dive into Okta Workflows.

Part 2: Extending Okta

Part 2 advances into the extended capabilities of Okta. Building on the foundational IAM principles covered earlier, this section introduces advanced configurations and features that enhance and scale Okta's utility. *Chapter 7, Okta Workflows*, details the automation of identity-related processes. *Chapter 8, API Access Management*, examines the protection of APIs with Okta's centralized control. *Chapter 9, Managing Access with Advanced Server Access*, focuses on managing secure server access at scale.

In this part, we aim to empower administrators with the knowledge to leverage Okta's advanced features, ensuring efficient and secure access management within complex IT ecosystems.

This part has the following chapters:

- *Chapter 7, Okta Workflows*
- *Chapter 8, API Access Management*
- *Chapter 9, Managing Access with Advanced Server Access*

7
Okta Workflows

Okta Workflows offers no-/low-code automation functionality for administrators. With the use of integrations, APIs, and events, Okta can centrally orchestrate every identity decision. It allows admins to be more on top of, have more visibility of, and be able to solve manual error-prone processes for the benefit of an organization, administrator, security, and – foremost – the end user.

In this chapter, you will learn more about the following:

- What Okta Workflows is
- Using Okta Workflows
- Integrating applications and functions
- Workflows export backup
- Delegated admin workflows

Let's start by looking at what Okta Workflows is and what different options we have.

What Okta Workflows is

When we talk about Workflows and Okta, we typically look at the separate no-code console we find in Okta (more on that later). However, we can also work with different types of hooks; let's look at these first.

Using workflow capabilities

The workflow capabilities within Okta expand across three areas – **inline hooks**, **event hooks**, and **automation**. These areas have different functionalities and different options.

Inline hooks

With inline hooks, you can call your own custom code with help from Okta's REST API. The outbound calls are triggered by events in your Okta process flows. Your custom code will be a web service with an internet-accessible endpoint. The service isn't hosted by Okta; it's hosted by you. The inline hooks use synchronous calls, which means that the process that triggered the hook/outbound call is paused until it receives an answer from your service.

So, how are these hooks added? Let's look at that.

> **Tip**
> Only super administrators can view and configure inline hooks.

Navigate to **Workflow | Inline Hooks**. Click **Add Inline Hook**, and then select what kind you want to use:

- **Registration**: This allows you to customize user registration requests in self-service registration
- **SAML**: This lets you modify assertions sent to SAML applications
- **Token**: This lets you modify tokens issued by your own authorization servers
- **Password Import**: This lets you import the passwords of users logging in
- **Telephony**: This is a method to utilize a third-party telephony service for SMS and voice services

To configure your new hook, you will need to enter the following information:

- **Name**: A name that describes the function of the hook
- **URL**: A URL pointing at the endpoint to call in your web service
- **Type of Authentication**: A choice between HTTP headers or OAuth 2.0
- **Authentication field**: The authorization header name
- **Authentication secret**: The field name's corresponding value string
- **Custom header fields**: An optional field name/value pair to send with the request

After saving, you need to pair the endpoint with the right Okta process flow. How to do this depends on the kind of inline hook you have set up (**Registration, SAML, Token, Password Import,** or **Telephony**). If you click on any of the types of hooks in the list in Okta, you will receive information on how to connect your specific type of hook, enabling it.

During the setup of an inline hook, you can choose to go with OAuth2.0 authentication rather than HTTP headers. By doing so, a slightly larger section will open.

The options you get here are as follows:

- **Client Authentication**: Here, you can choose to select the client secret or use self-managed keys
- **Client ID**: The client ID is one of the authentication credentials needed to connect with the service
- **Client secret**: This is a private value provided by the service, used to authenticate the identity of the application to the service or the self-managed key you created under **Workflows | Key Management**
- **Token URL**: The URL where inline hooks can exchange an authorization code for access and refresh tokens – for example, `/token`
- **Scope**: The scope that allows you to perform the actions on the hook endpoint that you want to access
- **Custom Headers**: Add a field name and value to send with the request

Key management, as mentioned under the **Client secret** bullet, is a separate section under the **Workflows** menu in the admin console. Here, you can manage the keys you want to generate for your services. Management is limited to renaming and deleting keys.

A generated key looks like this:

```
{
  "kty": "RSA",
  "alg": "RSA",
  "kid": "e86a0cf3-0df6-4c5e-aeeb-7fab2b1dfe15",
  "use": null,
  "e": "AQAB",
  "n": "w21EOpj1Mnm6jqLaM2FtfjR9cZU0u3agvA
Ts1EDuucEUW0-I52U3sN8n4MYGZC0DRiwtOhtVEt_
u7aXqKo2roUR3N11uced5sCQW9AaUT35lvKVVUKgvccS_VO7k9Zkn8qGYVBv72vTnH1QW
nsSAP3sHykNpK1hyziYBe2DbldO4ZmJE7nPIStWz160C-dccPbei4azYWyVOgHcYSZtg-
by0L4QLezkOShloSnZ_ZzDrjSkAI3FZefr-GFBYufNSSzclJRrMxe7zy-D0cpTdOHQ-7NB
o0Ar2cbBYIbQsH18EjKGR28NjT2OkC829w3JVJlMbGr1LLHMS9ZFtDLMVQQ"
}
```

This JSON-type file can be used to generate and manage the **JSON Web Key Set** (**JWKS**), which supports OAuth 2.0 client authentication.

> **Important note**
>
> Check out this help center section of Okta to understand how to further implement inline hooks for your business needs: `https://developer.okta.com/docs/concepts/inline-hooks/#currently-supported-types`.

So, what do you use these hooks for? These hooks are great to extend and expand the possibilities for you as an administrator to fulfill end user needs in one single event. That means that you can extend logins into applications with more or custom SAML information, using the SAML hook. Alternatively, perhaps you have a custom telephony service that is used for more than just Okta and you want to incorporate that; with the telephony hook, you can add that process.

Let's look at event hooks, which are somewhat similar but also very different.

Event hooks

Event hooks are like Webhooks. They send Okta events that are interesting to other systems, via HTTP POST, when they occur. Possible use cases for this kind of functionality could be the following:

- Sending a notification in a Slack channel when something suspicious occurs with a user

- Adding a customer to all systems in your marketing stack, after they sign up for your service

- Triggering an Okta workflow when a self-service event happens, additionally checking the user's context

Exactly as with inline hooks, you need a web service with an open endpoint. When a specific event occurs in your Okta org, HTTP POST is sent to this endpoint. As opposed to inline hooks, event hooks are asynchronous calls, and the process is not paused while it waits for the response from your web service. The setup, however, is exactly the same. By navigating to **Workflow | Event Hooks** and clicking **Create Event Hook**, you get to enter information in similar fields as those for inline hooks. The following fields are available in the setup window:

- **Name**: A readable and understandable name for the trigger

- **URL**: The URL this trigger will send information to

- **Authentication field**: An HTTP header-based authentication field

- **Authentication Secret**: The secret required to set up the HTTP header authentication

- **Custom Header Fields**: Any additional headers that are required by your service

- **Subscribe to events**: The option to select the event(s) on which you want the hook to trigger

Not all events are capable of triggering an event hook. In the **Subscribe to events** section, you are presented with a multi-choice list of events that are capable of triggering the hook.

> **Tip**
> Okta has more in-depth information on event hooks here: https://developer.okta.com/docs/concepts/event-hooks/#which-events-are-eligible. The catalog from the link has over 800 events that Okta publishes in the system logs. It includes explanations of each. Be aware that *not all events are eligible* to be used with the event hooks functionality. Okta flags those in the catalog with an event-hook-eligible tag.

Once you have added your event hook, Okta will ask to verify the ownership of the endpoint. This is to make sure your endpoint is allowed to be accessed and gives a response. You might be required to skip this step if the endpoint isn't set up yet.

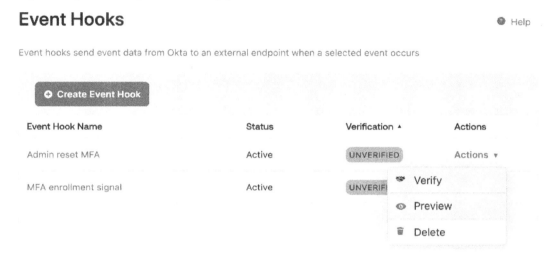

Figure 7.1 – Actions for event hooks

Once back in the **Event Hooks** main window, you will find your newly created event hook present, with a dropdown with some options:

- **Verify**: This option will (re)try to verify our endpoint URL
- **Preview**: Here, you can try and review what information is present in the event
- **Delete**: This option will delete the event hook

Let's investigate the **Preview** section. Here, you will find the information you entered during the setup of the trigger, but there is also a section that provides information on present data available in Okta. If none is present, then the section will generate example data.

Configure Event Hook request
The Event Hook that is being previewed.

Name	Admin reset MFA
URL	https://www.myendpoint.com
Event Type	Reset all MFA factors for user by admin (user.mfa.factor.reset_all)
System Log Event	There are no events for "Reset all MFA factors for user by admin". We have populated an example event below.

Figure 7.2 – A hook with available example data

The preview window under the selection pane will show a JSON body of the event. This allows you to understand what information will be sent to your selected endpoint service:

Preview & Deliver Event Hook
The outbound call Okta sends to the external service.

JSON   Edit

```
{
    "eventType": "com.okta.event_hook",
    "eventTypeVersion": "1.0",
    "cloudEventsVersion": "0.1",
    "source": "https://oktaadministration.okta.com/api/v1/eventHooks/who7rjsaa5pl4UAnx417",
    "eventId": "14cbe57e-7402-4795-a11b-15e33b65f6cc",
    "data": {
        "events": [
            {
                "uuid": "745070c9-e743-49be-a890-f18990584ac5",
                "published": "2023-10-28T15:19:20.930015Z",
                "eventType": "user.mfa.factor.reset_all",
                "version": "0",
                "displayMessage": "Reset all factors or authenticator enrollments for user.",
                "severity": "INFO",
                "client": {
                    "userAgent": {
                        "rawUserAgent": "Mozilla/5.0 (Macintosh; Intel Mac OS X 10_15_7) AppleWebKit/537.36 (KHTML,
                        "os": "Mac OS X",
                        "browser": "CHROME"
```

● Deliver Request

Figure 7.3 – An example of hook JSON code

This pane is a scrollable window with a lot of information, based on the event.

By clicking **Edit**, you can alter existing data for this test. This allows you to customize the information. Do note that this will not be a permanent change, and the body, as is, will always entirely be sent to your endpoint. If you want to save your edits, click on **Save**.

Now, to test this trigger, click on **Deliver Request** at the bottom of the JSON window. If the trigger is set up successfully, a note shows that the request was delivered successfully.

> Tip
> Okta currently has an early access feature in development that will allow you to filter on selected events for your event hook. This makes the event hook even more granular and allows you to be very specific on how the event hook will behave. More details can be found here: https://help.okta.com/oie/en-us/Content/Topics/automation-hooks/add-event-hooks.htm#Create.

Let's now move on to automations.

Automation

Automation is a section that allows simple actions to get triggered on different conditions.

Any new automation starts with a *time-based element* and will look at *one or more groups*. Additionally, you can add the following triggers to the automation – **User Inactivity in Okta** and **User password expiration in Okta**. These conditions combined in any way can set off different actions in the automation. You can add an action to *send an email to the user*, and/or *change the user's lifecycle state* to suspended, deactivated, or deleted. An automation setup can look like this:

Figure 7.4 – An automation flow to deactivate a user after 30 days of inactivity

In this automation, we have set up a deactivation flow if the user has been inactive for 30 days. The automation runs every day at 11:59 P.M. and it checks the entire organization group as the potential user population. If it finds a user meeting these conditions, the user's state is set to **Suspended**.

After saving the different triggers and actions and naming the automation, it can be activated and will run in the background.

Depending on the size of your Okta org, it can take up to 24 hours before the automation starts evaluating. These small automations can help automate simple tasks.

So, all these options – inline hooks, event hooks, and automations – have specific use cases and are available in every Okta org. Even though their usage might not be very elaborate and, in some cases, require a third-party service to trigger, they are useful to extend your automation strategy.

Let's go through other things we can do within Okta in the next section on Okta Workflows, Okta's advanced workflow engine built to automate every step of your IT business. We will also go through how to incorporate some of the previous functions into Okta Workflows and have them work together.

Using Okta Workflows

Okta Workflows is a GUI-driven no-/low-code automation tool with a lot of possibilities. This large pool of functionality allows Okta to be capable of managing different aspects of a user lifecycle more granularly. This differs quite extensively from the simpler automations we talked about in the previous section. Workflows allows you to incorporate dozens of applications, as well as your own functionalities as part of a workflow.

Workflows can do a lot. Let's look at a few use cases:

- **The provisioning and de-provisioning of app accounts**: Okta Workflows can automatically detect and act on newly added accounts. These newly joined employees, with their Okta account, will be assigned to the required applications, be granted the necessary entitlements, and even receive folder shares based on who they are and what their role is. Additionally, a message can be sent to their manager to make sure they are welcomed correctly. Conversely, Okta Workflows can suspend accounts, transfer over any digital assets to the required accounts or users, grant a grace period to allow manual work on the suspended user, and eventually deactivate the user within all and any connected applications.

- **Using logic and timing to sequence actions**: Using Workflows grants you the opportunity to get work done in advance. Using options such as creating deactivated accounts in applications allows you to make sure work can be done upfront. Once onboarding time arrives, Workflows will activate an account within Okta and activate application accounts as well. When a user leaves the company, they can still have access to payroll for personal administrative reasons and, after a year, the account will be closed entirely.

- **Conflict-resolving capabilities**: Workflows can have logic built in to detect and resolve conflicts when it comes to user accounts – for instance, creating unique usernames for applications, such as Slack, to make sure deactivated existing accounts aren't reactivated for a new user.

- **Using notifications for all types of events**: Using communication tools can help bring information to the correct people. Making sure managers are notified on Slack that a new employee will start or sending emails to IT to notify them about factory problems are all functionalities you can leverage with Okta Workflows.

- **Expanding logs and APIs**: With the use of exports and CSV files, Okta can not only send details periodically but also send details of events to third-party systems, ensuring all details surrounding users, applications, and systems are up to date and directly accessible for the right people.

For Okta to truly get a grip on all aspects of a user's identity within the different applications, new integrations need to be set up. This means Okta doesn't use the integrations already in Okta but needs to redo the integrations again in the Workflows interface.

Your first Workflows contact

First, you need to have access to the Workflows app itself. Okta comes with two applications, shown as follows:

Figure 7.5 – Applications in the Okta admin console

- **Okta Workflows**: This is the app to access the Okta Workflows console. This needs to be assigned to users, and only organization or super-administrators have enough privileges for it to be assigned.

- **Okta Workflows Oauth**: Even the Okta Workflows Engine needs to connect to your own Okta org. This app will be used to set up an integration. It will have to be assigned to the administrator who will set up the integration, allowing it to connect.

Once you have assigned the apps, you can find access to the Workflows console under the **Workflow** settings menu:

Workflow

Automations

Inline Hooks

Event Hooks

Delegated flows

Workflows console [↗]

Key Management

Figure 7.6 – The Workflow menu section

This feature will appear for any admin who is an organization administrator or super-administrator.

When you access the Workflows console, you will find that no integration has been set up. In your Okta integrations, a preset **OpenID Connect** (**OIDC**) app will have been created to set up the environment.

To start, follow the **settings** windows to integrate Workflows with Okta:

1. In the admin console, go to **Applications** | **Applications**.
2. Select **Okta Workflows OAuth**, and then open the **Sign On** tab.
3. Open a second browser tab, and in the admin console, go to **Workflow** | **Workflows** console.
4. In the **Workflows** console, go to the **Connections** menu and click **New Connection**.
5. In the **Connection Nickname** field, enter the display name that you want to appear in your connector list.
6. In the **Domain** field, enter your Okta org's domain, without `http://` and `-admin`, if applicable. For example, if the URL is `http://organization-admin.okta.com`, your domain is `organization.okta.com`.
7. In the admin console, copy the client ID from the Okta Workflows OAuth app. Return to **Workflows console**, and paste the ID into the **Client ID** field in the **Connection** window.
8. In the admin console, copy the client secret from the Okta Workflows OAuth app. Return to **Workflows console**, and paste the secret into the **Client Secret** field of the **Connection** window.
9. In **Workflows console**, click **Create**.

And you're done! You have added your Okta org as an integration in Workflows.

To integrate other compatible applications with Workflows, Okta provides step-by-step instructions that you can follow. Detailed explanations of these integrations are beyond the scope of this book and can be found within the Workflows interface.

Now, you can trigger events and create actions in Okta and any other integration you have set up. Let's look more deeply into these events and actions that workflows use.

Okta Workflows flows

To be sure you understand all the elements within Workflows, we need to be clear on the different names within the Workflows product:

*   **Workflows**: The Okta product used to automate business logic.
*   **Flows**: Flows are the workflows that are built to do the heavy work with integrations.
*   **Flowcards**: Flowcards are the steps in a workflow. These steps are visualized from left to right on the **Flow** page.

- **Event**: The event is the trigger from where a flow starts; there can only be one event in a flow.

- **Actions**: Actions are flowcards that do something in a flow, such as sending commands to the flowcard integration.

- **Functions**: Functions are cards that allow you to change how a flow interacts with moving data.

A complete flow with flowcards could look as follows:

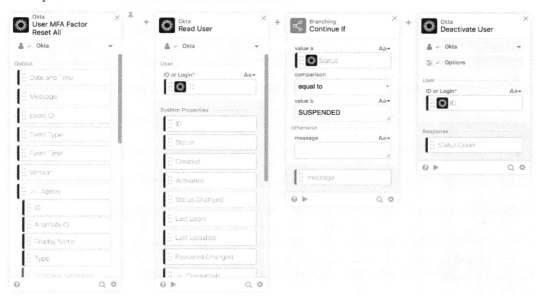

Figure 7.7 – Flow with Flowcards

In the preceding screenshot, you can see a sample flow. The first flowcard is the trigger card. This flowcard allows the entire flow to trigger. The second flowcard is an action flowcard, and it searches for the user in Okta based on the triggered event. The third is a function flowcard, determining whether the flow is allowed to continue if the condition is met. In this example, it uses a **Continue If** function. Finally, the last flowcard is another action flowcard, deactivating a user in Okta.

The data moving between the different flowcards allows the flow to handle, determine, and use data in any way you see fit.

Flowcards have input fields and output fields. Input fields are mapped against other fields in previous flowcards. Output fields generate what you think is needed for that flowcard. This can be created by the event, action, or function you use. Flows have a user-friendly drag and drop mechanism. By simply dragging any field into another flowcard's input field, you can map the data from these two fields. Fields can be used multiple times and can be used to connect to different input fields on other flowcards. This makes it super-easy to reuse data from one specific flowcard in any other:

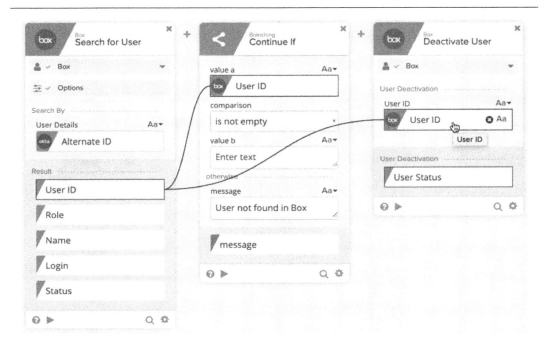

Figure 7.8 – Mapping data from one field to multiple others

Additionally, you can add note flowcards to the flow to expand more on what the actions are doing, ensuring that everyone else understands the flow in its entirety.

Platform features

Okta Workflows comes with some additional features that help you expand its possibilities even more:

- **Tables** are data stores within your flows. They can generate data during flow executions, store data for reporting, or create constants tables to be reused in different flows to recall information. All of this is stored within the Okta Workflows interface and available without re-authorizing the user's session.

    Tables can be exported and saved as a csv file, to be sent (with a flow) to whom it may concern – for example, sending security a monthly report on bad login attempts, or showing offboarding statistics to department heads and HR. All of this can be done with the help of tables.

    Tables can also be accessed within a flow to get the information needed and add it as context, used as information that needs to be transformed, or used to simply delete the info in a table. By adding a function card for the table, you can do whatever you like with the data in it.

- **API endpoints** are other types of triggers that can kickstart a flow. Using a third-party system with the right security access can start a flow with data sent along with it. Let's say your HR system doesn't have any integration out of the box with Okta but does have API capabilities. With some simple scripting, you can use the Okta Workflows API endpoints to create, update, or even deactivate new users. Based on the content sent along within POST call, you can allow a flow to use the start date to wait on the action for creation, or you can have the deactivation be prescheduled and run once the date is met.

  By changing the exposure in the flow settings, endpoints of the workflow can become more open to the public. If so, you can allow other services to trigger, and perhaps give information back on data from various applications, or allow services to register new users with your Okta. This can also be done by third parties that you do not control but who you would like to give automated access to your systems.

- **History** is available per flow and is stored for up to 30 days. This allows you, as an admin, to check whether everything went OK or fix issues if a flow didn't behave as expected. As flows can have sensitive data in them, allowing the storage of history requires an opt-in confirmation. You can do this within the flow by checking the **Save all data** checkbox in the **Save** dialog box, or by clicking on the **Enable Save Data** link in the right pane of the **Flow History** page. You can disable this any time you want. This might be relevant when **Personally Identifiable Information** (**PII**) moves within your flow and you need to debug when creating the flow. Once you have determined it's working as expected, turning off the flow history can be a good step to take.

Okta has a lot of different use cases and tutorials to help you start your first Workflows experience. It is recommended to read through `learn.workflows.okta.com` and check out its growing library of examples and flows that it walks you through.

App integrations

Applications are the heart of workflows. Integrating them allows you to understand the situation of a user in the app and act on it. Okta has an ever-growing library of applications, ranging from HR apps to MDM and specific document apps, such as Google Sheets, or communication services, such as Slack. As you might expect, all of these have their own advantages, and the usage of Workflows allows for unlimited possibilities to combine them:

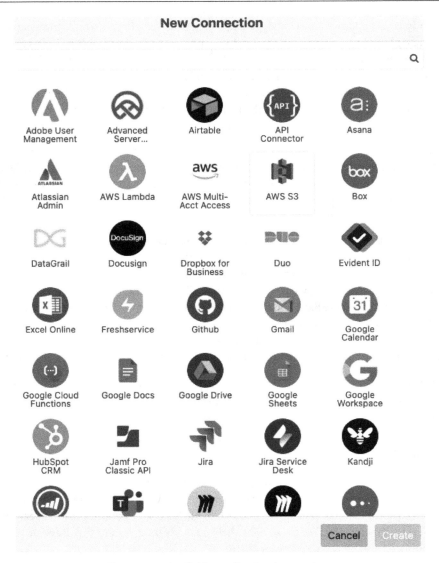

Figure 7.9 – Available application integrations

As each app requires its own setup, a detailed page for each application is maintained by Okta. Also, each app has its own library of triggers and actions. You won't always find a specific action for your use case, but in most cases, Okta also has an API action card you can add, and you can specifically call an API endpoint for that application. This allows you to do more, even if Okta doesn't have the pre-built action available:

Figure 7.10 – The setup of a custom API action for Google Workspace

Next, we'll take a look at the Workflows Connection builder and how this feature can help us.

The Workflows Connector builder

Workflows Connector Builder is a functionality in Okta that allows you to build your own application integration. Let's say your organization has a custom platform and you need to integrate it for identity-driven workflows. Instead of using custom API cards and triggers, you can create a fully functional integration, like any other app, and determine the triggers and actions you want to publish.

> **Note**
>
> As this is a relatively new and very advanced feature of Okta, we will not examine its usage entirely, as it will most likely change or be updated after the publication of this book. However, we will go over the basic requirements and settings here so that you have a basic understanding. Additional documentation can be found here: `https://help.okta.com/wf/en-us/Content/Topics/Workflows/connector-builder/connector-builder.htm`.

Building blocks

Connector Builder consists of the following **building blocks**:

- **Connectors**: These are the actors that interact with third-party applications or your own integration. Connectors can have events and actions.
- **Cards**: Cards are used to generate the functionality you want to present to Workflow builders. Each card can be individually defined in how it works. Some cards are events, while others are actions. These cards can be used in a regular workflow.

- **Authentication**: Authentication can be a requirement for a user to be allowed to use a connector. Depending on their scope, some or all cards might be available to the user building a workflow.

- **Options**: Options contain settings and values that you set when a connector is created. Some basic information and details can be added to the connector.

- **Inputs**: These fields can be determined by the developer of a connector. Inputs are ingested by the connector and internally used or sent to the external interface. Some might be required, while others are optional. As a developer, you can also allow certain or all data types, such as `Text`, `Number`, `True/False`, `Date & Time`, `Object`, and `File`.

- **Outputs**: These are similar to inputs, except outputs send back data to the workflow of a user.

- **Dynamic fields**: Dynamic fields, unlike static fields, vary, based on the connected account, and they allow for greater flexibility, as they are not constrained by the connector definition and can differ, based on custom datasets specific to a third-party service account.

During the setup of your first connector, you will be asked to give it a descriptive name and additional information to understand more about what the connector is used for.

A warning is given that (at the time of writing) built connectors cannot be moved or exchanged with other Okta Workflows environments. If you have multiple Okta orgs, this means you will need to build a connector in each one:

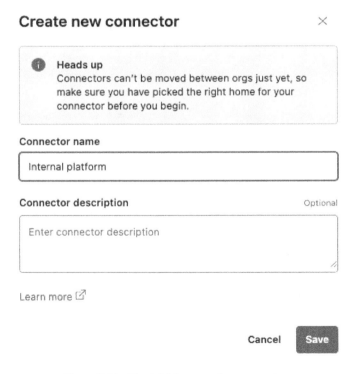

Figure 7.11 – The initial setup of a connection

Once you have created a connector, you will be presented with a basic window highlighting your connector. Here, you can see some basic settings of the connector and edit these:

Figure 7.12 – The settings for a built connector

You can update the settings for your connector, as shown in any connector during setup and usage.

Underneath this window, you will find a section to set up the required authentication method of your connector. This will be relevant for the user during the setup of the connector:

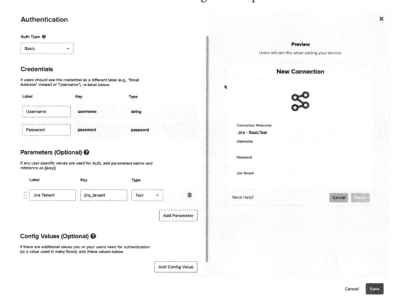

Figure 7.13 – Authentication options for a connector
(The textual detail in the above figure is minimized and is not directly relevant for the display
of the graphic. Please refer to the Free eBook download to access the detail in the graphic)

Here, we can choose between the following authentication types:

- **None**
- **Basic**
- **Oauth2.0**
- **Custom**

Each of these has its own requirements to be set up, and the preview window to the right will show the different end user experiences. Depending on your application, it might use any of these, where, of course, the custom authentication type will give you the most flexibility to set up authentication.

Options and functionality

The builder contains several options and functionality that allow you to build a connector with not only everything you need, but also everything you already know from regular Workflows. Technically, a connector also contains *internal* workflows that will handle different actions, events, data, and security requirements. All of this is compacted into your build, and once deployed, it is completely fixed in place and allows you to utilize the different events or actions in your regular Okta Workflows. To understand this, Okta has divided it into several topics:

- Flowtypes
- Dynamic options
- Extensible input fields
- Functions
- **Custom API Actions (CAPIA)**

> **Note**
>
> We will not discuss these subjects, as they vary with each integration and are beyond the scope of this book. We do recommend reading through the topics in the Okta help center to understand the usage of each of these, as they will be key to building your connector. This is a great place to start for those topics: `https://help.okta.com/wf/en-us/content/topics/workflows/connector-builder/connector-builder.htm`.

Building, testing, and deploying

Once you commence and start your build, you will need to test all flows, actions, cards, inputs, and outputs. This will make sure that the required and expected outcomes are given, based on the inputs a user eventually will pass along in an Okta workflow.

Using the builder flow history allows you to review and check the outcomes. If all seems well, you are ready to deploy your connector.

As said at the beginning of this section, you cannot share connectors between different Okta tenants. A connector can only be deployed to your own environment.

Once you have created a first action flow, you can create a test version. This test version will be applicable to be deployed. If you click on the menu at the end of the test version, you can choose **Deploy test version**:

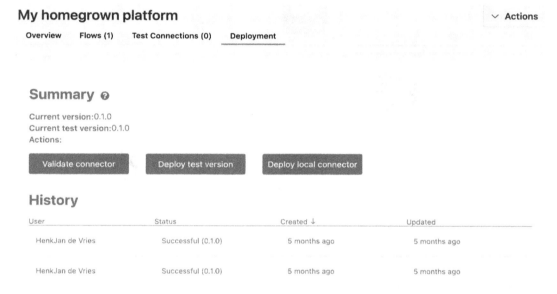

Figure 7.14 – The version history of your connector

Once you deploy your version, the **Private deployment** window will highlight the details of the deployment:

Figure 7.15 – Deployment information about your connector

Now, you will be able to find your deployment connector in the workflows connector list:

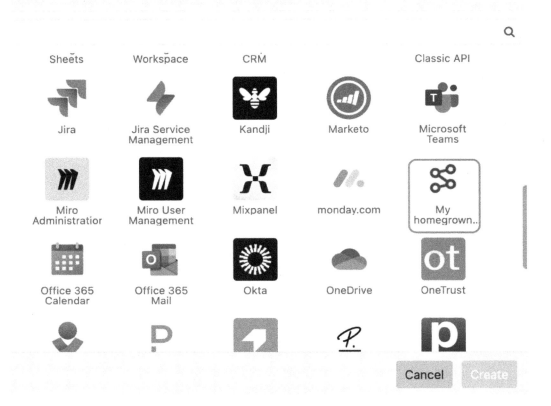

Figure 7.16 – Your built connector will be available among the others in your Workflows console

Fantastic! We have just run through how to start, create, edit, set up, test, and deploy a connector.

However, there is one more thing – besides deploying the connector to your private environment, you are also allowed to submit the connector to Okta.

Okta will review your connector and determine whether it can be publicly deployed. This can be of advantage if you are a software provider and want to integrate Okta with your services using Okta. The process your connector goes through has additional requirements, beyond just the connector itself. The requirements are as follows:

- The user documentation link for the connector
- The customer support email address

- Sufficient data in the Okta org for connector evaluation

- The file with exported test flows

- The document outlining tests covered in exported flows

- The API documentation link for connector building

Now, let's return to Okta Workflows and go over some additional functionality that it has to quickly help you set up and manage your workflows.

Templates

One of the neat functionalities in Workflows is templates. This catalog is ever-growing. Here, you find common use cases that can be handled by Workflows, and you can easily add a template from the collection to your Workflows console by clicking the **Add template** button. Each template provides setup instructions and a GitHub repo, which you can also download if needed.

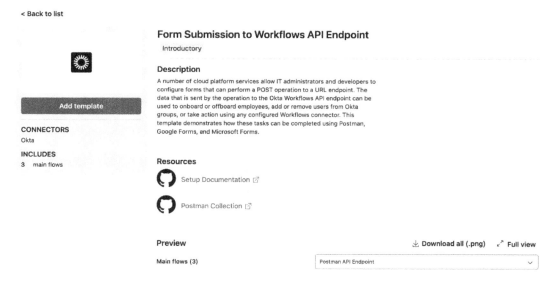

Figure 7.17 – The interaction of a workflow template

The template catalog is divided into different categories, such as **Popular**, **Introductory**, and **Connector**. It's also possible to search for templates by, for instance, entering a certain application. If you are missing a connector, you can click the **Suggest a template** link that appears in every collection.

Exporting workflows

Sometimes, you might want to export your workflow. It could be because you want to back it up, or you want to share your smart solution with someone else. You can do this both on a singular flow or a complete flow folder, although the latter probably is the most useful. Simply find your folder, hover your mouse over the folder name, click the three dots at the end of the row, and select **Export**. This file can be shared with someone else, who would need to create a new folder and follow the same steps but instead click **Import**:

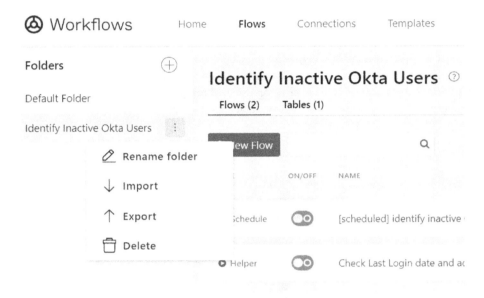

Figure 7.18 – The possibility to import and export flows

Now that we have looked at these smart features, let's dive into delegated admin workflows.

Delegated admin workflows

By default in Okta, you need organization or super-administrator privileges to access the Workflows console. There might be cases where you want a user to be able to run a workflow but without giving that user access to all available automations within that console. For these cases, delegated flows are perfect. In this scenario, you build a flow in the Workflows console and delegate it to another administrator, who can run it directly in the Okta administrator console.

To do this, there are a few prerequisites:

1. The workflow starts with the **Delegated flow** card:

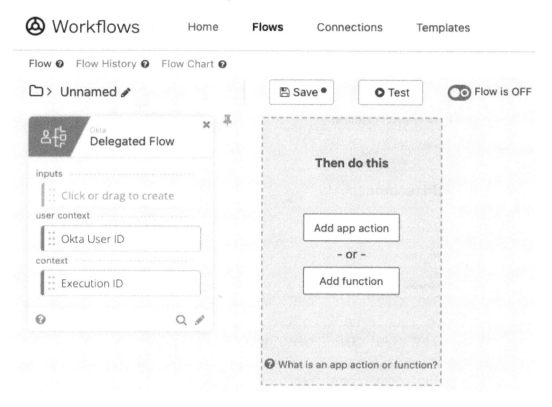

Figure 7.19 – The workflow with the delegate trigger card

2. The administrator with the delegated flow needs an admin role that contains workflow management, or a resource set that contains the delegated flow as well as the **Run delegated flow** permission. You can set this by going to **Settings | Security | Administrators | Resources**. Here, you can create a new resource set:

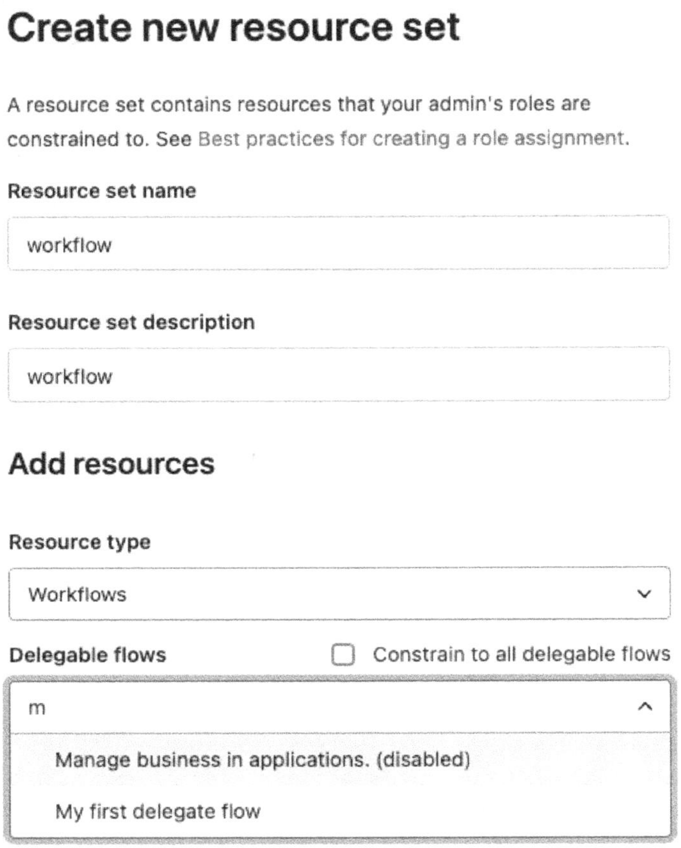

Create new resource set

A resource set contains resources that your admin's roles are constrained to. See Best practices for creating a role assignment.

Resource set name

workflow

Resource set description

workflow

Add resources

Resource type

Workflows   ⌄

Delegable flows   ☐ Constrain to all delegable flows

m   ⌃

Manage business in applications. (disabled)

My first delegate flow

Figure 7.20 – The workflow resource set options for admins

Once we have completed these steps, anyone building a workflow can delegate the functionality of the workflow to the admins allowed to start that workflow.

The benefits of delegating a workflow are that you can allow the admin to add data to the workflow as part of the trigger card. It means that you can add input fields in the delegate card, which will be shown as a popup for the delegate admin:

Figure 7.21 – The delegated workflow trigger card with input fields

As fields cannot be set to **Mandatory**, be aware that you need to correctly and fully describe the fields and their usage, as your workflow could fail based on bad input.

Once you have built your workflow, you can allow admins to run it.

If an admin has specific delegate access, it could be that the resource set needs to be expanded to allow the new workflow to start. If the resource set allows access to all workflows, the new workflow will be visible once the workflow is created. You do that by checking the **Constrain to all delegable flows** option. As shown in *Figure 7.22*, admins with access will see workflows under the admin console **Workflow | Delegated flows section**:

Figure 7.22 – The resource set options for workflow delegation

This window will list all available workflows, and each will show the name, the description given to the workflow, and a **Run** button to start the workflow.

If we do this for the given example, we will see the input fields we determined in the workflow in *Figure 7.23*:

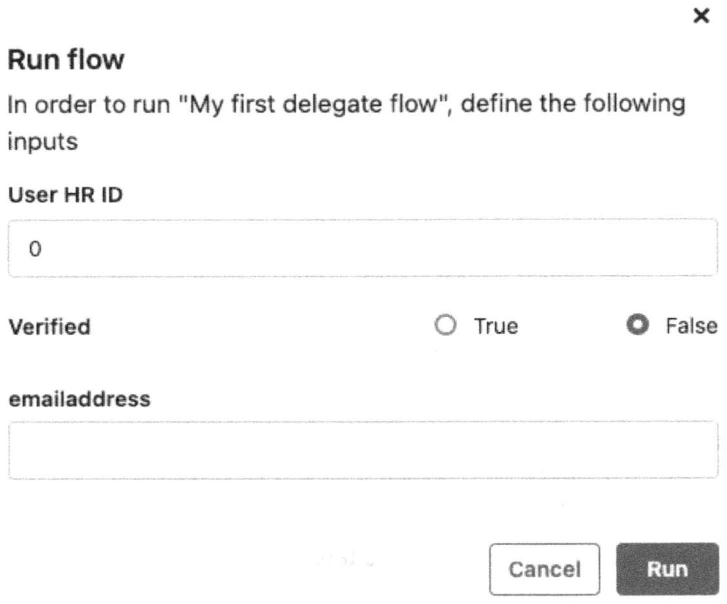

Figure 7.23 – The delegated admin view of a workflow with input fields

Once the admin has given the correct details (or not), the workflow will kick off and run. Once this happens, the workflow captures more information you can use. In the **Flow History** section of the workflow, you can see additional information on the admin's user ID and an execution ID.

Figure 7.24 – Input after a delegated admin ran a workflow

By having this information, you can use the Okta user ID to refer back to if, for whatever reason, the input was wrong, the workflow failed, or it successfully finished. The execution ID can be used for logging and auditing.

With that, you can now create a workflow and allow delegated admins to start them, allowing the workflows to be run when needed, securely based on the access rights, without providing access to the Workflows console.

Summary

In this chapter, we investigated how we can go that extra mile with automation. We've been through the simple but powerful automation options available directly in Okta, such as the various hooks. You learned how to add your Okta tenant as an integration in the Workflows console and the different elements that, combined, make a flow come to life. We also dived into the latest functionality of Connector Builder, learning how and why to use it. Lastly, we explored how to use templates, how to export and import workflows so you can easily share them, and how to work with delegated admin workflows.

In the next chapter, we are going to look at Okta's API Access Management.

8
API Access Management

So far in this book, we've looked at Okta's fundamental functionality. When we looked at giving users access, it was to applications. In this chapter, we're taking a step into more advanced features, such as the **application programming interface** (**API**) management of Okta and access to the APIs of external applications. This can be for an organization or Okta's APIs, as well as access to self-developed **OpenID Connect** (**OIDC**) applications. This is not a feature that every organization needs, but it's a feature that gives that little extra to the organization that needs it.

In this chapter, we will look at the following:

- API terminology
- Managing Okta with APIs
- API access management fundamentals
- API access administration

API terminology

There is some terminology that we need to go through to be able to understand all aspects of API management and API access management:

- **API product**: An API product is an application comprising multiple API endpoints. These endpoints serve various needs and use cases but share a common authorization server. API products are what users log into using OIDC with an ID token.

- **API**: APIs consist of endpoints that facilitate data exchange between systems based on requests and access permissions.

- **Authorization server**: An authorization server is the heart of OAuth 2.0, generating access tokens by utilizing Okta's scopes, claims, and access policies. In Okta, it's common to create one server per API product, although multiple products can share one. The server is designed to address specific use cases rather than individual endpoints.

- **Scopes**: Scopes are operations performed on your API endpoints. They are built into the application, and access is requested from the authorization server with the setup claims and policies.

- **Claims**: Claims are statements that authorize user actions within an application. Typically, they're not added to ID tokens, which focus on authentication. Instead, claims are included in access tokens generated by the authorization server. They can be standard (for example, email, name, or role) or custom, containing specific user or application-related data.

- **Tokens**: ID and access tokens are used differently. ID tokens carry information about the user and are used to log in and access a system using OIDC. Access tokens are dynamic and utilized to gain access to resources based on granted scopes within the access token.

- **Payload**: The information is sent along with the API call to the receiving server with additional information regarding the required actions.

Let's get an understanding of what we can do with APIs and Okta.

Managing Okta with APIs

The use of APIs has been increasing and has become a large part of any organization's footprint. Within all departments, APIs are used to share, transfer, move, read, change, delete, and adjust data from one system to another.

We might have to start by looking at what an API is and why Okta's functionality in this area is needed. Back in the early days, a web program was hosted on a web server and the browser only displayed its content through HTML sent from the server. These days, you might have apps on your smartphone or single-page apps, both that run code on your device or the client. These apps connect with a backend service, usually exposed through an API. Simply put, you can say that services and applications that handle smaller tasks and connect and interact with each other through APIs are called microservices. As this newer model of applications becomes more and more common, finding a way of managing these APIs becomes more critical. The opportunity for applications to utilize outside information from other applications is beneficial to the application builder because they don't have to gather, store, and manage that information themselves. Using API integrations allows applications to receive or pull in data that is required for their service, but have the user be in charge of what is and isn't allowed. As mentioned in previous chapters, Okta was built with an API-first strategy. This means most admin-related interface actions can also be configured using Okta's ever-growing API catalog.

Having access to Okta's APIs allows other systems to manage Okta, read information within your Okta org, and change or update information.

> **Important note**
>
> You can find out more about Okta's API catalog here: `https://developer.okta.com/docs/reference/`.

Let's take a look at how we can use Okta's APIs.

Using Okta's APIs

Using Okta's APIs allows you to orchestrate a lot of possible manual work in Okta in a more managed and automated way. You can also simply do a specific call to Okta to make sure the action is done. Sometimes, a repetitive task can become quite tedious in the administrator interface, and using Okta's APIs can help resolve that.

Preparing to use Okta's APIs

Various code languages can be used to work with APIs in Okta, such as Python or PHP. If you're not familiar with any coding language, you can utilize the **Postman** software to see examples of how to send API calls to Okta since it's low code and available to anyone. Postman is a software development tool and is used to test API calls. How to work with it and install it is explained at www.postman.com.

> **Important note**
>
> Okta delivers all their available APIs in convenient Postman collections, which are quick and easy to import into Postman. You can find the collections here: https://developer.okta.com/docs/reference/postman-collections/.

You can go to the collections page on Okta's developer site and import all available collections to use.

As many different languages can be used to work with Okta's APIs, we can't go through everything here. The examples in this chapter have been completed using curl.

Next, we need to understand how we can use these APIs. Okta's API endpoint requires a token to authorize the action you want to complete.

Tokens

To authenticate requests to the Okta API, API tokens are used. Only administrators can issue tokens. These tokens are based on the privileges that the administrator has.

> **Tip**
>
> Use service accounts to generate tokens so that permission for tokens doesn't unexpectedly change.

The validity of a token is 30 days, and this time is renewed when it's used for an API request. If a token is not used in 30 days, it can't be used again. If the admin account that created the token is deactivated, the token is also revoked. If the account is reactivated, so is the token.

You can find your organization's API tokens by going to the **Security | API | Tokens** menu. There, you will find a list of all your tokens. You will see the name of the tokens and, in front of them, a color marker to indicate their status. By hovering over the colored dot, you can read information about the status. The possible statuses are as follows:

- **Green**: The token was used in the last three days
- **Gray**: The token has not been used for three days, but it's not within seven days of expiring
- **Red**: The token is within seven days of expiring
- **Yellow**: The token is suspicious

Normally, a suspicious token is not associated with a known agent. You can investigate it by clicking on it; this will show you provisioning for the associated agent. For instance, the AD agent that's used to integrate with an AD directory will have a token to manage Okta's Universal Directory and all the users and groups in it.

To create a new token, click the **Create Token** button. On the first page of the setup, you will only have to give your token a name. Remember that if you want to create more tokens for different tasks, name them properly so that you can see which is which. On the next page of the setup, you will receive the token value.

> **Important note**
> Copy the token value directly when the token is created. After that point, the value will be hashed and you will never be able to see it again.

Once you've copied the value, you can use it in the designated service you want to connect with Okta. Click **Ok, got it!**.

If you have many tokens, you can filter them by type in the menu to the left. To revoke a token, simply click the trashcan icon next to the token's name.

Now that we have created a token, let's look at how to use it and send a call to Okta's APIs.

Example of tasks with Okta's APIs

To be able to work with Okta's APIs, a basic understanding of the usage of these APIs is good to have. Let's do that by illustrating some examples.

A company admin needs to quickly add some groups and wants to use Okta's APIs to do so. By using the API, the admin can create them without ever touching the browser interface.

The admin can state the name and description, which will be reflected in the Okta console groups overview. After sending this API request, Okta will respond with an answer. If everything is correct, the group will be created.

The call the admin executes will be similar to this:

```
curl -v -X POST \-H "Accept: application/json" \-H "Content-Type:
application/json" \-H "Authorization: SSWS ${api_token}" \-d '{
  "profile": {
    "name": "West Coast Users",
    "description": "All Users West of The Rockies"
              }
    }'
 "https://${yourOktaDomain}/api/v1/groups"
```

While the first part is required to make sure the API call is accepted and correct using –H as the statement for the headers, the second part simply states the actual creation of the group with the accompanying details.

> **Important note**
>
> To understand the basic usage and get an overview of all the elements that are required to use Okta's APIs, go to https://developer.okta.com/docs/reference/api-overview/.

A response will be sent back and it will state what is done. The first half of the response will include the ID that is created for the group, together with additional standard information that Okta sends along. The response will also show the group's profile, including its name and description:

```
{  "id": "00g1emaKYZTWRYYRRTSK",  "created":
"2015-02-06T10:11:28.000Z",  "lastUpdated":
"2015-10-05T19:16:43.000Z",  "lastMembershipUpdated":
"2015-11-28T19:15:32.000Z",  "objectClass": [   "okta:user_
group" ],  "type": "OKTA_GROUP",  "profile": {   "name": "West Coast
Users",   "description": "All Users West of The Rockies"  },
```

In the second half of the response, Okta sends several relevant links that can be used for additional calls or actions that the admin might want to make on the freshly created group after creation:

```
"_links": {    "logo": [     {         "name":
"medium",        "href": "https://${yourOktaDomain}/img/
logos/groups/okta-medium.png",       "type": "image/
png"      },     {        "name": "large",       "href":
"https://${yourOktaDomain}/img/logos/groups/okta-large.
png",      "type": "image/png"    }   ],    "users":
{     "href": "https://${yourOktaDomain}/api/v1/
groups/00g1emaKYZTWRYYRRTSK/users"    },    "apps": {      "href":
"https://${yourOktaDomain}/api/v1/groups/00g1emaKYZTWRYYRRTSK/
apps"    } }}
```

The responses from Okta can be different, depending on the request or API, but it gives information back that can be relevant for the next API calls or delivers an understanding of what the current situation is.

So, let's continue and create a new user with the basic details and add them to the previously created group. The API call for that would look like this:

```
curl -v -X POST \-H "Accept: application/json" \-H "Content-
Type: application/json" \-H "Authorization: SSWS ${api_token}"
\-d '{ "profile": {    "firstName": "Isaac",    "lastName":
"Brock",    "email": "isaac.brock@example.com",    "login": "isaac.
brock@example.com" }, "groupIds": [    "00g1emaKYZTWRYYRRTSK" ]}'
https://${yourOktaDomain}/api/v1/users?activate=true
```

What we did here is start again with the same required elements, including accompanying headers. Then, we created a user with a profile, adding their minimum required profile values. Secondly, we assigned the user to the previously created group. Lastly, we activated the user using the activation URL.

The response we get shows information about the user being created:

```
{   "id": "00ub0oNGTSWTBKOLGLNR",   "status":
"STAGED",   "created": "2013-07-02T21:36:25.344Z",   "activated":
null,   "statusChanged": null,   "lastLogin": null,   "lastUpdated":
"2013-07-02T21:36:25.344Z",   "passwordChanged": null,   "profile":
{    "firstName": "Isaac",    "lastName": "Brock",    "email":
"isaac.brock@example.com",    "login": "isaac.brock@example.
com",    "mobilePhone": "555-415-1337" },   "credentials":
{    "provider": {    "type": "OKTA",    "name": "OKTA"    } },
```

The second half of the response lists links to use by the user. These are quite self-explanatory:

```
"_links": {
      "schema": {
          "href": "${yourOktaDomain}/api/v1/meta/schemas/user/
oscuxbnkcNLVXoum3356"
      },
      "activate": {
          "href": "${yourOktaDomain}/api/v1/
users/00u5tiakg9PsvboKz357/lifecycle/activate",
          "method": "POST"
      },
      "self": {
          "href": "${yourOktaDomain}/api/v1/
users/00u5tiakg9PsvboKz357"
      },
      "type": {
          "href": "${yourOktaDomain}/api/v1/meta/types/user/
otyuxbnkcNLVXoum3356"
      }
    }
}
```

By incorporating these APIs, you can make specific work processes less repetitive and more automated.

> **Important note**
> Okta has a well-documented repository on all their publicly available APIs on their developer site. Please visit `https://developer.okta.com/docs/reference/` for more examples.

Now, let's take a look at how we can use trusted origins within Okta.

Trusted origins

If you are thinking of creating an alternative interface to manage and handle Okta's APIs, you need to make sure you configure your trusted origins. If you want to implement Okta's login widget on a custom login page, **cross-origin resource sharing** (**CORS**) is required. Check out Okta's reference page about their custom sign-in widget: `https://developer.okta.com/code/javascript/okta_sign-in_widget/`.

CORS allows AJAX calls to be made from different domains than where the scripts are loaded. Web browsers don't allow these actions according to the *same-origin security policies* (`https://developer.mozilla.org/en-US/docs/Web/Security/Same-origin_policy`). These same-origin security policies make sure services and sites don't get access to or use cookies that another website might have stored, thereby stopping any malicious activity. But there are legitimate reasons for this – these rules apply to the combination of protocol, domain, and port used. So, you might have a website at `https://myshop.com` and use `https://api.myshop.com` as a way to interact with your APIs. These two would not be able to communicate based on the same-origin security policies.

This is unless CORS definitions have been set up and allow the browser and the server to interact with each other through a cross-origin request. By using CORS, you can allow your web page with a self-hosted Okta sign-in widget to interact with Okta.

Let's see how we can set CORS up.

When doing cross-origin web requests and redirects, they all need to be whitelisted. You can do this by adding a trusted origin, which is a combination of the URI scheme, hostname, and port number of a page. Click the **Trusted Origins** tab under **Security** | **API** | **Trusted Origins**:

Figure 8.1 – The Trusted Origins menu

Next, you need to click **Add Origin**:

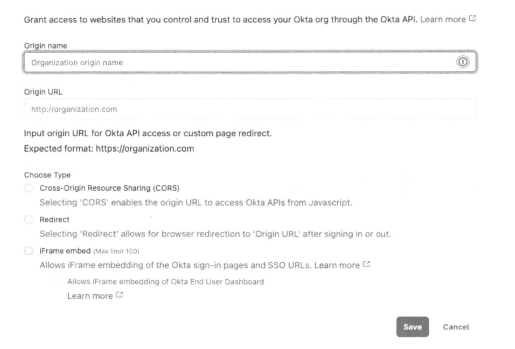

Figure 8.2 – Settings for a trusted origin

Provide the following information to create a trusted origin:

1.   Give the trusted origin a name.

2.   Enter the URL for Okta API access or custom page redirect.

3.   Select whether you wish to give access to **CORS**, **Redirect**, or **iFrame embed**.

What's the difference between CORS and redirects? Let's have a look:

*   **CORS**: XMLHttpRequest is sent from JavaScript on your website to the Okta API using an Okta session cookie.

*   **Redirect**: After signing in or out, the redirect allows your browser to redirect you to this trusted website.

*   **IFrame embed**: **Trusted Origins** in iFrame embeddings permits specific trusted origins to embed Okta sign-in pages and resources, enhancing security compared to the previous customizations-based iFrame embedding, which allowed any resource to be embedded on any site. **Trusted Origins** restricts embedding to trusted sources only.

After clicking **Save**, you'll be done!

For more information on using your CORS setup in your environments, we recommend going to https://developer.mozilla.org/en-US/docs/Web/HTTP/CORS and checking out how to implement it.

Rate limits

There are rate limits on how many API calls can be done within a certain amount of time. This is to protect Okta's service for all customers and is usual for **Software-as-a-Service** (**SaaS**) providers. Rates are divided into three sections:

*   Default rate limits

*   Concurrent rate limits

*   End user rate limits

> **Note**
>
> All the different calls and their rate limits can be found here:
>
> https://developer.okta.com/docs/reference/rate-limits/.

With that, we took a quick dive into Okta's APIs; there is a lot to say about them, and we can't include all the details in this book. We highly recommend going to https://developer.okta.com and creating a developer account. Follow all the tutorials and best practices they provide there to get up to speed on how to use Okta in the best way with Okta's APIs. Now, let's take a look at Okta's other API product, API Access Management.

Fundamentals of API Access Management

Using APIs is beneficial because they are automatable and can be programmed to do what is needed. In many cases, APIs are used by users to help their work be more automated and remove repetitive tasks. By connecting the APIs from different applications, users can see their data in different places, interact with it, and manipulate it where they want and how they like.

On the other side, developers and IT might invest in creating custom services and/or applications to make their lives, or that of their colleagues, better. Creating these applications usually entails adding APIs to open up data streams to collect and bring it all together.

Lastly, if your organization's business model is to build services or web products, chances are they'll be using APIs to connect to other applications, partners, systems, and so on.

All of these APIs require different needs, approaches, and management.

According to Okta (`https://www.okta.com/resources/whitepaper/api-security-from-concepts-to-components/`), you can divide API security into five levels of API management. We'll discuss these levels next.

Level 1 – no security

It's essential to understand what an API is and why Okta's functionality in this domain is crucial. Often, services start by serving data, but neglecting security is a risky approach. An internal project collecting data for the sales team may eventually evolve into a tool that's shared with partners and the public. Relying on the privacy of APIs initially is a common but misguided practice. When applications become public-facing, private APIs can still be vulnerable. Okta terms this approach the *no security method*. Concealing APIs within applications might seem secure, but once exposed to the public, they can become targets for exploitation.

Level 2 – using API keys

API keys are increasingly used for access control, allowing developers to work based on their access rights. Developers create API keys with specific permissions, ensuring their work aligns with the necessary security measures, which is a step up from having no security at all (Level 1). However, this approach has its limitations.

The challenge lies in the potential over-granting of permissions when the same key is used for public-facing access. While the key itself may seem secure, using it across multiple services can create numerous entry points with varying levels of access.

Reusing keys across applications complicates key rotation and renewal processes, making changes difficult to implement. If these keys fall into the wrong hands, due to factors such as team members leaving or inadvertent public sharing, it can become a significant security concern. While implementing a policy to use keys for single use cases is advisable, ensuring strict adherence can be challenging, leaving the organization uncertain about maintaining the highest security standards.

Level 3 – OAuth 2.0

OAuth 2.0 tokens empower users to define precise access and usage rights when developing APIs. These tokens allow you to set the specific level of access that token users are permitted to have. Notably, each token comes with an expiration time or date. For instance, a simple read request in a logging system might only require read rights with an extended expiration period, while a service capable of modifying CRM data may demand more extensive write permissions and a shorter token lifespan to prevent overuse.

The advantages of using scopes are twofold. First, tokens only possess the rights they've been configured with, avoiding the risk of excessive permissions associated with an administrator's account. Second, tokens have an expiration, imposing a time limit on potential attackers trying to access the system or data. Once expired, an attacker can't regain access without compromising user authentication as well.

Level 4 – API gateways

API access gateways are invaluable tools for seamlessly connecting diverse APIs within an organization. They empower IT architects to finely control access across different layers, while developers can effortlessly link microservices through the gateway, streamlining API management. Gateways excel in enforcing policies, facilitating logging, and supporting auditing, essentially acting as a centralized hub for APIs. This approach simplifies architectural complexity, making connections more organized and less convoluted.

Many API gateway vendors offer tools for creating and, in some cases, rotating API keys. A subset also provides OAuth 2.0 capabilities, utilizing user profiles for secure key management and access control. This ensures that developers can confidently use their keys, knowing they are handled securely and can be rotated when necessary. Users benefit from profile access scopes, granting them access to services as needed, and optimizing their interactions.

However, it's important to note that API gateways operate as external services with their user directories and management systems. They may lack a comprehensive view of a user's context and access within the organization.

> **Important note**
> Okta has some great information on using API gateways. Check out their digital book on the subject: `https://developer.okta.com/books/api-security/gateways/`.

Level 5 – API gateways and API Access Management

Okta plays a crucial role in enhancing security and access management, whether it's integrated with API gateways or used independently. With Okta, you can securely manage users, authenticate them, and authorize actions based on their context at any given moment.

When connected to the gateway, Okta adds granularity to user trust levels, allowing users to operate within defined policies and access rights. Notably, not every organization has an API gateway. In such cases, Okta's API Access Management comes to the rescue, enabling you to connect applications using OAuth 2.0 and OIDC, all while leveraging your Okta Universal Directory.

This service offers several benefits:

- Create Okta-hosted custom authorization servers to manage API endpoints for various client apps and roles
- Configure custom scopes and claims, aligning them with user profiles
- Utilize OAuth for token-based access instead of credentials
- Ensure API protection according to the latest security standards

In addition to API access management, Okta allows you to control access to APIs using rules, providing a comprehensive solution for managing user access and authorization.

> **Important note**
>
> There are many best practices for working with Okta API Access Management. To read about them all, go to `https://developer.okta.com/docs/concepts/api-access-management/`.

Now that we've understood the value of Okta's API Access Management, let's learn how to use it and set it up for an application.

API access administration

So, let's go into the Okta administrator panel to set up some of the features that we examined in the previous section. Navigate to **Security | API**. Here, we can see that we have three tabs we can work with:

- **Authentication Servers**
- **Tokens**
- **Trusted Origins**

This is what it looks like in the admin panel:

API

Authorization Servers   Tokens   Trusted Origins

Figure 8.3 – Available tabs for API management

Since we discussed **Tokens** and **Trusted Origins** earlier in this chapter, we will now only focus on **Authorization Servers**. If you don't have the API Access Management product enabled, you will only see this menu for the default org authorization server, as explained next.

Authorization server

Let's begin by understanding the purpose of an authorization server. An authorization server is essentially a tool that generates and validates OAuth 2.0 or OIDC tokens. It serves various roles, such as providing authentication for OIDC applications, granting access to specific API endpoints using scopes, and authorizing web services. In simpler terms, when using OIDC or OAuth 2.0, the authorization server verifies a user's identity and issues either an ID or access token. Each server has a unique issuer URI and signing key for tokens, ensuring secure boundaries.

There are two different kinds of servers available: org and custom authorization servers. The **Org Authorization** server comes by default with every Okta tenant. This authorization server is used to allow **single sign-on** (**SSO**) into Okta and get API access tokens for Okta's APIs. It's used to do SSO with Okta or to receive an access token to Okta's APIs. The server cannot be customized; it's only for Okta to consume or validate tokens. The access tokens from this server cannot be used by your applications.

For the **Org Authorization** server, clients can use the following endpoints for metadata-related information of your Okta tenant, programmatically:

```
OpenID: https://${yourOktaOrg}/.well-known/openid-configuration
OAuth: https://${yourOktaOrg}/.well-known/oauth-authorization-server
```

The **Custom Authorization** server is what you create and use to secure your APIs. You can create multiple servers, with different scopes, claims, and access policies. Okta provides one default **Custom Authorization** server, pre-configured, including a basic access policy and rule.

So, how do we set this up? In the **Authorization Servers** tab, click **Add Authorization Server**. You will then be asked to fill in the following information:

Add Authorization Server

Name

Audience

Description

Save   Cancel

Figure 8.4 – First configuration for a new authorization server

Fill in the following information:

- **Name**: Give your server a descriptive name
- **Audience**: This is the URI for the OAuth resource that consumes the token
- **Description**: Optionally, you can give the server a description

When you click **Save**, you will create the server and get more options for the setup:

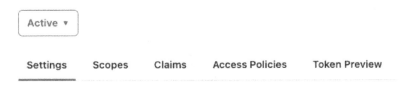

Okta Administration App

Active ▾

Settings   Scopes   Claims   Access Policies   Token Preview

Figure 8.5 – Available menus in a server

If you look closer at the **Settings** menu, you will see the configurations we just made while creating the server. You will also see that you can set whether **Signing Key Rotation** should be **Automatic** or **Manual**. This is set to **Automatic** by default; **Manual** should only be used if a client is unable to automatically poll the server to update the list of signing keys. We will look at key rotation in more detail at the end of this chapter.

Before moving over to the individual section of the **Authorization Server** menu, at the bottom of the **Settings** page, you will see a section named **Trusted Servers**. Here, you can add other authorization servers as trusted servers and accept tokens from these trusted servers for this authorization server. Adding a server is as simple as clicking on the **Add Server** button and selecting the server(s) you want to add:

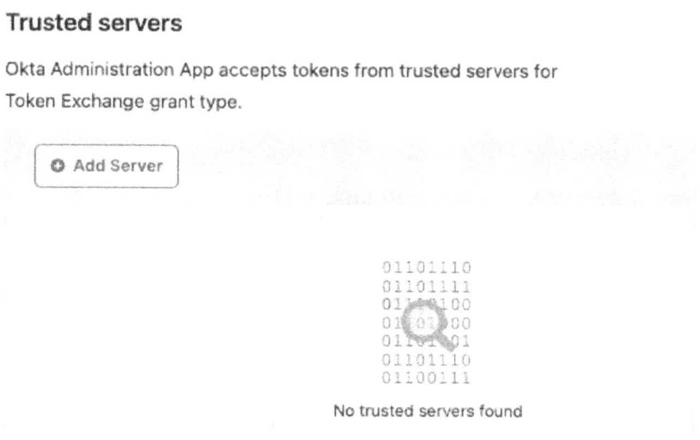

Trusted servers

Okta Administration App accepts tokens from trusted servers for
Token Exchange grant type.

⊕ Add Server

```
01101110
01101111
01101100
01101100
01101101
01101110
01100111
```

No trusted servers found

Figure 8.6 – Adding a trusted server to the authorization server

Now, let's look at the next tab on the page for your newly created server, named **Scopes**. This section already comes with a pre-populated list of reserved scopes that Okta adds by default. To create a new scope, click **Add Scope**:

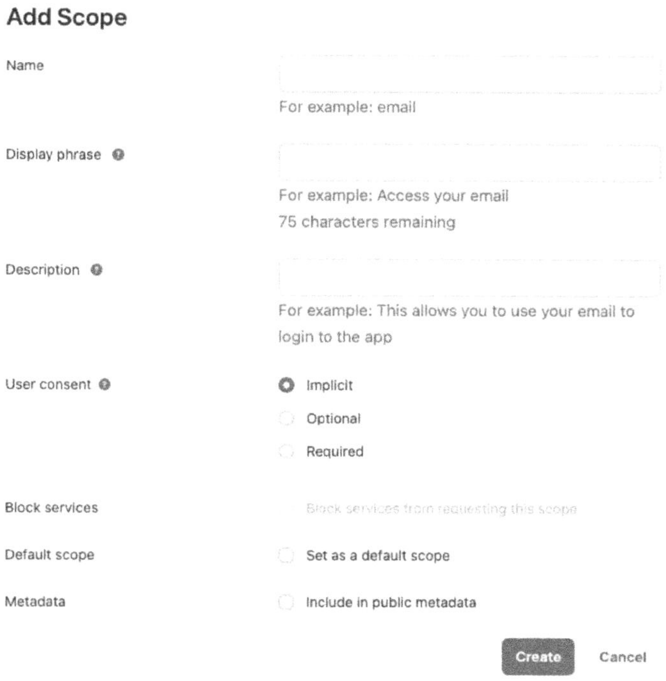

Add Scope

Name	
	For example: email
Display phrase ❼	
	For example: Access your email
	75 characters remaining
Description ❼	
	For example: This allows you to use your email to login to the app
User consent ❼	◉ Implicit
	○ Optional
	○ Required
Block services	Block services from requesting this scope
Default scope	○ Set as a default scope
Metadata	○ Include in public metadata

Create   Cancel

Figure 8.7 – Settings to add a scope

You must enter details in the following fields:

- **Name**: Give the scope a name – for instance, `email`.

- **Display phrase**: A descriptive phrase can be given to help the reader understand.

- **Description**: Describe what the scope will be used for.

- **User consent**: An option to determine if this scope requires any type of consent

- **Block services**: When **Optional** or **Required** is chosen in the previous setting, **Block services** will become available to be set as a secondary scope option.

- **Default scope**: Check this box if you want Okta to authorize requests to applications that don't have specified scopes. If so, for a request that passed the access policy, Okta returns all the default scope in the access tokens.

- **Metadata**: Check this box if you want the scope to be publicly discoverable.

Click **Create** to finish the scope configuration. On the main page, you will see a full list of all your scopes.

Next up is **Claims**. Claims are divided into two categories – **ID Token** and **Access Token**. To create a new claim, click **Add Claim**:

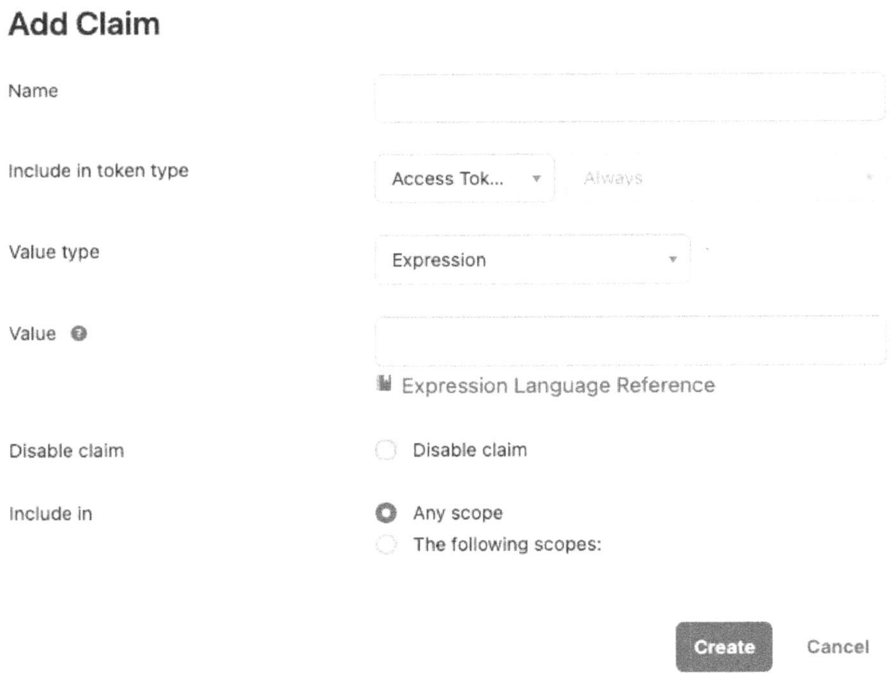

Add Claim

Name	
Include in token type	Access Tok... ▼ Always ▼
Value type	Expression ▼
Value ❓	
	📖 Expression Language Reference
Disable claim	◯ Disable claim
Include in	⦿ Any scope ◯ The following scopes:

Create   Cancel

Figure 8.8 – Setting up claims

Let's go through this setup:

- **Name**: Give this claim a descriptive name.

- **Include in token type**: Choose between **ID Token** and **Access Token**, depending on your use case. If you choose **ID Token**, you also get to choose when the authorization server is to provide a claim in the token; if you choose **Access Token**, the field will be set to **Always**:

Figure 8.9 – Token type menu when ID Token is chosen

- **Value type**: In this drop-down menu, you can select whether you will define the claim with a group filter or with Expression Language. If you select **Expression**, you get to enter your expression in the field value below. If you select **Groups**, you get to filter groups in the **Filter** field. For example, you can select just the sales team by selecting the sales team group, or be even more granular and use the Okta Expression Language to filter the correct users or groups for this claim:

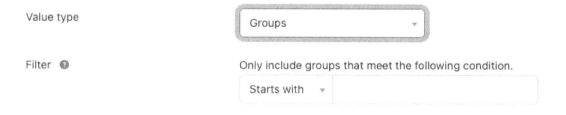

Figure 8.10 – If you select Groups instead of Expression, the field below it changes

Further down, we have two more options:

- **Disable claim**: If you want the claim to be disabled for a while – for instance, for testing or debugging

- **Include in**: Choose this option if you want the claim to be for every scope, or select the scopes you want it to be valid for

Click **Create** to finalize the setup of your new claim. If you have many claims set up, you can filter them by typing in the menu to the left. By using the pen and trashcan icon to the right of each claim, you can edit or delete your claim.

Next up, we have access policies. These let different services access your server and its scopes and claims. Move to the **Access Policy** tab and click **Add Policy**:

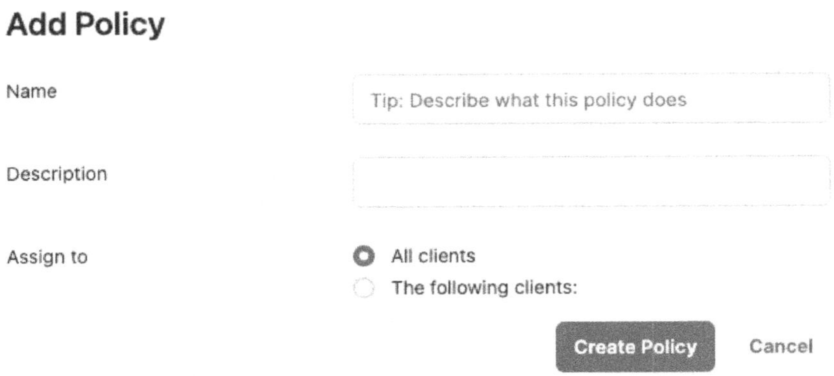

Add Policy

Name   Tip: Describe what this policy does

Description

Assign to   ● All clients
                        ○ The following clients:

                                        Create Policy   Cancel

Figure 8.11 – Setting up a new access policy

The setup is fairly straightforward:

- **Name**: Give the policy a descriptive name.

- **Description**: You can add a description, which is especially important if you have several that do similar things.

- **Assign to**: If you want your policy to apply to all clients, leave the option set to **All clients**. If you want to select clients, change this to **The following clients:** and enter the clients whom this policy is aimed at.

After that, click **Create Policy**; with that, you're finished! On the screen, you will see a list of all your access policies, similar to what it looks like for policies for passwords and other policies. In the list to the left, you can drag and drop your policies to prioritize them. For each policy, you can select whether you want to **Deactivate**, **Edit**, or **Delete** it. Also, as for other policies within Okta, you have to create at least one rule. Let's look at that now. Click **Add Rule**:

Add Rule

Rule Name

TIP: Describe what this rule does

IF Grant type is

Client acting on behalf of itself

- ✓ Client Credentials

Client acting on behalf of a user

- ✓ Authorization Code
- ✓ Implicit (hybrid)
- ✓ Resource Owner Password
- ✓ SAML 2.0 Assertion
- ✓ Device Authorization
- ✓ Token Exchange

AND User is

- ◉ Any user assigned the app
- ○ Assigned the app and a member of one of the following:

AND Scopes requested

- ◉ Any scopes
- ○ The following scopes:

THEN Use this inline hook

None (disabled) ▾

AND Access token lifetime is

1   Hours ▾

AND Refresh token lifetime is

Unlimited ▾

but will expire if not used every   7   Days ▾

Create rule   Cancel

Figure 8.12 – Configuring an access policy rule

Let's dive into it:

- **Rule Name**: Select a descriptive name

- Under the **IF** option, we have the following option:

  - **Grant type is**: You can choose whether the client is acting as itself or as a user. It's possible to select both, but if it's as a user, select any or all of the methods.

- Under the **AND** options, we have the following:

  - **User is**: You get this option if you select **Client acting on behalf of a user** in the **IF** statement. You will be able to select any of the users assigned to the app.

  - **Scopes requested**: Select the scopes that are granted if the user meets the conditions stated.

- Under the **THEN** options, we have the following:

  - **Use this inline hook**: If you have inline hooks set up, you will be able to call upon them here. If not, the only option is **None**.

  - **Access token lifetime is**: Here, you can decide what lifetime a token has before it's revoked.

- Under the **AND** option, we have the following option:

  - **Refresh token lifetime is**: The default is set to **Unlimited**, but you can select **Minutes**, **Hours**, or **Days** and set a number. You also get to select how long until it will expire if it's not used within its lifetime.

With that, you have created a rule. If you add multiple rules, you sort them, just as with the other policies. When a client request comes in, it starts from the top and when it matches one policy and/or rule, it doesn't move further down. Also, as with all policies, you can select whether the rule should be active or not, edit it, and delete it.

Lastly, we have the **Token Preview** menu in the **Custom Authorization server** section:

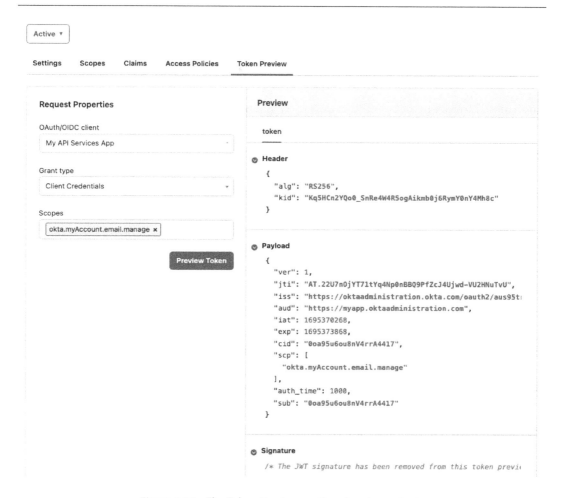

Figure 8.13 – The Token Preview section showing output

Testing your authorization server configuration is a crucial step to ensure that your OAuth 2.0 or OIDC setup functions correctly. In Okta, we've simplified this process by introducing the **Token Preview** tab, which allows you to experiment with various settings and observe the generated tokens.

The **Token Preview** tab on the **Authorization Server** page allows you to select configuration settings and examine the resulting tokens, including the following:

- **Access token**
- **ID token**
- **Refresh token**
- **Device secret**

The benefit of the **Token Preview** tab is that it provides a practical way to experiment with different configuration settings for your authorization server and observe the resulting tokens. It will allow you to streamline the process of configuring and testing your authorization server, and help you achieve a more secure and efficient OAuth 2.0 or OIDC implementation for your applications or integrations.

With that, we have set up our authorization server, allowing an outside application or service to delegate authentication to Okta, and letting Okta manage the claims and scopes for that app. Let's look at key rotation.

Key rotation

Key rotation is used to replace an existing signing key with a new cryptographic key. It is considered best practice in the industry to rotate these keys periodically. Okta automatically rotates keys four times a year.

> **Important note**
> This standard rotation can be changed by Okta without notice.

Authorization servers can be set to manually rotate keys instead of automatically. Since rotating keys is considered best practice, it is wise to investigate whether the change to manual is truly needed. Manual rotation requires admins to go into the admin console and click on **Rotate Signing Keys**. If you go to your authorization server, in the **Settings** tab at the top, you will find the button to do so. This button will only appear if you first set the authorization server to manual rotation:

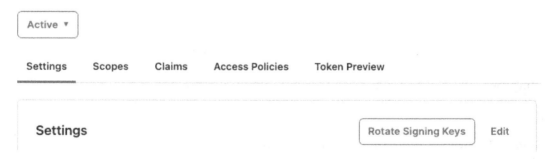

Figure 8.14 – The manual Rotate Signing Keys button

At the bottom of the **Settings** tab, you will see the **Previous**, **Current**, and **Next** keys:

Valid Keys

Next   ZosOuxh7PNhyA4v1QmHDDVoC02qwfVbLBRjCAEEIr60

Current   iNRMyQjPR3-Z4HUKzi1C_iqugTYOoC732AYlyo_akYA

Previous   Kq5HCn2YQoO_SnRe4W4R5ogAikmb0j6RymY0nY4Mh8c

Figure 8.15 – Rotated signing keys

These actions can also be done using Okta's APIs. This allows the developer to rotate if necessary, simply using code, instead of having the IT team and/or security do this for them and passing the new key along.

> **Tip**
>
> More information on how to use Okta's APIs to get and rotate signing keys can be found here: `https://developer.okta.com/docs/reference/api/authorization-servers/#get-authorization-server-keys`.

Summary

This chapter probably got your head spinning with abbreviations and links. But what we have tried to do is give a brief but full overview of what you can do with Okta's APIs. Understanding how to use them and what possibilities you have was key. You learned how to do some administrator tasks, such as adding a user, without using the administrator console, which can make some tasks less repetitive. We also provided extra reference links to outside sources to get into more detail where needed. On the other side, we went through Okta's API Access Management product to get a clear view of how to use Okta as your API access system and how to set it up. You learned about the important things to think about if you have APIs that need protecting, thus giving your organization a chance to increase its security using Okta. In the next chapter, we will investigate and uncover the possibilities of using Okta's Advanced Server Access product and how you can benefit from it.

9
Managing Access with Advanced Server Access

Okta's **Advanced Server Access** (**ASA**) is a product Okta added to its core functionality that added privileged access features. With ASA, you can extend Okta to your server fleet. With Universal Directory, you get a single source of truth for your server accounts. With Lifecycle Management, you can automate the provisioning of these accounts. With **single sign-on** (**SSO**), you can create a simple and reliable authentication for your workflows. Lastly, you can fully utilize the contextual **multifactor authentication** (**MFA**) controls for your server accounts. In this chapter, we will go through why a product such as ASA is needed, as well as what you need to do to set up and manage ASA.

To understand this fully, in this chapter, we'll look at the following topics:

- ASA – a high-level overview
- Setting up ASA
- Managing your ASA environment
- Automation

ASA – a high-level overview

Throughout this book, we have only spoken about managing applications. With ASA, Okta expands its touch surface by securing access to the server infrastructure. By doing so, the road to zero trust becomes a reality for more parts of your business than just users, applications, and devices. Also, as cloud adoption becomes an increasingly important DevOps job, making sure automation is the driver to it all is where Okta fits in.

Managing servers in your organization as part of your infrastructure, or as part of your business model, means that your developers and/or administrators need to have access. This access is normally given using privileged accounts, either using the **command-line interface** (CLI) with **Secure Shell** (**SSH**) or with privileged accounts accessing the server with **Remote Desktop Protocol** (**RDP**). These accounts are granted access based on the role of the accessing user, but over-privileged access can quickly become a problem. Commonly, you will see that besides possible individual user privileges, access to more critical tasks is done using shared admin credentials. These, of course, have more access rights, but also allow a lot more access to the entire infrastructure. Security can be at risk at that point. Implementing a zero-trust strategy will help you and your team shift from network-related security to the application side.

Security nowadays is mainly managed by the user, not the **Infrastructure-as-a-Service** (**IaaS**) vendor. As these services become more and more difficult, you have to make sure that you meet all the compliance regulations for your services. Making a mistake can lead to immense problems. On the other hand, having your DevOps engineers manage dozens, perhaps even hundreds or thousands, of servers and microservices requires a lot of access. All these admin and user credentials require some sort of oversight, and when your fleet of systems grows, so will your user credential stack. Managing this can become a giant on its own in terms of work and time. As we mentioned previously, adding more and more privileges to accounts is more common than not. Developers might be given the same access to a range of servers, while they might require different rights in each of them. Auditing all of this becomes a large problem. Using cloud services allows for the fast adoption and expansion of different systems for different needs. Access management becomes increasingly harder to manage with this expansion, especially when automation comes into play. What if the admin leaves – how are you certain that they have no access to systems anymore? Lastly, while we always want to make end users happy, developers are even more important. They *will* find ways to make life easier, and that usually entails bypassing security if needed. So, we have to make sure both security and productivity go up; otherwise, it's doomed to fail.

So, what's behind this ASA? Let's take a look at some practical elements.

Users who log in using their local SSH tools will find that they need to store a **Rivest-Shamir-Adleman** (**RSA**) **public-key cryptosystem** key for authentication. This key can be used for different privileged roles for that user. The main concerns are that these RSA keys are static and hosted locally. This can comprise a range of security issues:

- It has no awareness of the user
- It doesn't consider the context
- It trusts the entity it's on, regardless of what is done with it
- There's no possibility to provision or deprovision users while scaling the fleet

ASA can help on these fronts as it is an identity-first management system for servers. It works across cloud and on-premises environments. The unique outstanding element in this strategy is the use of an *ephemeral credential mechanism*. These dynamic credentials are created on demand for the user, based on context and with the required task access. It allows you to make sure that your users can only access that server when and how they need to with just the right set of privileges to fulfill the job. This makes sure we can enhance our setup by doing the following:

- **Increase access security** by not giving out the keys to the castle
- **Set rules for access and tokens** so that we don't have to have credentials valid for a long time
- **Better scalability** and possibly automation
- **Dynamic access from Okta** rather than statics keys being stored on local machines
- **Complete syslogs** on who accesses what, when, and where – and with that, increasing auditing capabilities

These ephemeral credentials are tightly created and expire in minutes, leaving no room to share, phish, or otherwise lose them altogether. By using Okta's Identity Cloud, they are utilized and backed by all the context Okta delivers to make sure policies are enforced. Adding more MFA can increase security while still keeping access simple.

While this is quite revolutionary, other vendors might have similar features in place. What makes Okta so unique is its ability to combine all contexts and truly set the identity of the user in the center of it all. This will allow a zero-trust approach to become reality and make life more secure, more productive, and easier to manage.

How ASA works

ASA operates as a bidirectional system, requiring two-way access. On one hand, your system device must be able to reach the servers, while on the other hand, the servers should be readily available to the designated users.

Every server that needs to be accessed needs to enroll in ASA. This is done using an enrollment token to securely add the server to ASA. On each server after enrollment, a lightweight agent called `sftd` runs and manages the local user and group accounts and any given entitlements and captures all login events for ASA's system logs. It also makes sure it regularly communicates with Okta to make sure any updates are instantly mirrored in the servers since it works locally with regular files such as `/etc/sudoers` and `/etc/passwd`.

On the user side, a small client is installed to allow communication between the user and Okta. The client agent also comes with CLI commands to help ease its usage. It integrates with local SSH tools.

The user logs in using the CLI and gets redirected to Okta for authentication. Policies and MFA will apply, all the while looking at the context of the user and possible enrolled device context.

Once authentication has been granted, the CLI can show which servers the user has access to. By using $ sft list-servers, the accessible servers are listed. Accessing these servers requires no extra or new commands. By simply using the $ SSH {server name} command, the client application will create a short-lived **Certificate Authority (CA)** token with the right scopes and grant access immediately. If the user wouldn't have logged in first with Okta, the command would have kickstarted an authentication process through the primary browser after the SSH command.

This authentication is bound to the machine and user, creating a secure and strong session that limits access from other systems and devices. Based on the role and group, the user has access to the machines that are part of the project the user is assigned to.

A project is a collection of different resources with their own configuration. They are set up with additional access controls and policies. At least one project is needed in ASA.

This authentication will not use RSA keys, so there isn't any SSH folder and there are no authorized key files present on the machine. Authentication is limited to the access and scope of the ephemeral certificate that's minted during authentication by the client. This allows you to have auditable trails that can be traced back to the user because of the group assignments, permissions, and **Superuser Do (SUDO)** entitlements that are set and managed by Okta.

Collections of servers are managed in ASA by projects. Projects contain the groups to which users are assigned, the tasks users are allowed to perform, and details and events of the past. Users and groups are managed by Okta; make sure the correct users are assigned to the correct projects, for instance, using rules. These assigned groups and users are locally provisioned to the projects' servers. Granting extra admin rights in the project will add SUDO privileges to the provisioned users on the Linux servers.

Sometimes, users might need to perform specific actions on servers, but you do not want to give them full admin access. By assigning entitlements to groups, users are allowed to run commands, without having the full rights to the server.

Let's say your support team needs to be able to restart Apache on servers. Before, they were granted access with SUDO entitlements because the management of the team was too cumbersome and affected by changes. Now, using ASA, the users, individually and as a group, can have specific entitlements.

The support group that's assigned to the project with the accessible servers allows them to do the following:

- Access the server they need access to
- Be provisioned to the servers with those entitlements
- Have enough rights to run the commands

With this, we can enforce least privileged access for users, making sure the zero-trust approach is upheld.

So, now that we know what ASA is and why it's needed, let's have a look at how to set it up.

Setting up ASA

Setting up ASA is not particularly difficult, but it does require an understanding of the infrastructure it will eventually integrate with.

A few different steps must be followed to start using ASA:

1. Configure ASA in Okta.
2. Enroll server(s) with the enrollment token and install the agent(s).
3. Connect your team's server ASA.
4. Configure your servers.

Let's go through them in order, starting with configuring ASA.

Configuring ASA

ASA is its own product, and to be able to use it in your organization, you need to purchase it separately.

To start using ASA, you need to configure the product in your Okta tenant. The product is available as an application, so you must start as you would when adding any application:

1. Go to **Applications | Applications**.
2. Click the **Browse App Catalog** button.
3. Search for Okta Advanced Server Access, click on it, and then click **Add**.

In the following general setup area, you get to fill in an application label and application visibility:

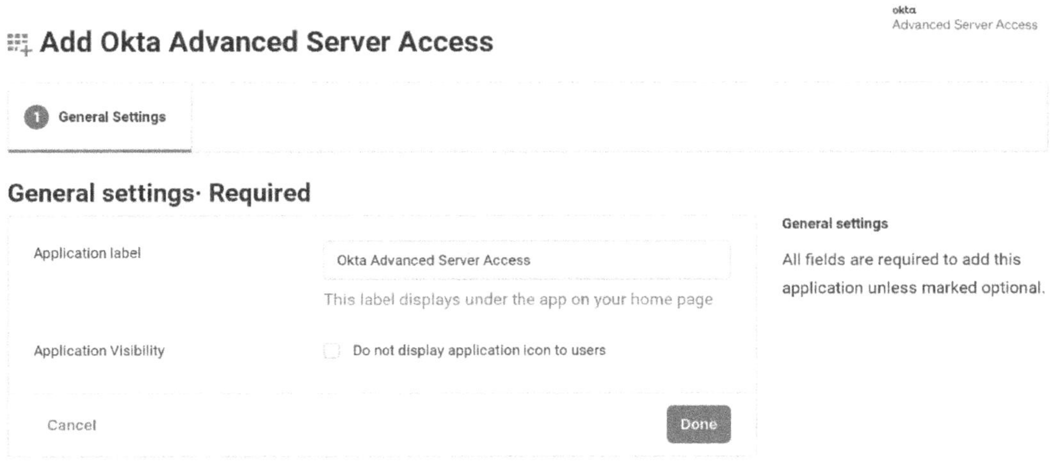

Figure 9.1 – General settings of the Okta ASA application

By clicking **Done**, you will finalize the installation. Now, it's time for the settings.

> **Important note**
> You have to start by assigning the application to yourself and any additional administrators.

To assign the application, do the following:

1. Go to the **Assignment** tab, click **Assign**, and select **Assign to people**.

2. Search for your name, then click **Assign**.

3. Then, you get to choose whether you want the username to remain as your Okta username or if you want to change it to something else.

4. Click **Save and go back**, then **Done**.

Now, it's time to navigate to the ASA home page at `https://app.scaleft.com/`. Open this link in a new tab; you will need both this and your Okta tenant. To set up ASA on the website, do the following:

1. Select **Create a new team**.

2. Select a team name. This could be your company name. If you are just testing ASA, add `PoC` or `trial` to your name, to make sure you don't misuse a team name.

   After this, you will see a section containing the information you will need in Okta. Go back to your Okta tenant tab and select **Sign on** for your ASA application. Click **Edit** and scroll down to **ADVANCED SIGN-ON SETTINGS**:

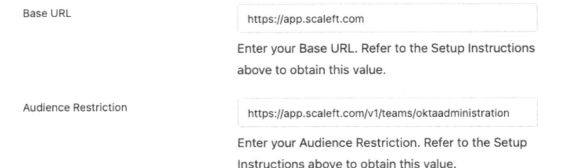

Advanced Sign-on Settings

These fields may be required for a Okta Advanced Server Access proprietary sign-on option or general setting.

Base URL

https://app.scaleft.com

Enter your Base URL. Refer to the Setup Instructions above to obtain this value.

Audience Restriction

https://app.scaleft.com/v1/teams/oktaadministration

Enter your Audience Restriction. Refer to the Setup Instructions above to obtain this value.

Figure 9.2 – Information needed from the ASA website

3. Copy and paste the **Base URL** and **Audience Restriction** values from the ASA website, then click **Save**.

Scrolling up to the SAML2.0 settings, click the blue **Copy** button for **Identity Provider metadata**:

Metadata details

Metadata URL   https://login.oktaadministration.com/app/exk8jb8qw2
                                405VZiH417/sso/saml/metadata

     📋 Copy

Figure 9.3 – Link for metadata

This will copy the metadata URL so that it can be used on the ASA website:

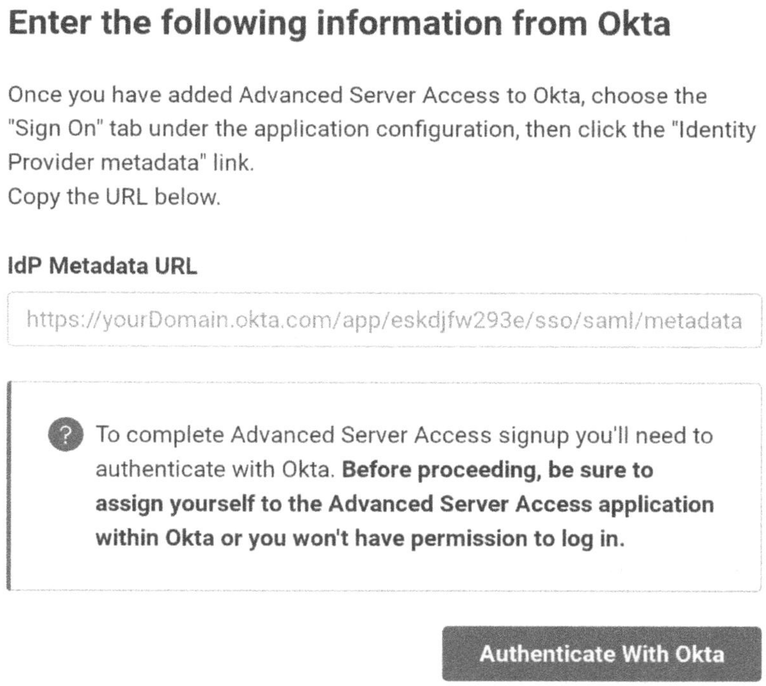

Enter the following information from Okta

Once you have added Advanced Server Access to Okta, choose the "Sign On" tab under the application configuration, then click the "Identity Provider metadata" link.
Copy the URL below.

IdP Metadata URL

https://yourDomain.okta.com/app/eskdjfw293e/sso/saml/metadata

> (?) To complete Advanced Server Access signup you'll need to authenticate with Okta. **Before proceeding, be sure to assign yourself to the Advanced Server Access application within Okta or you won't have permission to log in.**

Authenticate With Okta

Figure 9.4 – Setup on the ASA website

4. Paste the URL in the **IdP Metadata URL** field.
5. To verify the connection, click **Authenticate With Okta**.

When your verification is done, you will have completed the installation! Now, we will look at how you enroll a server.

Enrolling a server

For ASA to interact with a server, an agent must be installed on the server, and the server must be enrolled in a project on the ASA portal. The agent is working on the project to manage the server. With just default settings, the agent manages user accounts on the server, and client certificate authentication for SSH or RDP is enabled.

To enroll servers, you must use an **enrollment token**. So, what is an enrollment token? It's a Base64-encoded object containing metadata that the agent uses to configure itself. To create an enrollment token, we need a project, so let's start with that. In the dashboard on the ASA portal, click **Projects | Create Project**, where you have to enter the following information:

- **Project Name**: Give your project a name, preferably something so that you understand what server it's referring to.
- **Gateway Selector**: This allows you to add any gateways required for the project.
- **User management**: If you require preauthorization for users, check this box. With this, ASA will issue credentials to users who have been authorized previously. This is optional and requires a specific window of time for a user to be granted access to servers within the project.
- **On Demand User Time to Live (TTL)**: Here, you get to choose whether you want to create users on the server when the server is enrolled, or on-demand when the user tries to access the server. For the first use case, leave this option as **Disabled**; in the second case, select the time stating how long the account will live before it's removed from the server.

> **Important note**
> If you want to use the on-demand account creation process, the agent must be accessible on port 4421 of the network hop.

- **Traffic Forwarding**: This allows you to forward all traffic in the project through the selected gateways. Additionally, you can select **Record forwarded SSH sessions** and **Record forwarded RDP sessions**.
- **SSH Certificate Signature Algorithm**: This allows you to select a public SSH certificate algorithm key. This option defaults to the *ssh-ed25519 algorithm*, but admins can configure the project to use ssh-rsa to support legacy servers.

Once you have created your project, you will be brought to a new window showing your configuration. From here, you can manage the following within the project:

- **Details**
- **Groups**
- **Users**
- **Servers**
- **Enrollment**
- **Preauthorizations**

Figure 9.5 shows these options:

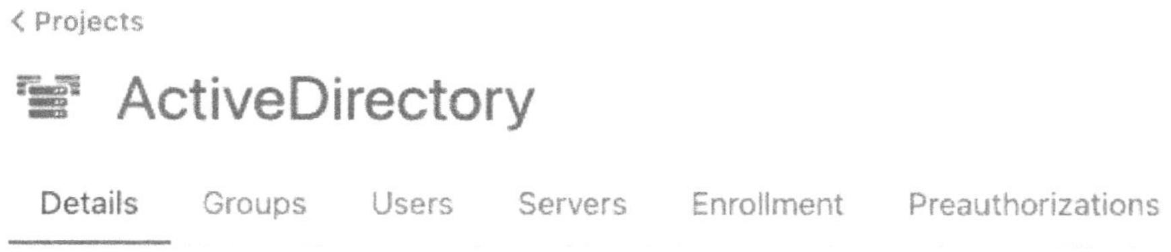

< Projects

ActiveDirectory

Details   Groups   Users   Servers   Enrollment   Preauthorizations

Figure 9.5 – Project sections

Now that you have your project, you can create an enrollment token. In the project you just created, go to the **Enrollment** tab. Scroll down and click **Create Enrollment Token**.

Give it a description based on what it will be used for. For instance, for a trial, you can name it `ASA trial token`.

You will get a notification that your token was successfully created. Copy the token. If you have a configuration management system, you can use it to store the token; otherwise, write it to a file on the server. Depending on the server type, your token can have different paths:

- For Linux: `/var/lib/sftd/enrollment.token`
- For Windows: `C:\windows\system32\config\systemprofile\AppData\Local\scaleft\enrollment.token`

Now, it's time to install the agent on your server. The installation process is the same for any server type, but the naming and code differ. The steps are as follows:

1. Find the required repository to install the server agent from.
2. Add the signing keys to your keychain or configure trust for the signing key.
3. Install the server tool package, including the agent.

These steps are initiated by code and are unique per server type. For all the code snippets that you will need, go to https://help.okta.com/asa/en-us/content/topics/adv_server_access/docs/install-agent.

For a Windows server, the process is even easier:

1. Start by downloading the ASA server tools. These can also be found at the preceding link.

2. Double-click the download to install the **Microsoft Installer** (**MSI**), a Windows installer package file type.

That's it! Now, you can check whether the servers have been enrolled. On the ASA website, go to your project and click on the **Servers** tab. Your server will appear under the tab if it was enrolled successfully. Now, let's move on and look at the ASA client.

ASA client

To do calls using code, you can use the ASA client. By enrolling a client in your team, the client can perform actions on your behalf. The client can be installed on platforms that Okta supports. See this link for an up-to-date list of platforms: https://help.okta.com/asa/en-us/content/topics/adv_server_access/docs/sft.

Once you have clicked through the installation, it's time to enroll the client in a team. In the client, run the following command in the client terminal:

```
sft enroll
```

This command opens a web page where you get to select what team to connect the client to. Once you've selected the one you want to use for this client, click **Approve**. The command window in the client will let you know if the enrollment was a success. If the enrollment was successful, you will see the client on the ASA website. In the menu to the left, click **Clients**; you will see your client there.

So, what can we do with the client? There is a lot, and we won't go into everything here. Use commands to get help, see versions, use a specific account or team, and so on. Commands are in the following form:

```
sft [global options] command [command options] [arguments...]
```

These are the global options you can use in any command:

- Display help: -h, --help
- Display version: -v, --version
- Provide an alternative config file path: --config-file
- Use a specified account: --account
- Use a specified team: --team
- Use a specified instance of the ASA platform: --instance

An example of a command option is to use `sft config` to configure your client. The client comes with a default configuration set to supply the best security measure you might need. If you still want to do your own settings, there is a full array of commands for this. You can find commands for the client at `https://help.okta.com/asa/en-us/content/topics/adv_server_access/docs/setup/configure-scim`.

Setting up gateways

In the realm of Okta's ASA, the use of gateways plays a crucial role in enhancing both availability and security. These gateways can function as standalone replacements for SSH bastion servers or work alongside them. They also facilitate SSH session capture, providing administrators with valuable information on access activities.

These gateways offer high availability through various mechanisms, ensuring uninterrupted access to servers without the risk of a single point of failure. They also surpass traditional SSH bastions in terms of security due to their **zero-trust design**, **logical access management**, and **native identity provider (IdP) integration**.

With zero trust, access credentials are never directly given to clients, minimizing the risk of compromised devices granting attackers direct server access. The use of gateways allows for easier monitoring of access attempts, enhancing overall security.

Logical access management is streamlined through labels, simplifying access control and reducing complexity when managing different security requirements for various servers and bastions. Gateways can be labeled based on specific criteria, ensuring the right gateway is used for accessing servers that meet defined requirements.

Moreover, gateways integrate deeply with Okta's ASA, ensuring user authentication through Okta's IdP. These combat vulnerabilities present in SSH bastions as gateways guarantee that access to servers is protected by Okta authentication.

Now, let's learn how to install and configure gateways and use session capturing.

Installation

There are a few requirements for installing an ASA gateway on your servers:

- It needs to be able to download packages from scaleft.com
- It needs to be able to listen to incoming connections from clients
- It needs to be an SSH target host
- It needs to have enough storage to store the session logs
- It needs to be running a **Network Time Protocol** (**NTP**) and be correctly syncing to external NTP pool servers

The installation depends on what OS you want to install the gateway on. You can find specific instructions per OS here: `https://help.okta.com/asa/en-us/content/topics/adv_server_access/docs/install-gateway.htm`.

Typically, first, you need to add the repository key and then update or create a file or list of artifacts.

Once you've been through the instructions for your specific OS, you need to generate a gateway setup token. This token includes metadata to enroll in the gateway. Start by accessing the ASA admin portal:

1. Navigate to **Gateways**.
2. Click **View All Setup Tokens**.
3. After that, click **Create Setup Token**.
4. Then, enter **Description** information for the token.
5. Using **Labels**, specify server access control for a project. Enter a key-value pair and submit it by clicking *Tab* or *Enter*. You can add as many as you would like.
6. When you are done, click **Submit**.

The next step is to configure the gateway.

Configuration

There are two ways to configure the gateway – either via the command line or the configuration file. Let's investigate these two options a bit more.

By using `service`, you can run the gateway `sft-gatewayd` service, while with `support` you can collect local system information to hand over to Okta support if needed. If you need help, simply input `-h` or `--help`, and if you need to know what version is running, type `-v` or `--version`. Lastly, with the `--syslog` command you force system logging.

If you would prefer to work with the configuration file, you can find it at `/etc/sft/sft-gatewayd.yaml` after installation.

Note

You must restart the gateway after making changes for them to take effect.

Next up are options you can set for different purposes. We will go over them separated by their subject. They will need to be added to the `sft-gatewayd.yaml` file and require the correct usage of indentation:

- Setup token options
- Log options
- Connection options

- LDAP options
- RDP options
- Session capture options

> **Note**
> We will write the sub-elements per option section in **Option: DefaultValue – Description** format for better visibility. **Option: DefaultValue** can be used in the configuration file.

Setup token options

The setup token option allows you to determine the way the gateway will enroll itself in ASA:

- **SetupToken: Unset**: This is considered an insecure method where the setup token will be stored in clear text. It is recommended to change the read permissions on the configuration file to keep access restricted.

- **SetupTokenFile: Linux: /var/lib/sft-gatewayd/setup.token**: For a smoother setup, it's recommended to specify the path to a separate file containing the setup token; in this case, you'll need to manually create the token file and add the corresponding token from the ASA platform. Once the gateway has been enrolled with a team, the token file will be deleted. Keep in mind that if the **SetupToken** option is configured at the same time, the gateway will prioritize the token specified there.

Log options

Log options are used to write logs to a pre-determined file and log the amount of information you set the level to.

For **LogLevel: Info**, additional log levels are **Error**, **Warn**, **Info**, and **Debug**. Okta recommends using the **Info** level.

Connections options

The following options are used by the gateway to establish and manage connections to and from the gateway:

- **AccessAddress: 1.1.1.1**: This setting designates the client-accessible network address (IPv4 or IPv6) for the gateway, utilizing either the specified address or, in its absence, the address from the network interface or cloud provider metadata.

- **AccessPort: 7234**: This specifies the port clients can use to access the gateway.

- **ListenAddress: 0.0.0.0**: This indicates the gateway's listening network address (IPv4 or IPv6), with the default behavior being to listen on all available interfaces.

- **ListenPort: 7234**: This specifies a port that's used by the gateway to listen for connections.

- **TLSUseBundledCAs: True**: This enforces the gateway's utilization of the bundled certificate store (rather than the OS certificate store) for securing TLS-protected HTTP requests, encompassing connections to the ASA cloud service. To revert to the OS certificate store, set this option to **False**.

- **RefuseConnections: False**: This setting controls gateway acceptance of SSH and RDP proxy traffic. When enabled, such connection requests won't be routed or listened to.

- **ForwardProxy: Unset**: Specify the outbound **HTTP CONNECT** proxy URL for connecting to ASA or use the **HTTPS_PROXY** environment variable.

LDAP options

These options manage the gateway's secure connections with LDAP servers, a configuration essential for AD-joined functionality, including default TLS initiation without certificate validation:

- **StartTLS: True**: This option enables TLS encryption for Active Directory/LDAP server communication. When disabled, communication with the server remains unencrypted. StartTLS is an LDAP extension that utilizes the TLS protocol for encryption and can't be enabled alongside UseLDAPS.

- **UseLDAPS: False**: This option activates the LDAPS protocol for encrypted communication. Note that this option cannot be concurrently enabled with the StartTLS choice.

- **LDAPSPort: 636**: When the UseLDAPS option is enabled, this port value is utilized for establishing the LDAPS connection.

- **ValidateCertificates: False**: This option validates certificates from the AD/LDAP server; if turned off, LDAP communication could be vulnerable to MITM attacks. When active, the gateway checks certificates at the TrustedCAsDir path, requiring valid certificates for each domain to enable them; without them, the gateway rejects connections.

- **TrustedCAsDir: unset**: This option defines the directory path housing the CA's public certificates, often managed within Active Directory via Group Policy. Certificates must be PEM encoded and readable by the `sft-gatewayd` user. Subdirectories are not inspected; any path can be used, with `/etc/sft/trusted-ldap-certs/` being Okta's recommendation.

> **Note**
> You must indent these options within an LDAP YAML dictionary using two spaces:

```
LDAP:


  StartTLS: ...
```

Caution: When both **StartTLS** and **UseLDAPS** are disabled, LDAP communication with Active Directory remains unencrypted; Okta suggests enabling **StartTLS** for encryption.

RDP options

These options govern RDP session management within the gateway, which is essential for directing sessions to agent-enrolled servers or AD domain servers; configuration is imperative for AD-joined functionality. To enable RDP connections, utilize the **Enabled** option alongside **TrustedCAsDir** or **DangerouslyIgnoreServerCertificates**; even without RDP support, AD-joined mode enables Active Directory server discovery:

- **Enabled: False**: This option manages gateway RDP functionality. Initially, this is deactivated due to it requiring additional setup; it must be enabled (set to **True**) before you can permit any RDP connections.

- **TrustedCAsDir: unset**: This option specifies the directory with CA-signed public certificates (often managed within Active Directory and distributed via Group Policy), requiring PEM-encoded certificates that can be read by the `sft-gatewayd` user, while subdirectories aren't scanned; any path is acceptable, yet `/etc/sft/trusted-rdp-certs/` is Okta's suggestion.

- **DangerouslyIgnoreServerCertificates: False**: This option limits gateway validation of server certificates for connecting to an RDP host; caution is advised in non-test settings but is necessary when the RDP host utilizes self-signed certificates.

- **MaximumActiveSessions: 20**: This option manages concurrent RDP sessions in the gateway, capping the number to avoid overloading. Surpassing this limit results in connection errors due to resource and performance considerations.

- **VerboseLogging: True**: This option manages the log level for internal RDP logs, aiding issue diagnosis but potentially cluttering logs. Setting this to **False** designates all internal RDP log messages as **Debug**.

Session capturing options

With the following options, you can fine-tune session recording:

- **SessionLogFlushInterval: 10s**: This option specifies the interval threshold for flushing and signing session capture logs

- **SessionLogMaxBufferSize: 262144**: This option sets the maximum buffer size for individual session capture logs

- **SessionLogTempStorageDirectoryt: /tmp**: This option determines the temporary storage directory for SSH session logs before uploading

- **LogDestinations: unset**: This option specifies where finalized session logs will be stored

Here's an example of this for Linux/BSD:

```
LogDestinations:
- Type: file
LogDir: /var/log/sft/sessions
```

- **LogFileNameFormats: unset**: This option enables custom naming formats for session recording log files. These are two default examples:

  - **SSHRecording**: `{{StartTime}}-{{.TeamName}}-{{Username}}`

  - **RDPRecording**: `{{StartTime}}-{{Protocol}}-{{.TeamName}}-{{ProjectName}}-{[.ServerName}}-{{.Username}}`

Now that we've determined how we set up the gateway with the configuration file and briefly went over the options for session capturing, let's take a closer look at it.

Session capturing

Session capturing is a powerful capability that allows teams to create secure and comprehensive records of individual SSH and RDP sessions. By capturing every action, command, and interaction within these sessions, it provides an accurate and detailed historical account. These recorded sessions serve multiple important purposes, such as helping with audits, enhancing training, and facilitating server monitoring.

In practical terms, session capturing involves recording the complete sequence of events within an SSH or RDP session. This creates a play-by-play recording that captures all user commands, system responses, and data that was exchanged during the session. These recordings are stored securely for later access.

The advantages of session capturing are significant. For audits, organizations can review recorded sessions to ensure compliance with security policies, industry regulations, and internal procedures. In training, captured sessions become a valuable resource for introducing new team members to real-world scenarios as they observe experienced users in action. Additionally, session recordings assist in server monitoring, allowing administrators to retrospectively analyze sessions for troubleshooting and issue resolution.

In essence, session capturing fosters transparency, accountability, and efficiency by providing a clear window into SSH and RDP sessions, contributing to enhanced security practices, knowledge sharing, and operational effectiveness.

Session capturing storage

Throughout a session, the gateway effectively manages temporary file storage at a designated location. When the session concludes, teams have the flexibility to store the completed session logs on the gateway's local storage or transmit them to external repositories such as **Amazon Web Services** (**AWS**) S3 or **Google Cloud Storage** (**GCS**).

> Tip!
>
> Refer to the *Session capture options* section for a detailed configuration.

The session logs themselves are thoughtfully structured, featuring a UTC timestamp, the ASA team name, and the corresponding user account. This naming convention results in filenames such as `YYYYMMDDTHHMMSS.SSSS-teamName-userName.asa`, illustrating the organized format of the captured session logs.

Signing and encryption

In the realm of security, ASA takes a proactive approach by signing session logs to ensure their integrity. This measure thwarts any attempts by malicious actors to tamper with log files and conceal their activities. It's worth noting that the system generates fresh signing keys approximately every 24 hours, further bolstering security.

However, it's important to clarify that ASA doesn't directly store or encrypt session logs. For enhanced security, Okta suggests leveraging automatic encryption by storing the logs within an encrypted cloud storage solution, such as a secure cloud bucket. Refer to the *Session capture options* section for in-depth configuration details and optimization.

Now that we understand the usage and relevance of session capturing, let's enable this on a project to see what it does.

How to enable session capturing on a project

Session capturing can be enabled on any project connected to an ASA gateway. When setting up a new project or editing an existing one, specifying the gateway selectors to one or more gateways will allow you to turn on session capturing. These gateways are then used to record the session logs.

So, let's update a current project and turn on the session recording options:

1. Go to **Projects** from the left main menu.
2. Create a new project or edit an existing project.
3. Under **Gateway selector**, add the labels that have been assigned to your gateways to multi-select gateways associated with this project.
4. Select **Enable traffic forwarding**.
5. Select **Record forwarded SSH sessions**, **Record forwarded RDP sessions**, or both.
6. Click **Submit**.

And done! This project will now start recording sessions with the given gateways.

Managing and accessing session logs

Once an SSH or RDP session concludes, the ASA gateway undertakes the crucial step of encrypting and then securely storing all the logs generated during the session. This robust security measure ensures that the integrity of these logs remains intact, preventing any unauthorized access or tampering attempts by potential attackers.

To engage with these encrypted session logs effectively, the ASA client plays a pivotal role. It empowers users to not only export and decode the logs but also enables them to meticulously verify and review the recorded information. The utilization of the ASA client serves as a paramount safeguard against any malicious alteration of the session logs by unauthorized entities.

To efficiently manage these session logs, teams can seamlessly utilize the `sft session-logs` command. This command provides them with the means to control and organize the logs, enabling a streamlined and organized approach to handling crucial session data.

Before we begin, the following is required:

- Ensure that you have successfully installed and enrolled the ASA client.
- Transfer the pertinent log files to a destination that is readily accessible by the ASA client.
- Adjust the read permissions of these log files in a way that grants the ASA client the necessary access. In Linux environments, this can be accomplished using the `chmod` command.
- Additionally, if you intend to review RDP session logs, it is imperative to first install the RDP Session Transcoder. This step is vital to ensuring a seamless and comprehensive examination of RDP session-related information.

> **Note**
>
> A key element that's required for RDP session playback is the **RDP Session Transcoder**. Please follow this link for the installation file for different OSs: `https://help.okta.com/asa/en-us/content/topics/adv_server_access/docs/rdp-transcoder.htm`.

Let's learn how to review two types of logs: SSH and RDP.

How to review SSH session logs

You have the option to utilize the widely used **asciinema** tool, which allows you to replay and revisit exported session logs. It's important to note that Okta doesn't actively maintain this tool, but the process of exporting session logs to a format compatible with `asciinema` is straightforward. Here, you'll find simple examples of commands that demonstrate how to effectively review these session logs. For more comprehensive guidance, you can refer to the detailed information provided in the **asciinema** documentation.

To begin, launch a terminal window and execute the subsequent command to export a session log in the `asciinema` format:

```
sft session-logs export --format asciinema yourSessionLog.asa --output
exportedSession.cast
```

By using this command, you will successfully convert the session log into the appropriate `asciinema` format and save it as `exportedSession.cast`.

After exporting the log, you can proceed to replay it using the following command:

```
asciinema play exportedSession.cast
```

Running this command will enable you to relive the session's sequence of events.

For your convenience, there's an optional step where you can print the exported log to standard output using the ensuing command:

```
asciinema cat exportedSession.cast
```

This provides an additional way to interact with the session log's content.

> **Note**
>
> Remember, these steps give you a concise overview of the process. If you require further insights or details, be sure to delve into the comprehensive resources available within the **asciinema** documentation: `https://asciinema.org/`.

How to review RDP logs

Once an RDP session has been captured and is stored within the ASA gateway, it becomes possible to convert the binary `.asa` format of the session into the more widely accessible `.mkv` video format. This conversion not only facilitates ease of viewing but also allows for more seamless sharing and analysis of the recorded content.

To initiate this conversion process, you'll need to utilize a terminal window. Execute the following command to export the session log in the `.mkv` video format:

```
sft session-logs export /path/source-file.asa --format mkv --output /
path
```

At the given `/path`, you will now be able to review the transformed `.mkv` file.

AD-joined advanced capabilities

AD-joined functionality within Okta's ASA introduces a comprehensive approach to enhancing secure RDP access. Specifically designed to leverage your organization's existing AD infrastructure, this feature streamlines and fortifies your server management practices.

Traditionally, ASA excels at automating the lifecycle management of user accounts tied to devices. This is achieved by creating and administering local accounts on individual devices, effectively streamlining the user provisioning process. However, with the AD-joined feature, this now changes. Teams now have the power to harness their established AD accounts, groups, and permissions to regulate and facilitate device access.

The significance of this capability lies in the seamless integration of AD-joined with your organization's AD environment. This synchronization enables users to leverage their AD credentials to gain entry into ASA-managed servers through RDP. By circumventing the need to maintain separate credentials, users experience a consistent and frictionless access journey.

In addition to the benefits associated with user authentication, AD-joined also centrally oversees and synchronizes the roster of available servers within the AD domain. This centralization eliminates the intricate task of manually tracking and maintaining server listings. ASA takes the reins, dynamically adapting to any connection alterations or server modifications. This automated tracking contributes to an accurate and up-to-date inventory, empowering administrators to have a real-time overview of their server landscape.

> **Tip**
> To learn more about the requirements and steps to utilize AD-joined functionality, please visit `https://help.okta.com/asa/en-us/content/topics/adv_server_access/docs/ad-overview.htm`.

With that, we've learned how to set up servers, clients, gateways, and enrollment. We also discussed how to set up gateways and session recordings, explaining how to review and audit these recordings. Now, let's take a look at how we can manage users, groups, and projects.

Managing your ASA environment

Now that we have established our first setup in ASA, and we understand how ASA works from a project perspective, let's dive into other management parts of ASA. For instance, what else can we manage within a project, how do we manage groups and users, and how do we allow users to have access?

Managing projects

In the previous section, we created a project so that we could create an enrollment token. If you want to secure anything in ASA, you will need a token. The project is used to connect a set of resources with a set of configurations. You can compare it to a domain in AD. The project will let you manage different kinds of servers or web applications. So, after you have created your project, as you did to create the enrollment token for a server, you want to add groups to it. But before we can do that, we have to create a group. Once you have integrated ASA with Okta using **System for Cross-Domain Identity Management** (**SCIM**), you can sync your groups and users from Okta, making your administration much easier. To set that up, follow the provisioning integration process from *Chapter 5, Automating Using Lifecycle Management*, or refer to `https://help.okta.com/asa/en-us/content/topics/adv_server_access/docs/setup/configure-scim`.

In ASA, we work with groups and team roles. Each group can be assigned a team role. Team roles can be any of the following or none at all:

- **Admins**: With this team role, users can manage other users, groups, and project resources
- **Reporting**: With this role, users get read-only access for reporting purposes

So, once you have synced your groups to ASA, you can edit the usage and details even more. When you go to the groups list through the left menu, you will see all the groups. By default, you have two groups – **everyone** and **owners**. The group owners have the **Admin** team role and by default, the person who created the ASA team belongs to this group. Any additional groups pushed from Okta will be listed here as well. To edit any settings, click on the group's name.

Under the **Actions** button, you can edit the group's team attributes. For example, you can edit the **Unique Group ID Number** (**Unix GID**) if there is a specific need to have the group be numbered differently, or the Unix name and Windows group name.

In the following example, we have pushed the **devops** group to ASA. While the naming of the group is consistent in ASA, it has been transformed to **sft_devops** for Unix and Windows. In this case, it only used the last part of the name after the last *space* to create the naming for Unix and Windows. Additionally, it added the `sft_` prefix to it:

✚ Update Team Attributes for 👥 devops

Overriding a group's team attribute values may cause unintended collisions. Groups with colliding attribute values will not be synced to servers.

ATTRIBUTE	TEAM VALUE
Unix GID *	180003
Unix Group Name *	sft_devops
Windows Group Name *	sft_devops

Figure 9.6 – Team attributes of a group in ASA

If you change any settings, don't forget to click **Update** to save your changes.

Back in the group's details overview, you can also assign a team role to your group. You can assign more than one team role to the group if that is needed.

Don't forget to click on **Update Roles** to save your changes.

Now that you have your groups, you probably want users to be added to them. As we explained in *Chapter 2*, *Working with Universal Directory*, you can push groups to applications. Users in those groups will be synced if they are also provisioned into the application under the **Assignments** tab in the application. The same goes for ASA: you need to assign users. Then, you can push these users into groups from Okta to ASA by using the **Push Group** function.

Just like the groups on the left-hand side menu, you can also click on users.

This will list the users that have been provisioned into ASA. Users aren't editable and will only show information on their profile that is relevant to ASA. ASA comes with a large list of attributes that can be synced from Okta to ASA. The following is the minimum that's required:

- First name
- Last name
- Full name
- Email

These user details will appear as follows:

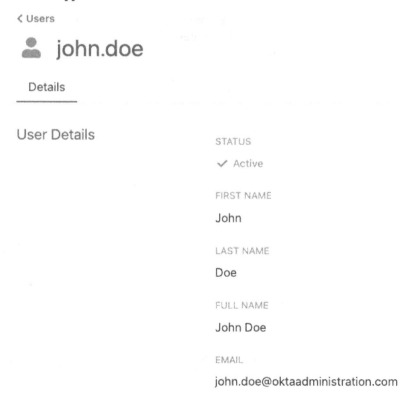

Figure 9.7 – User details in ASA

Additionally, ASA-created attributes are shown in the user overview. These can't be edited in ASA, but they can be managed from Okta:

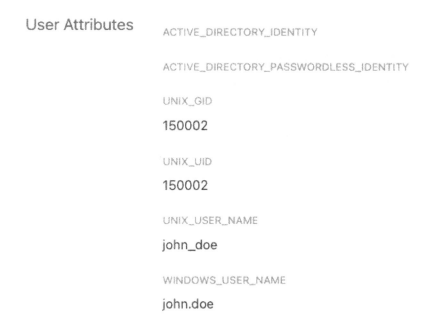

Figure 9.8 – User attributes in ASA

Lastly, on the user page, you will see the groups that the user has been assigned to:

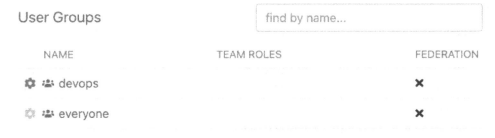

Figure 9.9 – User-assigned groups in ASA

With that, we understand how groups and users are synced. Now, let's go back to adding groups to the project:

1. Go to **Projects** in the left-hand side menu.

2. Select the project you want to add a group to.

3. Click the **Groups** tab in that project.

Here, you will see the different tabs that are available in a project:

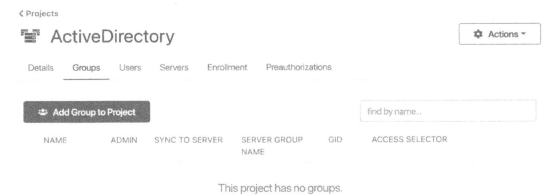

Figure 9.10 – Tab choices in a project

From this page, you can follow the remaining steps.

1. Click the **Add Group to Project** button.

2. Select what group to assign to this project from the **Group** drop-down list.

3. Select if the group is allowed access to **All Servers** in the project or **Specific Servers** you appoint here.

4. By selecting **User** or **Admin** in the **Server Accounts Permission** section, you can decide whether the accounts that are temporarily created will have user-level or administrative rights.

5. If you want your groups to be synchronized to the server(s) associated with this group and project, click the **Sync group to servers** checkbox.

The dialog box to add the group to your project looks like this:

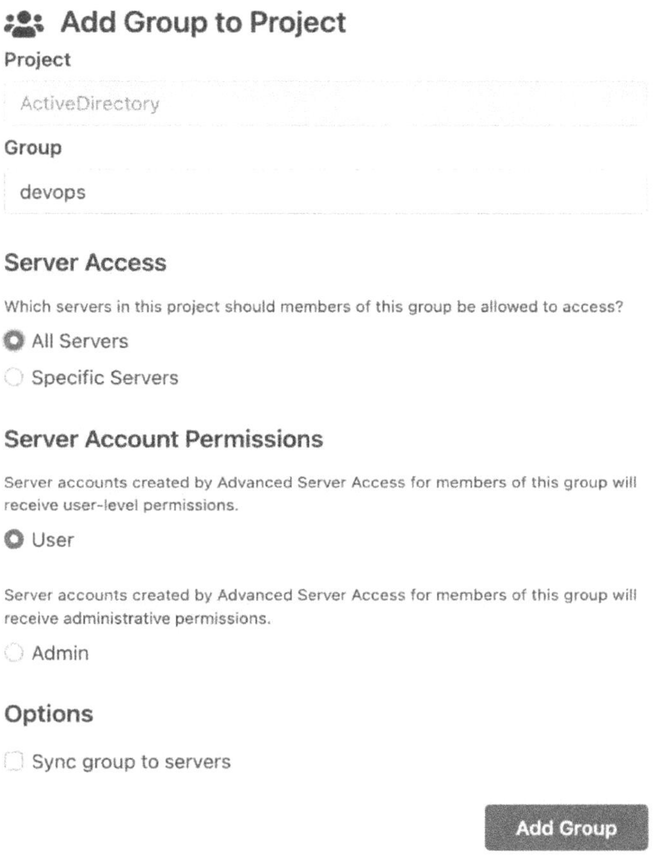

＊ Add Group to Project

Project

ActiveDirectory

Group

devops

Server Access

Which servers in this project should members of this group be allowed to access?

◉ All Servers

○ Specific Servers

Server Account Permissions

Server accounts created by Advanced Server Access for members of this group will receive user-level permissions.

◉ User

Server accounts created by Advanced Server Access for members of this group will receive administrative permissions.

○ Admin

Options

☐ Sync group to servers

Add Group

Figure 9.11 – Settings for adding a group to a project

And with that, you're done.

Now that the group has been added to the project, you can click it to view group-related information.

Additionally, at the bottom, you can select **Add Sudo Entitlements Binding**. To assign Sudo entitlements, let's understand what it is and how to set it up before we assign it to a group in a project.

Sudo entitlements

In the world of computing, sudo stands for **Superuser Do**, and it's a powerful command that allows users to execute administrative tasks on their systems. It's like having the key to the kingdom, giving you access to make significant changes to the OS and its settings.

On Linux machines, the sudo command allows regular users to perform actions that usually require superuser (root) privileges. These actions could include installing software, modifying system configurations, or managing user accounts. By using sudo, users can temporarily elevate their permissions to carry out these tasks safely and securely. It's like having a special pass that grants you limited time access to perform crucial tasks without having to log in as the all-powerful root user all the time.

Now, on Windows machines, we don't have a command called sudo like in Linux, but we have something similar called "sudo entitlements" or "elevated privileges." When you're an administrator on a Windows machine, you have the authority to access and change critical settings.

When you run certain applications or tasks that require administrator permissions, Windows will prompt you with a **User Account Control** (**UAC**) dialog. This is like a safety gate, asking you to confirm that you indeed want to use your administrative privileges for the specific action. This helps prevent accidental changes or unauthorized access to your system.

So, whether it's "sudo" on Linux or "elevated privileges" on Windows, these mechanisms give us the ability to perform essential tasks, but it's vital to use them wisely and responsibly to keep our systems secure and running smoothly.

These entitlements can be managed within ASA for users on the different servers they have access to, within a group. This means that ASA will make sure that users have the right privilege to execute a command for the given server, within the boundaries of that session.

Creating these entitlements within ASA can be done by going to the left panel and selecting **Entitlements**. Let's create our first entitlement for our project.

Click on **Create Sudo Entitlement**. The next window will have fields we need to fill and store:

- **Entitlement Name**: This is a single-line text, usually human-readable to understand what this entitlement does.

- **Description**: This field allows you to be much more expressive in what this entitlement does and is used for. Being as complete as possible will give a better understanding of whether this entitlement is one you would like to assign to groups or people.

- **Commands**: In the following section, you can determine what is allowed and run. The command needs to be a single-line function and must be one of the following types. As each command is considered a single execution, you can add more commands to an entitlement. Each command is set up with the following:

  - **Raw**: This sudo entitlement lets users execute only a specific command set by the admin during creation. The admin can choose any command, and users can't change it in any manner.

  - **Directory**: This sudo entitlement allows users to execute any command within a specific directory set by the admin during creation. The directory can be any valid Unix directory defined by a string starting and ending with the / character, including the root directory (/).

- **Executable**: This sudo entitlement allows users to run the executable chosen by the admin during creation. The admin can decide whether the command will accept any arguments, no arguments, or specific arguments. The command must be a valid Unix path starting with a / character.

- When you click on **Advanced Configuration**, additional options become available. These settings will apply to all commands in the entitlement:

  - **Run As**: To execute all the commands specified in the sudo entitlement as a particular non-root user, input the username in the **Run As** field. Additionally, disable **Enable NOPASSWD** if you wish to require a password for users to run sudo. By default, this option is selected, allowing passwordless sudo access. If you want to disallow commands from executing child processes, choose **Enable NOEXEC**. Finally, if you want to permit the overriding of environment variables for commands, select **Enable SETENV**.

- **Environment**: To fine-tune the environment variable settings for a sudo entitlement, you can use the **env_keep +=** and **env_keep -=** arguments. For more information, refer to your *system's sudo documentation*.

Once you are done, click on **Create Sudo Entitlement**. This will store your entitlement and allow you to assign it to a group or user. If you go back to your project, click into a group, and go to the bottom, you can now assign your newly created entitlement:

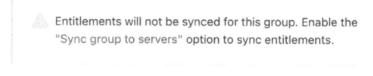

Figure 9.12 – Settings for adding a group to a project

Clicking on **Add Sudo Entitlement Binding** will present a new window where you can pick and choose the entitlement(s) you created and want to assign to this group in this project.

As *Figure 9.12* shows, if group syncing is not turned on in the group settings for the project, selected entitlements at the group level will not be synced to the server. Turning on group sync will make sure users can execute any assigned entitlement on the selected server(s).

Now we have set that up, let's understand the last part of a project – preauthorization.

Preauthorization is like having a watchful guardian stationed at the entrance of your server infrastructure. Just as this guardian scrutinizes a guest list before granting entry to the castle, preauthorization allows you to dictate who can access specific servers even before they attempt to connect. With ASA, we can manage a user's allowed moment to access infrastructure, and for how long, in that project. This forces the project to only grant credentials to specific users within a limited time frame.

Now that we understand what preauthorization is, let's set it up for a project.

Go to a project and click on the **Preauthorizations** menu at the top. Then, click **Create Preauthorization**. This will prompt you with a new window where you can set up the new preauthorization. Here, set the following options:

1. Select a user you want to preauthorize.

2. Select an expiry date of this preauthorization in the **Expires at** field, then set a **time** value.

3. Click **Submit**.

This can be time-consuming if admins need to do this for each user, on each project, and update it whenever the preauthorization expires. ASA also has integrations with Workflows and an API, which would allow you to benefit from all sorts of automations. That way, you can pre-program what type of preauthorizations are allowed, whenever it is required. Only have the project be accessible when needed, not simply allow everyone access all the time.

In the next section, we'll look at automation.

Automation

Automating the enrollment of servers in ASA is the best way to scale your infrastructure. This allows you to quickly manage all the servers across the board, along with the needed access per group and user. To make this happen, your infrastructure automation tools require a solution to allow your identity management to scale along with the infrastructure.

Using tools such as Hashicorp's Terraform (`https://www.terraform.io`) gives your admins options to create baked-in solutions that are run as soon as new servers are spun up. This allows enrollment automation to happen based on the common usage and access grants that are needed for those servers.

> **Important note**
> Okta also has a certified Terraform provider. To learn more and implement it, please visit `https://registry.terraform.io/providers/oktadeveloper/okta/latest/docs`.

Perhaps you have a service that requires its own server for each customer. Customers can sign up for free and you need to be able to create that server automatically. But you also want to make sure your users and admins can access that without having to manually get in or use shared credentials to gain access. By having the enrollment happen along with the creation, the server will automatically be enrolled based on the variables you added to the enrollment script. This will ensure the customer-specific server is added to the right project and group of admins. Perhaps the customers will start paying for the services and upgrade their server to a more supported one. This might require your servers to move over from one group to another and have different groups of support and admin users being able to access that server. This can then be done automatically, based on rules.

As there are quite a few scenarios with different tools and infrastructure vendors, we recommend taking a look here and discovering how to implement ASA within your cloud server fleet using infrastructure automation tools: `https://help.okta.com/asa/en-us/Content/Topics/Adv_Server_Access/docs/cloud-deployment.htm`.

Automation can be addressed further with Okta's solutions. As mentioned earlier, ASA has integrations with Okta Workflows. This integration is capable of creating the following:

- Projects
- Enrollment tokens
- Groups
- Preauthorizations

Together with regular Workflow management in Okta itself, you can build elaborate workflows that automate almost the entire privileged access management flow for users to gain access to servers and resources.

Additionally, if you add in Okta's IGA, you can build automation that would make sure that access is approved, auditable, and managed correctly within the suite of Okta.

Summary

ASA is a great way to extend your identity-centric management to your servers and infrastructure. It allows your DevOps engineers to be busy with what they need to do without securing, updating, and managing static keys and credentials. This chapter gave insight into its usage but also showed steps on how to set up, install, and enroll servers. We also discussed how users can install their clients to access their provisioned servers. We explained how project management can be done within ASA and we lightly touched on adding ASA as part of infrastructure automation using tools such as Hashicorp's Terraform.

With that, we have reached the end of this book; we hope you have found it helpful. Regardless of whether you were an Okta novice or you had already worked with Okta, we hope you have learned something new. If you used this book to study for a certificate, we wish you well on your exam. If you have any comments or want to share anything, please reach out to us. Take care and good luck in your Okta endeavors.

Index

Packtpub.com

Subscribe to our online digital library for full access to over 7,000 books and videos, as well as industry leading tools to help you plan your personal development and advance your career. For more information, please visit our website.

Why subscribe?

- Spend less time learning and more time coding with practical eBooks and Videos from over 4,000 industry professionals

- Improve your learning with Skill Plans built especially for you

- Get a free eBook or video every month

- Fully searchable for easy access to vital information

- Copy and paste, print, and bookmark content

Did you know that Packt offers eBook versions of every book published, with PDF and ePub files available? You can upgrade to the eBook version at packtpub.com and as a print book customer, you are entitled to a discount on the eBook copy. Get in touch with us at customercare@packtpub.com for more details.

At www.packtpub.com, you can also read a collection of free technical articles, sign up for a range of free newsletters, and receive exclusive discounts and offers on Packt books and eBooks.

Other Books You May Enjoy

If you enjoyed this book, you may be interested in these other books by Packt:

Practical Cybersecurity Architecture - Second Edition

Diana Kelley, Ed Moyle

ISBN: 978-1-83763-716-4

- Create your own architectures and analyze different models
- Understand strategies for creating architectures for environments and applications
- Discover approaches to documentation using repeatable approaches and tools
- Discover different communication techniques for designs, goals, and requirements
- Focus on implementation strategies for designs that help reduce risk
- Apply architectural discipline to your organization using best practices

Fuzzing Against the Machine

Antonio Nappa, Eduardo Blázquez

ISBN: 978-1-80461-497-6

- Understand the difference between emulation and virtualization
- Discover the importance of emulation and fuzzing in cybersecurity
- Get to grips with fuzzing an entire operating system
- Discover how to inject a fuzzer into proprietary firmware
- Know the difference between static and dynamic fuzzing
- Look into combining QEMU with AFL and AFL++
- Explore Fuzz peripherals such as modems
- Find out how to identify vulnerabilities in OpenWrt

Packt is searching for authors like you

If you're interested in becoming an author for Packt, please visit authors.packtpub.com and apply today. We have worked with thousands of developers and tech professionals, just like you, to help them share their insight with the global tech community. You can make a general application, apply for a specific hot topic that we are recruiting an author for, or submit your own idea.

Share Your Thoughts

Now you've finished *Okta Administration Up and Running – Second Edition*, we'd love to hear your thoughts! Scan the QR code below to go straight to the Amazon review page for this book and share your feedback or leave a review on the site that you purchased it from.

https://packt.link/r/1837637458

Your review is important to us and the tech community and will help us make sure we're delivering excellent quality content.

Download a free PDF copy of this book

Thanks for purchasing this book!

Do you like to read on the go but are unable to carry your print books everywhere?

Is your eBook purchase not compatible with the device of your choice?

Don't worry, now with every Packt book you get a DRM-free PDF version of that book at no cost.

Read anywhere, any place, on any device. Search, copy, and paste code from your favorite technical books directly into your application.

The perks don't stop there, you can get exclusive access to discounts, newsletters, and great free content in your inbox daily

Follow these simple steps to get the benefits:

1. Scan the QR code or visit the link below

https://packt.link/free-ebook/9781837637454

2. Submit your proof of purchase

3. That's it! We'll send your free PDF and other benefits to your email directly